CHICAGO PUBLIC LIBRARY
BUSINESS / SCIENCE / TECHNOLOGY
400 S. STATE ST.   60605

Bob Kimball, PhD

agement

Kimball has written an excel-
t overview of the art of man-
The book examines all aspects
ject from recruiting and hir-
:ipline and termination with
sis on motivation and devel-
ccessful team. The book sorts
e multiple managment theo-
ve come in and out of vogue,
s on what will help anyone
ccessful. This book is a must-
w managers or any leaders
hone their leadership skills
highly productive teams,
aying out of the corporate
"

ard, MBA
strict Sales Manager,
Pharmaceuticals

CHICAGO PUBLIC LIBRARY
HAROLD WASHINGTON CENTER
400 S. STATE STREET
CHICAGO, IL60605

D1468577

CHICAGO PUBLIC LIBRARY
BUSINESS / SCIENCE / TECHNOLOGY
400 S. STATE ST.   60605

NOTES FOR PROFESSIONAL LIBRARIANS
AND LIBRARY USERS

This is an original book title published by Best Business Books, an imprint of The Haworth Press, Inc. Unless otherwise noted in specific chapters with attribution, materials in this book have not been previously published elsewhere in any format or language.

CONSERVATION AND PRESERVATION NOTES

All books published by The Haworth Press, Inc. and its imprints are printed on certified pH neutral, acid-free book grade paper. This paper meets the minimum requirements of American National Standard for Information Sciences-Permanence of Paper for Printed Material, ANSI Z39.48-1984.

The Book on Management

BEST BUSINESS BOOKS
Robert E. Stevens, PhD
David L. Loudon, PhD
Editors in Chief

The Book on Management

Bob Kimball, PhD

Best Business Books®
An Imprint of The Haworth Press, Inc.
New York • London • Oxford

Published by

Best Business Books®, an imprint of The Haworth Press, Inc., 10 Alice Street, Binghamton, NY 13904-1580.

© 2004 by The Haworth Press, Inc. All rights reserved. No part of this work may be reproduced or utilized in any form or by any means, electronic or mechanical, including photocopying, microfilm, and recording, or by any information storage and retrieval system, without permission in writing from the publisher. Printed in the United States of America.

PUBLISHER'S NOTE
Identities and circumstances of individuals discussed in this book have been changed to protect confidentiality.

Cover design by Lora Wiggins.

Library of Congress Cataloging-in-Publication Data

Kimball, Bob.
    The book on management / Bob Kimball.
        p. cm.
    Includes bibliographical references and index.
    ISBN 0-7890-2500-0 (hard : alk. paper)—ISBN 0-7890-2501-9 (soft : alk. paper)
    1. Management. I. Title.

HD31.K4676 2004
658—dc22

2004004245

CHICAGO PUBLIC LIBRARY
BUSINESS / SCIENCE / TECHNOLOGY
400 S STATE ST.   60605

R03028 62524

CONTENTS

PART I: FOUNDATION

ABOUT THE AUTHOR

Bob Kimball, PhD, is Professor of Marketing at the University of West Florida in Pensacola, where he teaches Marketing Fundamentals, Professional Selling, and Sales Management. He is the author of the *AMA Handbook for Successful Selling,* co-author of *Selling in the New World of Business* (Haworth), and is the author, executive producer, and narrator of "Secrets of Professional Selling," a video sales training program. Dr. Kimball worked for thirteen years in sales and marketing with Coca-Cola USA and, for seven years, managed The Kimball Organization, specializing in developing and conducting sales and management training programs for a wide variety of firms in the southeastern United States.

PART I: FOUNDATION

Chapter 1

"Our Managers Can't Manage"

About three decades ago, during my early days in a Fortune 500 company, I was part of a task force charged with conducting a detailed situation review addressing every aspect of our company business. We identified opportunities in new products, new packages, and enhancements to our distribution system. We uncovered needs for revised policies and procedures, but one conclusion stood head and shoulders above all the rest: Our managers couldn't manage.

Since then, I've worked with and for hundreds of managers in all types and sizes of organizations. Consistently I hear the same refrain: Managers, by and large, are at best minimally competent at the job of managing. How can this be so? There are two reasons.

First, effective management demands the integration of a diverse array of personal characteristics and skills, all of them essential. Just as a chain is only as strong as its weakest link, a manager's overall competence can never exceed the competence of the weakest subset of all those personal and professional components. In fact, weakness in just one critical element may be enough to doom a manager to failure. Think about your car: It can be in perfect condition—except for one key part. Then you're stranded on the side of the road. Consider your computer: In tip-top shape except for one tiny chip, invalidating all its calculations. Or yourself: A perfect physical specimen—but just one little defect and you're on the way to the emergency room. It's the same thing with management: You can do all of it right but for one critical skill, such as knowing how to conduct interviews and make a hiring decision, and you will fail.

You've probably heard the fable of four people in a dark room with an elephant. Each of them holds onto a different part of the elephant—respectively, trunk, tusk, leg, and tail—and attempts to describe the total beast based upon this limited knowledge. Of course, everyone paints a different picture of the whole, none of them even close to accurate. Management is the elephant, and we must step back from it, turn on the lights, and examine it in totality to describe it. Then, we must observe its functions and habits, determine its capabilities, and ascertain what we can do to help it achieve its potential.

Many managers fail because they don't have the necessary comprehensive perspective and attendant competencies. For the same reason, many companies have failed with fads and buzzwords ranging from quality to empowerment. That's not to say that quality and empowerment were not important to their success. On the contrary, both are vital to success or, for that matter, survival; but each is only one piece of the elephant.

One of my colleagues was recently reminiscing about an incompetent manager who read *The One Minute Manager* (Blanchard and Johnson, 1982). For a week afterward, this person dropped in for the obligatory one-minute interaction every day. But nothing got better, so he gave it up. Don't get me wrong: *The One Minute Manager* is a great book, as relevant today as in 1982, but I'm sure its authors would agree that it will not, by and of itself, make someone an effective manager. For the same reason, individuals and companies fail when they look for the right buzzword or a magic bullet. If you don't like the elephant analogy, think of a jigsaw puzzle. Each piece is critical but only a part of the total picture.

Closely related to all of this is the second reason why managers can't manage: No one ever taught them how. If your company is like most, you have some sort of training program for entry-level employees beyond giving them a customer list and a set of keys. You evaluate candidates for education, skills, and aptitude as part of the hiring process, and you provide training and orientation to ensure their ability to handle the requirements of the job. If they perform well, what happens? They get promoted. Initially, a person may receive a promotion to another "doing" job, perhaps necessitating more formal or on-the-job training, but nevertheless a situation in which the employee succeeds or fails on the basis of how well he or she does the work. Inevitably, though, in most organizations, success as a doer means consideration for promotion to management, a veritable sea change in the essential nature of the job. Whereas in the past the basis of results was the personal accomplishment of tasks, now success means causing tasks to get done through others. Responsibility shifts from functions and developing accounts to developing people. The manager's role is no longer that of a player but that of a coach. Most important of all, one's status and identification can no longer be that of an employee. One must be perceived as a member of management—an officer, not an enlisted person.

For a person to succeed as a manager, this paradigm shift must take place on Day 1. Inexplicably, most organizations appear to assume that individuals promoted to management already know everything they need to know to succeed in management. They don't. They lack many vital skills and are completely oblivious to the relationship-based intangibles. By the time the new manager begins to get a working idea of what managers are and what managers are supposed to do, he or she is about six months into the job and has already failed.

Management is not a seat-of-your-pants talent. Management is a skill. It's both a "doing" skill and a "being" skill which one must learn all about and perfect. Because it's unlikely your organization will train you to be a competent and effective manager, this is a journey you'll have to take on your own. It's going to be both interesting and enlightening.

Chapter 2

"Gentlemen, This Is a Football"

Back in the days of the late, great coach Vince Lombardi, the Green Bay Packers had a most interesting beginning to pre-season training. All the players knew that at the first team meeting, the legendary coach would waste no time getting straight to the point. Many of the men, half Lombardi's age and twice his size, were openly fearful, dreading the encounter. The coach did not disappoint them, and, in fact, delivered his message in one of the great one-liners of all time. Football in hand, Lombardi walked to the front of the room, took several seconds to look over the assemblage in silence, held out the pigskin in front of him, and said, "Gentlemen, this is a football."

In only five words, Lombardi communicated his point: We're going to start with the basics and make sure we're executing all the fundamentals. The communication was effective: Lombardi openly confirmed what everyone already knew, that he would assume nothing about their skills and abilities, but he did not needlessly belabor the point. A touch of humor broke the tension without diverting attention from the issue at hand. And he was able to make this audience feel more comfortable while retaining his role as coach and status as management. It's a great example which illustrates what Lombardi was: an effective manager. Let's take a page out of the coach's playbook, then, building our foundation on the basic fundamentals of what management is.

MANAGEMENT: THEN AND NOW

Let's define management as planning, organizing, staffing, directing, and controlling the activities of others to achieve predetermined objectives for which the manager is ultimately accountable. That broad definition would have been appropriate ten years ago or eighty years ago, though what management means today is very different from ten or eighty years ago. Very few organizations around today operate under the paradigm used eighty years ago, though if we think hard enough we can probably come up with one or two that are running things about the same as 500 years ago and are still in business. Many more organizations, and who knows how many managers, however, are managing things about the same as ten years ago. Take a good look at them, because few will be around ten or even five years from now. The reason is simple: Business, and the management of people in business organizations, has undergone a radical transformation.

In case you missed it, the nature of the American economy has changed from eighty years ago, when Henry Ford's assembly line was the consummate business model. At the time, a line of people would stretch from River Rouge (Michigan) to Baton Rouge, all hoping for a shot at the unheard-of wage of five dollars a day for the privilege of spending ten or twelve hours giving a nine-sixteenths-inch bolt two and a half turns. And these people were glad to get the work. If you didn't like it, or you had the flu with a 102-degree temperature and couldn't get to work today, no problem, you were fired. Who's next?

Through the 1940s, the American economy was predominantly labor intensive, churning out physical products. The management guru of the day, Frederick Taylor, coined the term *scientific management* to describe workers as human cogs in an industrial machine. Through the 1950s and 1960s, the essential roles of management and workers were unchanged. More employees were moving out of labor and into the "professional" ranks, but such persons were referred to as "knowledge workers," whose input into the machine was knowledge rather than labor. These persons were the inspiration for the creators of *Star Trek: The Next Generation,* models for the Borg, intelligent entities with no free will. In this management system, also known as the military model, all thinking was done and all goals set at the top. Down through the layers of middle management, administrators worked out the details for execution of the strategy until, at the end of the chain, each doer carried out the assigned task: Turn that bolt. Peel those potatoes. Doers did not merely not think. They were specifically *trained* not to think and were disciplined if they tried to think or act independently. In this environment, the organization and its administrators were obsessed with policies, procedures, and controls. Knowledge workers spent countless hours writing manuals to spell out every last detail of every last thing. Paperwork and reporting systems ensured that no detail was overlooked and every task had been discharged on time according to specifications.

The obsession of control over workers doing mindless tasks was considered a satisfactory system through the 1930s. Of course, the United States at that time had 25 percent unemployment and was experiencing the worst depression since the barbarians sacked Rome, but if you had shelter from the rain and food on the table, who was complaining? The labor movement had shortened the workday, raised wages, and improved the physical workplace environment. The government had instituted the beginnings of a safety net. Was being a mindless automaton all that bad after all? Certainly not, especially for people who had no idea what a mindless automaton was.

The same old way of doing things worked out pretty well through World War II. One thing you can say about the military model: it gets the job done in crisis and wartime. Everything was peachy through the Eisenhower years, which carried us innocently through the 1950s. By the 1960s, though, the first cracks had begun to appear in the machine. Foreign competition, devastated by World War II, began to appear on the horizon, first from Germany with its challenge to the American automobile industry, the Volkswagen. America responded with the forgettable Chevrolet Corvair and Ford Falcon, but no big deal. We really wanted Mustangs and GTOs anyhow. Personally, I was out cruising around in a Malibu Super Sport and a Torino GT, the latter of which had a 390 engine which could comfortably hold the road but tear up fan belts at 120 miles an hour. I remember the first time I heard about a Japanese automobile. I actually laughed out loud and said to the bearer of the fact that this was a joke, right? A few years later, that joke was threatening to undermine the very fabric of America's auto makers and make the city of Detroit yearn for the good old days of the depression. Our side responded with the Citation and the Fairmont, in the tradition of the Vega and the Maverick, and, to phrase it diplomatically, the people were not impressed. Japan's invasion continued, expanding from autos to electronics and everything in between. American industry and American management suddenly awoke to the reality that what Japan had failed to achieve at Pearl Harbor it was winning in the marketplace. Something had to be done or, many predicted, America was destined to become a second-rate economic, and thus political, power. Most of us had never questioned the ways of doing things. Now we were forced to or perish.

Dr. W. Edwards Deming is the man most associated with the concept of quality and the Japanese style of management. In the 1980s, American management, desperate for answers, tried to out-Japanese the Japanese with quality circles, zero defects, and participative management, all of which, of course, were just pieces of the elephant, and none of which could fix a fundamentally flawed machine. In sum, the machine itself had to go.

In the new management paradigm, most mindless tasks can be performed more efficiently and more effectively by robots and other mechanical devices. It makes no sense to have a person turning bolts all day if that person is capable of skilled tasks, and, very possibly, in a radical shift from eighty years ago, that person may make the greatest contribution through his or her mind rather than physical actions. The micro level (an organization), and the macro level (the national economy) are the sum total of the productivity of all its mechanical devices and all its individuals. An organization or an economy can succeed only to the extent that every individual optimizes his or her productivity, which happens only when people think and make decisions rather than merely execute assigned tasks. The challenge to management was to let go of the controls and create an environment in which every individual could fulfill his or her potential.

Economic and technological changes have made this new management paradigm a prerequisite for survival. In today's global economy, it makes no sense for educated and trained workers in advanced countries to perform tasks and produce products that can be made more cheaply in less developed countries. As a result, economies of the advanced countries have shifted away from manufacturing products and have moved toward services, requiring competent employees that can think and initiate action.

Technology and the Internet spelled the end of middle management and staff support, most of whom were involved in moving paper and information from one layer of management to the next. Overnight, most of their primary functions became the routine tasks of a personal computer. As a result, the person at the end of the chain, at the point of encounter with the organization's customer, must think and make decisions because the middle manager who might have previously told him or her what to do is no longer around.

A final nail in the coffin of the old management machine is the fact that the best entry-level employees, new college graduates, are different from graduates of just a few years ago. Back then if you wanted a decent job you had to play ball with the establishment or perish. You wore the company tie, sang the company song, and did what you were told to do, even if your manager was an idiot who wouldn't let you think. Not so today. These twenty-somethings will get together and form their own organization and, taking advantage of every nuance of knowledge and technology, go about making a living on their own and perhaps, if they feel like it, putting you out of business in the process. They will not be treated as if they have no brains. They will question all policies and procedures which, let's face it, have probably outlived their usefulness, anyhow. And they will not tolerate being patronized. As Lyndon Johnson once said of J. Edgar Hoover, he would rather have him inside the tent pissing out than outside the tent pissing in. Any organization that manages its employees today the same way as it did ten years ago will miss out on the best and the brightest.

THE FIVE MAJOR FUNCTIONS OF MANAGERS

So, with all that in mind, let's take a quick overview of the five major functions of managers in this new paradigm. We'll revisit many of these points in detail later on.

Planning

Figure out where you are now and where you want to go. Please do not delude yourself into thinking you can do this by reading over marketing research reports in the comfort of your ivory tower. The truth is not in the numbers; it's in between the numbers. One of the classic marketing blunders of all time was made by a leading beverage manufacturer whose competitor was gaining share relative to its flagship brand. In a consumer survey, as a response to the question, "Which brand's taste do you prefer?" the competitor was gaining as well. The conclusion? Obvious! Consumers' tastes are changing, and trends in taste preference are driving trends in market share. Backing up this conclusion was the fact that in blind taste tests, the competitor consistently beat the leading brand, but a revised formulation by the leading company beat both the competitor and the leading brand's present product. The decision? Change the formula! The result? Disaster! How could it have happened?

When the leading manufacturer's marketing people got out of the office and into the stores, they made a disturbing discovery. Recent new product introductions had suffered a fatal flaw in execution: Rather than take shelf space from slow-moving competitive products, a fundamental objective in any new product introduction, most space for the new entries had come from the flagship brand. For a discretionary consumer nondurable product, reduction in shelf space portends one thing: loss of share. Next, they uncovered that the consumer research had been misinterpreted. When you ask people which brand they like best, they tend to respond with the brand they bought most recently. Taste preference wasn't driving market share. Loss of shelf space was driving market share and taste preferences!

In addition, the blind taste test data were not projectable. That is to say, results in a blind taste test were inconsistent with results when the products were identified. Outside the lab, in the real world, where products are identified, consumers hated the new formulation. Management discovered too late that they needed to get out in the field and talk to people at the point of encounter before formulating their plans.

As you plan and seek out future opportunities, keep in mind whatever differential advantages you have in your products, services, delivery system, and cost structure. Develop your strategies, policies, and programs around the differential advantages, and consider the likely competitive response. You'll then have to secure and manage your budget, the ultimate scorecard of your success.

Organizing

Having just pummeled the notion of managing through the administration of policies and procedures, let's clarify that point by saying that only an anarchist would advocate the elimination of all policies and procedures. Along the same lines, though you will emphasize flexibility and encourage individual initiative, there is still a need for an organizational structure and position descriptions. You will foster a culture of cooperation and teamwork, but you will also need explicit guidelines which define roles and objectives. Perhaps most difficult of all, you must have a way of assessing individual performance vis-à-vis explicit standards. An empowered team atmosphere is great as long as individuals can't use it to find a place to hide.

Staffing

Whether it's sports or business, managers can only be as good as their personnel and how well they're trained. Many organizations chug along with employees who never should have been hired in the first place or who underperform due to a lack of requisite training or skills. Should you be faced with such a situation, it must be addressed before you can ever expect your organization to accomplish much of anything. Staffing involves

1. Recruiting: figure out how you're going to identify and make contact with those persons you'd want to consider as employees
2. Selecting: a structured process for determining who you want to interview and how you'll go about making a hiring decision
3. Orienting: help employees become familiar with your organization, its people, its products, and its ways of getting things done
4. Training: be sure everyone has all the attendant skills necessary for peak performance
5. Developing: coach your people to help them achieve their personal and professional potential.

As you work on staffing, go beyond your area of direct responsibility. Seek out your management colleagues and explore any opportunities for forming cross-functional teams across formal organization boundaries.

Directing

In the old days of an organization obsessed with control, directing meant "delegating" in the sense of having employees act as your arms and legs, not brains, to accomplish tasks for you. The word *delegation* is out of vogue now, having been replaced with the more enlight-

ened term *empowerment,* which in essence means "effective delegation." In a team-oriented environment, that means coordinating all
the players to be sure everyone is on the same page and moving in the
right direction. To this end, an effective manager must establish and
maintain lines of communication throughout the organization, acting
as a facilitator of ongoing change and a person to whom all parties
can look for clarification of roles and resolution of conflict. When directing, the manager must go beyond narrow administrative functions
and become the leader who motivates team members to want to excel.

Controlling

Extending the actions of directing, controlling involves coaching
individuals and groups to facilitate their achievement of objectives,
then measuring and evaluating performance against the previously
articulated standards. Finally, after assessing results, provide rewards
for or take corrective action with the team or, most particularly, its individual members.

So, there are the basics, a very fundamental description of what
managers do. As we proceed, we'll go into these functions in much
greater depth but even more so will address the intangibles of effective management. It's not so much what managers do as what managers are, after all. But let's not get ahead of ourselves. We need to lay
the groundwork and complete the foundation first.

Chapter 3

How Do You Spell "Assume"?

You've probably heard that one. It's a-s-s-u-m-e because when you assume things you make an "ass" out of "u" and "me." In their highly acclaimed book *In Search of Excellence,* published originally more than twenty years ago, Peters and Waterman (1982) pointed out nunerous beliefs that conventional business thinking consistently assumed to be tried and true but that were patently false and a prescription for disaster. It's important to revisit these, as many managers and their organizations continue to cling to many or all of them to this day.

FALSE BUSINESS ASSUMPTIONS

Assumption 1: Bigger Is Better

Big is better because you can get economies of scale. Low-cost producers are the only surefire winners. Customers focus on cost in the final analysis, and survivors make it cheaper. All of these assumptions are false. In marketing, this is known as a production orientation. Customers *talk* price but they *buy* value. A firm that makes a product cheaper may be failing to develop new and innovative products and services which constitute value, for which people will gladly pay more, including the value of customer service and follow-up after the sale. Although the big guys get economies of scale for mass-producing commodities, the smaller organizations have the flexibility to act quickly and seize opportunities in the higher-margin niche markets, where specialization and customization create value worth paying for.

Assumption 2: Get the Facts

Get all the facts before you act. Analyze everything. Big foolish decisions usually can be avoided through good market research. All of these assumptions are false. This is the traditional business school mentality of "paralysis by analysis." It is management by algorithm, the idea behind which is that if I have all the facts, the correct decision will pop out. With this approach, managers spend their days accumulating data to be fed into a computer program, thus avoiding having to make any decisions for which they might be held accountable. If they can get away with it, this insulates them from ever making mistakes and becoming scapegoats to be led to slaughter. Few organizations still permit managers to do no more than assemble information, since that job can be done by a student intern for about eight bucks an hour. Beyond that, in the fast-paced business world today, there simply isn't time to analyze everything because windows of opportunity are very limited. By the time a manager completes a fully comprehensive analysis, the window has closed or the competitor has exploited the opportunity. Furthermore, no research or analysis will enable managers to spot new breakthrough opportunities since they haven't even been thought about yet. Consider for a moment the assumption of 1910 concerning the usefulness of the airplane for public transportation (If I was supposed to fly, I'd have wings.), the assumptions of 1945 about the future for television (Who would want to do anything more than read a magazine or listen to the radio?), or the assumptions of 1980 concerning the Internet and the in-home personal computer (Only the biggest 500 companies need a computer.). Effective managers get what facts they can within a reasonable time frame. They earn their high incomes by making educated guesses of where opportunities might be, and taking action.

Assumption 3: The Budget Is the Model

Budgeting can and should be used as a model for long-range planning. Insist on forecasts with hard numerical targets. There is no substitute for effective planning and massive commitment of resources. Again, all of these statements are false. It's tough to disagree with each of those points, but they can add up to more of those traditional business school shortcomings. Yes, you've got to have specific objectives and it's important to make your numbers. But what is "long-range planning"? On the battlefield, it's everything that happens up until the first shot is fired. In business, it's all those things until the Mississippi floods or your competitor gets bought out by a conglomerate. Long-term plans and objectives are all well and good, but only to the extent that they affect what I'll do *today*. Effective planning is essential, as are sufficient resources. No one will dispute that. But even more important is flexibility, which authorizes employees to modify those plans and redirect resources as *they* deem necessary. At any given moment, after the first shot is fired, events may transpire that never could have been imagined when you did your long-term plan and employees did their weekly and daily plans. Your people have no time to get back to you, ask you to modify the strategy, and wait for you to return it to them. They need to act now.

Assumption 4: Decision Making Is a Manager's Most Important Job

The manager's job is decision making, making the right management decisions and the tough ones. Implementation and execution are of secondary importance. Again, this idea is false. Many managers respond that decision making, implementation, and execution are all of *equal* importance, but this idea is still false. Implementation and execution are of *primary* importance. This flies in the face of the beliefs of most managers who assume that strategy begins with objectives and then works its way down to tactics for achieving the objectives. But what good is a great strategy if it can't be readily executed—if it can be executed at all? You will be far more successful with a basic and unsophisticated strategy that can be fully and properly implemented. Beyond that, it's likely that you could have a significant differential advantage in some aspect of production or implementation and that a strategy should be developed from the bottom up. I ran across that firsthand with a consumer products company whose headquarters was directing its distributors to put marketing emphasis on a particular package in a highly competitive marketplace. I was speaking with one of the distributors who told me that he was planning to go against the wishes of headquarters and instead fight it out head to head with more traditional packages. His reason? Both he and his major competitor would need to have outside facilities produce products in the new innovative package. But whereas the competitor also had to rely on outside facilities for the traditional package, this distributor produced it on-site, yielding a significant cost advantage. By focusing promotional activity on the package on which he had a differential cost advantage, he was able to build market share, enhance profitability, and deprive his competitor of resources which could have been employed elsewhere. Along the same lines, your company may enjoy a differential advantage of unique product or service features or some form of favorable positioning. Build your strategy *up* from your advantages, not *down* into uncertain execution and implementation.

Assumption 5: Control Is Everything

Specify the organization structure in detail, write clear job descriptions, ensure that every possible contingency is accounted for, and issue orders. Having control guarantees a positive outcome. This is false. Recognize the obsession with control, hallmark of the old management school? Sure, maintaining strict control *will* minimize mistakes, if that's your objective, rather than achieving anything positive today. A while back, I was doing business with an established company that had a headquarters sales-and-marketing staff of 160 people. My first reaction was that 160 seemed a very large number for what had to be done by those individuals. Looking a little deeper, I discovered that none of these people was allowed to send any correspondence, written or electronic, to anyone outside the building, including their own field salespeople, without approval by a person on the staff of the vice president of marketing. If, as happened fairly frequently, that person was out of town for a few days, everything ground to a halt until he returned and could get around to sorting out the several thousand messages awaiting his return. The vice president of marketing could claim with pride that virtually no mistakes were made under his tutelage. I'm sure that was of great comfort to him when a new division president came in and sacked him and 140 of his staff.

Extreme measures of control will minimize mistakes. They will also stifle creativity, prevent employees from reaching their individual potentials, and drive out your best and your brightest. The effective manager is not obsessed with preventing or punishing mistakes; he or she recognizes them as the necessary, often unpleasant, price of developing high achievers willing to make decisions. As a manager, set boundaries and parameters on individuals and teams so that the inevitable mistake will be a hand grenade and not a nuclear explosion. Expect all of your employees to learn from their mistakes and not make the same mistake twice.

Assumption 6: Incentives Yield Performance

Get the incentives right and performance will follow. Straightforward monetary incentives will give very large rewards to top performers and weed out the 30 to 40 percent deadwood who don't want to work. These statements are all false, and not over the 30 to 40 percent figure, either. Yes, money motivates, but only to a point, and its kick is usually only short term. Often it's nothing more than keeping score in a game in which intangibles are a far more effective motivator. An effective manager goes beyond paying people for reaching a stated goal and firing people who don't. Motivation comes about when people love their jobs and can't think of anything they'd rather be doing, whether or not they were being paid for it. This level of commitment takes more than money and cheerleading, and it's the very essence of management, which we will explore later in the book since everything else must be done right before you can get around to motivating employees who are fully committed to the organization.

Assumption 7: Finance People Are Good Managers

A manager who understands finance can manage, since people, products, and services are resources that must be aligned to get good financial results. This idea is false. Finance is the analysis of money and assets, whereas management is the process of a manager and his or her employees working together and communicating with one another with the objective of achieving results. You can't treat employees as if they were entries on a balance sheet. Finance people and accountants often distrust persons in marketing and sales. Your job is to make them comfortable with you, to see you as someone with an eye on watching expenses and achieving bottom-line results. That done, you'll minimize any negative influence they might have on the morale of your employees.

Assumption 8: Increasing Earnings Equals Security

As long as earnings quarter by quarter never stop growing, a company's position is essentially sound. This is another false idea. Since you may have invested in a few of them, there's no point in naming the several companies who were prominent in their fields, consistently improving their earnings, until investors suddenly discovered the reason for the earnings growth: In essence, management had been liquidating the business for years, failing to invest in the future and milking the cow until it finally ran dry. These folks apparently figured that by the time the chickens came home to roost, they'd have moved on to greener pastures on the strength of all their achievements. Earnings growth is one—but only one—measure of a firm's health.

Peters and Waterman (1982) noted these false assumptions more than twenty years ago, which makes it truly astonishing that they persist to this day. We grow too soon old and too late smart. Should you be clinging to any of these notions to this day, perhaps it's time to step back and remember how to spell "assume."

Chapter 4

"What Did You Do Today, Dear?"

Having just shot down several false assumptions that are a prescription for management disaster, let's take on another myth of effective management, namely that the harder one works, the more one gets done. That myth may be basically true for someone digging a ditch, and it's marginally true for a doer such as an outside sales rep, but it's patently false for a manager. Since your mission is to achieve results through others, how hard you work is beside the point, because there is no direct relationship between hard work and positive accomplishment. Inept managers who believe their results are proportional to their activity generally live by the credo that when you lose sight of your objectives, all you need to do is redouble your efforts. Let's look at a case study describing just such a manager, Creighton Barrel from the Bulldawg Beverage Company. As you may surmise, in case studies I've changed the names of the players and their companies, but the situations portrayed are real.

CASE STUDY:
BULLDAWG BEVERAGE COMPANY

Creighton Barrel is a marketing manager with the Bulldawg Beverage Company. "How do you do it?" he is often asked by his co-workers. "We've never seen anyone who works as hard as you do." *This will be another rough day,* he thought as he turned off the expressway ramp at 6:15 a.m. *There's always so much to do at this time of the year, but today I've got to finish that report for Mr. Johnson and at ten a.m. Clay Potts is coming in for his performance review.*

Creighton got to his office at 6:30 a.m. and sat down at his desk. This was his favorite time of the day: No one else had yet arrived and he had a chance to get things done without all the interruptions that bothered him during the day. After waking up with a cup of coffee and reading through the past several days' e-mail and the morning paper, he glanced at the three-inch-high stack of mail and memos in his IN basket. *Better go through that first,* he said to himself. *I haven't looked at any of it since Friday.* But as he got halfway through the stack, he began to shake his head. So much he had to do, and it seemed like everything had to be done yesterday. Creighton then realized it was nearly 7:00 a.m. and decided he'd better check to be sure all the trucks had gotten out on time. He knew there was trouble the moment he caught sight of a truck with its hood up. The driver/salesman was furious: Maintenance had failed to fix his alternator, and now he was going to be late getting out. Creighton and the driver/salesman had just started walking toward the maintenance building when Hap Hazard, the route supervisor, stopped them. "All the trucks went out this morning without any two-liter Bulldawg Cola," he said. "I guess the production center didn't send us a shipment this week." *Oh, no,* thought Creighton, *that's the third time this month.*

It was 7:45 a.m. by the time Creighton and the driver/salesman located a replacement alternator and a mechanic to install it. Back at his desk, Creighton immediately phoned the production center. The manager had not yet come in, so Creighton left an urgent message for the manager to call him back as soon as he arrived.

Creighton decided he'd better get started on the report for Mr. Johnson and began assembling papers from several piles on his desk. He found everything but the monthly chain sales report; it just didn't seem to be anywhere. *No problem,* he thought, *Anita Weekov will be in at 8:30 and I can get a copy from her.* In the meantime, some of the office staff was coming in and this was a good opportunity to take a quick break, have a second cup of coffee, and talk about the company's team in the Metropolis Softball League.

At 9:10 a.m., Creighton was back at his desk with Anita's copy of the chain sales report, but he couldn't find his calculator. *I had it here yesterday,* he thought, *someone must have borrowed it.* His secretary had arrived and he asked her to see if she could find out who had his calculator or whether he could borrow one from someone else. She volunteered to add up the figures herself, but Creighton said no, he could do it himself in the time it would take to show her what to do.

Just before 9:30 a.m., Dusty Rhodes called to remind him of the United Way meeting in a few minutes. *United Way meeting?* Creighton recalled that he was going to be one of the pledge chairpersons in the campaign, but he knew nothing about a meeting. Dusty mentioned that an e-mail had been sent out a week before; as Creighton reviewed his messages, he found it. *Must have missed that when I went through those messages earlier this morning,* he thought to himself.

It was 10:15 a.m. when Creighton returned to find Clay Potts waiting for his performance review. Creighton apologized for being late and for having to delay further by returning the callback from the production center manager, who was again away from his desk. Creighton left another urgent message for the manager to call again.

The performance review was very hurried since Creighton had to attend an 11:00 a.m. meeting to preview promotions that were going to be offered by Bulldawg Beverage Company next season. Also, in the middle of the review, the production center manager called back and said that the two-liter

Bulldawg Cola had been shipped out earlier that morning and should have already arrived. Creighton called Hap to check it out, but Hap was away from his desk.

The 11:00 a.m. meeting lasted until 12:10 p.m., and a follow-up meeting was scheduled for a week later when the marketing managers could get together again to review that day's discussion and talk about organizing a committee to establish procedures for deciding points to be addressed in developing promotion guidelines. After a quick lunch, it was 12:30 p.m.—no time to do much since Creighton was scheduled to go out and meet the store manager at a Winn-Dixie grand opening at 2:00 p.m. But it was just enough time to write all the office employees' names on the United Way pledge cards and distribute them around the office.

The driver/salesman had just finished building the 500-case extra display when Creighton arrived at the Winn-Dixie at 1:55 p.m. Creighton was shocked when he saw it: 250 cases each of Diet Bulldawg Cola and Bulldawg Yello two liter. The driver/salesman explained that he'd wanted the display to be 50 percent Bulldawg Cola as specified, but he changed the order when he found the plant was out of two-liter Bulldawg Cola. Creighton called the plant to talk to Hap and waited on hold until Hap could be located, fifteen minutes later. Creighton finally talked to Hap, verified that the two-liter Bulldawg Cola had arrived at the plant, and arranged to have a truck loaded with 250 cases sent to the Winn-Dixie. By the time Creighton and the driver/salesman rebuilt the display and Creighton got back to the plant, it was nearly 5:00 p.m. The next hour was frantic as Creighton tried to make phone calls and meet with the other marketing managers before they all went home.

A little after 6:00 p.m., Creighton sat down at his desk, alone in the office again. *This place is a madhouse,* he thought to himself. *I never get a chance to get anything done. Now at last everyone is gone and I can get to that report for Mr. Johnson.* Just then, Creighton realized that he never had gotten a replacement calculator, so he checked around the office trying to find one. No luck. By the time he had added up all the figures manually, it was nearly 7:00 p.m. *Looks like another late dinner again tonight,* he sighed. *It's going to take me at least a couple of hours to finish writing this report. I wonder if I have a package of crackers in my briefcase.* He opened the briefcase and found no crackers, but he did relocate his calculator.

Analysis

I suspect you've run across a few Creighton Barrels, and to some extent you may have just a little of him in you. Most people would agree that Creighton is extremely dedicated to his company and his job. He cares and he works hard. When he gets home at night and is asked, "What did you do today, dear?" he probably speaks with pride of all his activities. But Creighton is extremely ineffective in the role of a manager, a classic case of a good doer being promoted to management. He is simultaneously busy while consistently wasting time, guilty of all ten classic time wasters.

TEN CLASSIC TIME WASTERS

Time Waster 1: Phone Interruptions and Visitors

Most managers spend a good portion of their day dealing with others, in person or by phone—perhaps too much of their day. Although it's not as personal, e-mail may be far more efficient and effective for many or most communications, particularly those dealing with explicit points of content. Back in the olden days, executives at General Motors had to go through a secretary and make an appointment to speak to the person in the office next door. That's a bit too formal and impersonal. But many managers today still won't e-mail someone ten feet away, believing they need to seem more personable by getting up, sticking their head around the corner, and asking, "Are you busy?" The other person will respond, "No," even though he or she is. If you feel awkward about sending such short-distance e-mails, bounce the idea off your colleagues before you initiate it as a routine procedure. Chances are, they'll see it makes a lot of sense, and you'll all get more done every day.

Even though you may increase your utilization of e-mail, the phone, of course, is still going to ring. That does not mean, however, that you should answer your phone every time it rings or have an "open-door" policy in which colleagues and employees can walk in whenever they wish. You want to be accessible, but you won't ever get top priorities done if you're being interrupted every five minutes. One of the most important management activities of Creighton's day was the performance review for Clay Potts. It was unconscionable that he was late and then played phone tag in the middle of the meeting. You can just imagine how focused and motivated Clay was when he walked out of that fiasco.

When you're dealing with a top priority, close your door and let voice mail pick up your calls. Make sure everyone understands that means you are not to be interrupted except for a genuine emergency. One of our managers set the boundaries when he was in a conference with a colleague discussing a very sensitive situation. The phone rang, and he let voice mail pick it up. The person calling chose the "If you would like to speak with a human" option and got his secretary, who phoned the manager to let him know someone was holding. He also ignored her call and let voice mail pick *it* up. She tried a second time with the same result. She then walked down the hall and tapped on his door. He ignored it. Finally, she procured a passkey, opened the door, stuck her head in, and said, "You have a phone call." He glared at her and replied, "No shit." Please understand that I in no way advocate tokens of disrespect and the use of profanity. That said, word of this event spread quickly and employees had no doubt what was meant by the closed door: Don't interrupt unless the building is on fire and flames are lapping at the door.

Many managers minimize the impact of this time waster by setting aside set hours for "phone time," when they make and return calls. Best times for this are just before lunch or at the end of the day, when people are less likely to linger with superfluous conversation. In a short time, folks become acclimated to phoning you or expecting your call between, say, 11:00 a.m. and 12:00 p.m. or 4:00 and 5:00 p.m. Along the same lines, establish a "reception hour" when you're generally available for people to pop by briefly.

You'll get a lot more done all day by having a "quiet time" for setting and working on top priorities. Do this first thing. If office hours are 9:00 to 5:00, it might work out well to have quiet time from 8:00 to 9:00 followed by reception hour from 9:00 to 10:00. Yes, we just agreed that managers are not paid merely to work hard, but coming in an hour early does not mean you can leave an hour sooner. Do another quiet time between 5:00 and 6:00, and let the traffic clear up a little.

When dealing with others by phone, in person, or even via e-mail, get to the point straightaway. Of course, a little banter and small talk is fine, but add a minute of chatter to every contact of the day and you'll be lucky to be out the door before 7:00.

Many managers prefer to hold meetings in their office, familiar territory where they feel the advantage of home turf. The problem with that is that it's easier for you to get out of someone else's office than it is to get them out of yours. You may be able to control the environment more effectively by going to their cubicle, meeting in the halls, or, at the least, remaining standing while in your office.

Time Waster 2: Paperwork/Messy Desk

Nowadays, this time robber is also known as "e-mail." Remember how technology was supposed to relieve you of all those mundane tasks? Unfortunately, the system that used to produce twenty pages of memos a day now churns out 150 e-mails, with attachments. Creighton had no way of organizing all that information, had no idea how to extract data and reports from the decision support system, if there was one, and acted like a tail trying to wag the dog.

As with telephone calls and drop-ins, establish a system for e-mail, checking it no more than two or three times a day. Generally, you'll find that only a small percentage of paper memos and e-mail messages—perhaps as few as one in five—require more than a few seconds to handle. Set them aside until you can dedicate the necessary time. As for the rest, do a quick reply, forward to someone else, or delete. Read all the interoffice spam if you wish, but don't plan on leaving the office before 7:30 p.m.

Insist on executive summaries of no more than one page. Attachments and appendixes may be added, but a busy manager, properly empowering his or her people, will seldom read them.

Creighton's desk was a mess. It should have been cleared of everything but the project at hand with a filing system, electronic or manual, and procedures for reviewing and deleting files.

You will encounter detailed reports and articles from your company, customers, and industry, in written or electronic form. Some you don't need to see at all. Trash 'em. For the others, scan the index or table of contents and then scan the report or article for an overall view. That may be all you need. If necessary, go back and read carefully only the appropriate sections.

Time Waster 3: Socializing/Wasting Time of Others

There's nothing inherently wrong with a little socializing and wasting time, at the appropriate time and the appropriate place. Creighton, unfortunately, chose to do his at what should have been his quiet time, first thing in the morning. Similarly, as we've noted, friendly small talk is all well and good as long as the several minutes times several people don't add up to several hours. As a related point, beware of those people who consistently impose on you with socializing and gossip. Some need to talk about their problems, some enjoy talking about others' problems, and some just like to sit around and complain all day. As in the example of the manager who established the ground rules concerning his closed door, you need to draw the line with people who want to drop by and chat too frequently. There's no need for a serious discussion. Simply always be busy and have no time to talk with them. They may feel hurt, but that's okay. It's better than them hurting you.

Time Waster 4: Failure to Delegate Unnecessary and Unimportant Tasks

Creighton spent most of his day doing things that readily could have been done by someone else. One has to wonder what his secretary and other subordinates were doing all day. Apparently not much to help Creighton achieve his objectives.

Working as teams and being a team player are popular concepts, sort of like parenthood. Who can possibly be against them? Creighton failed as a manager, though, when he took a valid concept too far. I'm sure he felt like a team player at the Winn-Dixie store. But doing a task that could have been handled by an unskilled laborer was simply not the best use of his time. Similarly, he was in the office doing mundane clerical tasks that could have been handled by others with minimal training. Perhaps Creighton just hates to ask someone to do something he can do himself. Perhaps he feels that asking someone to add up figures or fill in donation cards is inconsistent with the theme of empowering teams. But none of that is at issue. Here, we are looking at the assignment of basic tasks, and only one thing is at issue: the economics of differential advantage. If someone else who makes less money than you can do the task as well as you, that person should handle it, not you. I know of one manager who put in two hours on the copier rather than ask the six-dollar-an-hour intern to do it. His rationale was that he didn't have all that much to do at the time and hated to put the intern on the copier while he sat in his office twiddling his thumbs. My suggestion to him would be: Go in your office, close the door, and think about what you *ought* to be doing for the next two hours. Can't think of anything? Then you better start looking for work. Your present company certainly doesn't need you, and sooner or later they're bound to figure that out.

Time Waster 5: Lack of Planning/Shifting Priorities

Creighton demonstrated one of the most fundamental characteristics of an incompetent manager, or an incompetent doer, for that matter, by spending his day reacting to events as they occurred instead of starting off with a little quiet time to review priorities and create an action plan. It would even have been a valid use of his time, when he arrived at 6:30 a.m., to go down and meet with the driver/salesmen *before* they left on their routes if the purpose of the visit had been to glean information about the state of the marketplace and to get input on management issues that needed his attention. As it is, Creighton has no idea where he's going, but he's making great time.

Time Waster 6: Crisis Management/Recurring Crises

The world's most organized person cannot plan every activity for every minute of every day, because unexpected events are bound to happen and unforeseen crises will pop up. Realistically, if you can free an hour or two a day to dedicate to your personal top priorities, you may be doing pretty well. That said, there is no excuse for enduring recurring crises from the same people and the same sources. Creighton appears content to react to crises emanating from the production center instead of taking a proactive stance and initiating action to prevent the same problems in the future.

Time Waster 7: Ineffective Communication

Interpersonal relationships, including the profession of management, are all about communication. The content component of communication must be complete and explicit. The relationship component must generate respect and trust. You're going to encounter numerous aspects of communication throughout this book, especially those intangibles of leadership and motivation we'll discuss in Part III. At this stage, discussing foundation, let's take this concept only so far as to observe that no one seems to deal with, or communicate particularly well with, anyone else at Bulldawg Beverage Company. Creighton doesn't appear to have any significant contact with his people throughout the day and so is failing to utilize or develop them. He seems to enjoy playing phone tag rather than leaving explicit messages detailing what he needs from the person he's calling.

These are symptoms of managers each running their own little duchies, holding onto their proprietary information as if it were a security blanket. People are isolated with no free flow of information throughout the organization.

Time wasters 1 through 7 are the most basic, and no one can be effective without conquering them. Speaking with managers, I generally find they believe these time wasters are characteristic of many of their colleagues but not of them. Since *everyone* seems to believe that, some personal assessment may be in order. If these time wasters are endemic throughout your organization, stop right here and fix this dysfunctional management style before going any farther.

Time wasters 8 through 10 reflect the organizational system and will be dealt with in detail later in Part I. Time waster 8 is meetings, the subject of Chapter 5. Time waster 9 is duplication of effort or no specific responsibilities, a function of ineffective delegation, which will be covered in Chapter 6. Finally, time waster 10, decision by committee, describes an admirable and necessary concept—teams—which has been improperly implemented. We'll go into that as part of Chapter 12, the capstone of Part I. At a quick glance, though, you can see that Creighton was guilty of all these, giving him a perfect ten for ten in the time-waster department. You may also get an inkling that Creighton in not atypical of other managers at Bulldawg Beverage and that this organization needs a lot of work on its foundation.

Chapter 5

Meetings

Since management is all about causing things to happen through others, interpersonal contact and communication skills are basic to your foundation. We just noted that for the sake of efficiency it might make sense to utilize e-mail for specific points of content. But for the intangibles, especially organizing, leading, and coaching, generally you'll deal with colleagues face to face. Whether your contact is with one person or several dozen, you're having a meeting. If that meeting is not handled properly, your effectiveness is bound to be impaired. Furthermore, if you have empowered a team to handle a project and they get together, without you, to meet, they, too, best understand the fundamentals of managing meetings. If they don't have that knowledge and skills, all your good intentions at empowerment are likely to be for naught.

The following case study consists of transcript highlights of a community organization meeting called to plan a fund-raising activity. It's a good example of some of the things that can happen in meetings.

CASE STUDY: THE PLANNING MEETING

Amy Attacker, Dan Downer, and Irving Introvert are all seated around a table. It's 7:10 p.m.

DAN: Has anyone heard from Corey Comedian?

AMY: He's only ten minutes late. That's pretty good for him.

DAN: I called Wanda Wanderer this afternoon. She said she'd be here.

AMY: If Wanda doesn't show up in five minutes, I move we kick her off the task force.

DAN: She probably got lost in traffic again.

AMY: It's ten past. We're supposed to start at seven. Anybody that's late twice in a row, to hell with them. Irving, second my motion.

IRVING: What motion?

AMY: Just second the damn motion so we can call the question.

IRVING: Second.

AMY: Call the question.

[Wanda strolls in.]

WANDA: Hi, y'all. Did I miss anything?

DAN: No, it looks like Amy just withdrew her motion.

AMY: I'm not withdrawing it. I'm tabling it until the next meeting.

WANDA: What are we going to do tonight?

DAN: The same thing we didn't finish last week and the week before: the charity fund-raiser.

WANDA: Oh, when is it?

AMY: In two weeks, dummy. Where have *you* been?

DAN: If we ever get it organized. I'll end up having to do it all myself at the last minute.

[Corey bursts into the room, doing a shuffle and tipping his cap.]

COREY: Hey, hey, hey!

AMY: It's about time. I haven't got all night.

COREY: Oh, planning something big later this evening?

AMY: If I were, that would exclude you.

WANDA: What are we going to do for the fund-raiser?

DAN: We were talking about a luau, but people don't like to dress up except at Halloween. And no one likes Hawaiian cooking.

COREY: Who cares? We're going to have three kegs.

WANDA: I can bring chow mein.

AMY: This is a luau, not the Chinese New Year, you idiot.

DAN: I don't think a dinner is a good idea, anyhow.

COREY: Maybe we could hold a Richard Nixon look-alike contest and charge everyone five bucks' admission.

AMY: This is for charity. I move we make it ten bucks.

WANDA: What if everybody brought a covered dish?

AMY: I made a motion. Second it, Irving.

IRVING: Second.

DAN: Don't you think we ought to talk about it for a while? This is stupid.

AMY: Call the question. If we vote to charge everyone ten bucks admission, we can forget about the fund-raiser, and this meeting, and go home.

DAN: It makes more sense to let people in for nothing and charge them ten bucks to leave.

AMY: [raising her hand]: All in favor.

WANDA: Maybe we can do a car wash.

COREY: If we do a car wash, make sure Irving brings his truck so we can put a keg in the back.

AMY: That'll be just great. All you guys getting drunk at a charity fund-raiser.

COREY: We'll cover it with a blanket. Nobody will see it.

DAN: [raising his hand]: All opposed. Vote is one to one with three abstentions. The motion fails.

WANDA: What if we had a bake sale?

COREY: That'll work. I'm on a strict high-carb diet.

DAN: Dinner, talent show, car wash, bake sale. One group or another is always doing them. Maybe we should think it over and see if we can come up with any better ideas by next week.

AMY: Is that a motion?

DAN: I guess so.

AMY: Second it, Irving.

IRVING: Second.

AMY: All in favor.

[Amy, Corey, and Dan raise their hands.]

AMY: Opposed.

[No hands are raised.]

DAN: Then I guess we'll wrap this up next week, same time, same place, same dull people.

WANDA: Are we doing the car wash?

Analysis

The planning meeting illustrated what can happen when different and often incompatible personalities overshadow the stated purposes of a meeting. In this example, it appears as though Dan was the nominal meeting leader, if there was one at all, though Amy seemed to dominate the conversation. For a meeting to be successful, the meeting leader, supported by other group members, must recognize and effectively deal with the personalities that can detract from group efforts and positive accomplishments. Let's look at the five meeting demons one at a time.

Amy Attacker wants to dominate others to further her personal agenda. She always has an answer and is not interested in the opinions of others. To counter her influence, direct questions on the current topic to others, perhaps cutting her off diplomatically with something along the lines of "That's a good point. Does anyone else have some ideas on that?"

Corey Comedian is constantly joking around and distracting others. He just can't grow up and be serious. Treat him like a recalcitrant eighth grader without patronizing him, seeking his input on specific points of content. Compliment him on positive actions and input.

Dan Downer has negative attitudes about group members, ideas, and activities and is always pointing out why something won't work. Put him on the spot by soliciting his ideas and suggestions for what he thinks *would* work, and get others to make comments that counter his negativity.

Irving Introvert lacks the confidence to take a role or say anything, responding only to questions directed at him. Speak with him before the meeting and help him plan for involvement. Follow that up by positively reinforcing his comments and actions.

Finally, *Wanda Wanderer* will suddenly bring up irrelevant points. She appears to lack awareness of the group's purpose or its agenda. Don't allow her to derail the meeting topic. Get her back on track with a comment such as, "That's interesting and we may want to discuss it later. But just now . . ." or ask her direct questions about the topic at hand.

THE SIX RULES FOR MEETINGS

With an awareness of the relationship issues, structure the meeting itself with the six rules for meetings.

Rule 1: Send out a notice on the specific agenda and participants well in advance of the meeting. Then, stick to the agenda and use its legitimacy to keep certain personalities on topic. Many disruptions can be cut off at the pass with a simple "You raise a valid point, but that's not on our agenda today."

Rule 2: Participants attend *only* those segments which apply to them. We've all been subjected to the agony of being in a meeting in which two people engaged in a twenty-minute debate that concerned only them. Have them get together and hash things out before or after the meeting. Or similarly, there's a two-hour meeting with twenty people and only half the meeting time is relevant to everyone. Let's say you have a two-hour meeting with twenty people scheduled from 8:00 to 10:00 a.m. If one hour of that applies to everyone, set that part of the agenda between 8:00 and 9:00. Then, consistent with continuity, schedule other segments of the agenda ranked according to a topic's applicability to the greatest number of people. Some people can leave at 9:00, others can split at 9:30. A few can break out at 9:00 and return between 9:30 and 10:00. As long as you have a specific agenda and follow it, everyone can make better use of their time and no one is sitting through a meeting segment that has nothing to do with them.

Rule 3: Start and end on time. This, of course, is absolutely essential if you're going to have an agenda and stick to it. The problem is, invariably it's the scheduled start time and certain key players have yet to arrive. This requires one simple solution: Start without them. Lock the doors at the exact scheduled start time and force latecomers to knock on the door and walk sheepishly to their seats. If decisions need to be made according to the agenda, and missing parties have not made prior arrangements or submitted a proxy, proceed without them. At the very first meeting of any team, the meeting leader needs to make it absolutely clear this is how things will be handled. Many members may not believe he or she is serious about starting on time and enforcing the consequences. It may take one explicit example, but after that people will find a way to be there when they're supposed to be there.

Rule 4: Send an e-mail summary *that day* of all decisions and each individual's assigned activities and deadlines. This will avoid any misunderstandings that can arise in a meeting's oral communication format.

Rule 5: If the meeting is with employees of an organization, for profit or not for profit, calculate the total dollar cost of the meeting in the e-mail summary, including everything from salaries to sandwiches. Double each person's salary to account for benefits, related business expenses, and fixed costs: An employee making $50,000 a year really costs the company more like $100,000. Divide that by 2,000 hours a year: That employee costs the company fifty dollars an hour. Add it all up. If the cost of the meeting exceeds its contribution to the company's bottom line, it shouldn't have been held. Likewise for a committee or task force: Dissolve it or maybe just outsource it and its entire function.

Rule 6: This is the last one, but it supersedes all the others. Ask yourself whether the meeting is necessary in the first place. How much can be delegated or handled with phone calls or e-mail?

In his book *On Managing,* Mark McCormack (1996), whom you will meet in Chapter 10, has some additional points on holding effective meetings. First of all, a corollary to Rule 6: When in doubt, don't call a meeting at all. Then, don't let yourself get locked into meetings as a matter of tradition. Do you have a weekly staff meeting mostly because you've always had a weekly staff meeting? Periodically shake things up, changing who's there, the meeting format, and its place, time, and length. He suggests you not let people get too comfy, because it just prolongs the meeting. Consider having wooden chairs and skip the refreshments. Finally, McCormack urges managers to go into meetings with an open mind receptive to suggestions. Be able to say, "You're right. I never considered that." Roughly translated, you are communicating, "I'm wrong."

Chapter 6

Delegation: The Big "D"

The Big "D" is delegation, and it's the very essence of effective management, which is, as we've described, causing action through others. Delegation is all about accomplishing results for which we are ultimately responsible, through the activities and efforts of our subordinates. Delegation is, always has been, and probably always will be the bedrock upon which management is built. However, *how* we delegate is different from a decade or two ago, reflecting the fact that how we manage is now different from a decade or two ago.

As noted earlier, the word *delegation* has been replaced by *empowerment,* but empowerment is nothing more than effective delegation. The bottom line is if you're a competent manager getting the most out of your people, delegation and empowerment are one and the same. A few pages back, we were describing people as resources whose minds hold the potential for an individual's optimum contribution to meaningful achievement. If by "delegation" you mean using only your people's arms and legs to carry out assigned tasks, you're not making the best use of those resources. Instead, if you turn over every aspect of a project to others and allow them to work together to make decisions and implement solutions, that's empowerment. And that's teamwork. And all that is just a little bit scary.

At this very outset of discussing the big "D," it's important to address a few fundamentals. First of all, to do it right, delegation means letting go. By delegating you will have less control and involvement over day-to-day activities. Individuals or the team may take different approaches to tasks and reach different conclusions than you would have, and mistakes will be made. You probably don't want to know that so you might have read over it quickly, hoping it wasn't there, so let's reiterate: Giving up control, and permitting others to use their minds, means that mistakes will happen. But it's not all bad. If people never make decisions and never try anything, you'll minimize mistakes, but nothing much of significance will be achieved. Allowing for mistakes ultimately results in far more meaningful accomplishments. Effective managers accept mistakes as part of the price of achievement and excellence, realizing that "zero defects" equates to low brain utilization and even lower morales. To keep it all in proper perspective, manage mistakes and their attendant costs by clearly articulating boundaries in which the employees operate. Within those boundaries, employees run with the project and implement decisions. Before going outside those boundaries, however, they need to run it by you.

KEY CONCEPTS FOR EMPOWERED DELEGATION

There are four key concepts for empowered delegation.

Concept 1: Responsibility

You pass decision-making responsibility to the individual or team. Keep in mind, however, that delegation does not relieve you of the ultimate responsibility.

Concept 2: Resources

You must ensure that your people have whatever financial backing and training necessary to succeed. They must have all necessary accessibility, cooperation, and support from persons both inside and outside the organization. Most critical of all, they must have access to any and all information pertaining to the project at hand. This important point causes discomfort to many managers who tend to withhold information from employees who do not have a narrowly defined "need to know." This belief is predicated on the assumption that secrecy is necessary to prevent proprietary information from reaching the competition, and that *is* a valid concern. That said, the failure to share information openly, even the fact that profitability is projected to decline and layoffs may be necessary in six months, communicates to employees that you really don't trust them and that you're not all in this together. Most important of all, opening information to your employees enables them to make optimum use of that brainpower you're paying them for.

Concept 3: Authority

This is power, a resource which empowers employees to enforce decisions that are made. Whether authority is bestowed by you or by a higher-up in the organization, it must be made clear that compliance and cooperation is respectfully requested and expected. Let me share a couple of stories that illustrate this in both a negative and positive light. My first experience was a negative one. I was working with a large multinational corporation, dealing with Mr. K., who had just taken the newly created position of corporate marketing director. This corporation had a U.S. division. The U.S. division had a close working relationship with corporate management, communicating openly and sharing information. In contrast, the international division was fiercely independent, ran its own show, and provided corporate management little more than basic sales and financial data on a monthly basis. Mr. K. believed he needed more timely information to identify problems sooner and assigned me to create a system for daily reporting of sales and financial information from the international division. I met with the international division marketing director and presented a proposal for such a system. He said it all looked good to him, but a month later nothing was happening, so Mr. K. asked me to follow up. Again, the international division marketing director assured me that everything was coming along. But after another month, still nothing had changed, and an increasingly impatient Mr. K. called me in and demanded action. I called the international division marketing director again, about my sixth follow-up, and asked if we yet had a timetable for program implementation. There was a pregnant pause of about five seconds, and then he said, "Bob, can I speak frankly to you?" Taken somewhat aback, I said, "Sure, Ted." He replied, "Bob, we're not going to do it. We don't report to any corporate marketing director. We report to the president of the company himself, no one else!" A great learning experience and example of delegation's 3rd key concept. The president had created the position of corporate marketing director but had given him no power of enforcement. The international division was not about to accept a role subordinate to the corporate marketing director, and the president, who may well have realized that he maintained his position at the behest of the international division, was not about to engage in a game of chicken. Your humble narrator, another rung down the ladder, had no way of making anything happen. The corporate marketing director should never have given me responsibility with no authority, but in retrospect I learned the valuable lesson of never again allowing myself to be put in the position of not having a complete understanding of my authority or lack thereof. In a subsequent situation, when a national sales manager commissioned me to oversee a project with his field sales reps, the first time I heard "Says who?" a light went on, and I had the manager notify his reps that I was operating under his auspices and that their cooperation was expected and appreciated.

Concept 4: Accountability

Clear, observable, measurable performance standards and deadlines constitute accountability. Throughout this book, I'll talk about the need of having employees work together toward the achievement of shared objectives. That's what teamwork is all about, and working in teams is a great idea unless the team deteriorates into decision by committee and/or teams give individuals a place to hide. When you create a situation in which more than one person is responsible for a project, be sure to have accountability for each individual as well as the team as a whole. I've seen numerous examples in which team members do peer evaluations to assess individual performance, but personally I believe that's a management cop-out. Peer evaluations are seldom completely objective, tainted by personal popularity and nonperformers covering one another's ass. You, the manager, must conduct individual performance reviews. You, the manager, determine what raises individuals get or whether they are to be retained by the organization at all. Thus, you, the manager, must find a way of quantifying the contribution of each individual under your sphere of responsibility.

Now that I've covered the basics of delegation, take a look at another case study. As you read through it, consider this manager's dedication and competence, and informally evaluate his effectiveness as a delegator.

CASE STUDY:
CONSOLIDATED CUPCAKE CORPORATION

Douglas Furr is a branch manager for the Consolidated Cupcake Corporation. It was 11:15 a.m., Tuesday, and he was busily preparing to clear his desk before leaving for the airport to catch the 1:30 p.m. flight to Tampa, where he was attending a management seminar that would last until Friday noon. The first thing he noticed was the partially completed sales report from the previous weekend. All he needed were the Kroger figures, and to get them he called Marilyn Crabbe, the marketing manager. Marilyn was out back, so Doug left the message, "Important: Call or see me about Kroger sales before you go to lunch."

Next, Doug leafed through the papers from his IN basket to see what needed to be handled before he left. There were three items: A meeting at 10:00 a.m. Wednesday to organize holiday promotions; an invitation from his college alumni board to attend a dinner the following Monday to honor a retiring professor; and a request from the vice president of marketing for a report on annual sales by product in Piggly Wiggly stores for the past three years.

First, he called his assistant Jim Schourtz about the Wednesday morning meeting. Jim was out, so he sent an e-mail message: "Please plan to attend the holiday promotion meeting, Wednesday morning at 10." *Good,* thought Doug. *I can see him when I get back and find out what happened.* Next Doug composed a memo on his computer to the college alumni board, saying that he was very sorry but had other commitments for Monday and would be unable to attend. His secretary was at lunch, so Doug printed it out and attached a note, "Please put this in today's mail," and left the memo on her desk. The final item, Piggly Wiggly sales, was no real problem, although Virginia Hamm, who generated those figures, had been out of the office for a couple of days and wouldn't be back until tomorrow. It took Doug only ten minutes of clicking through computer files to find the data and just three or four minutes to transcribe the figures. He then composed and printed out a memo to the vice president saying that he'd attached the requested information, adding a quick note to his secretary to deliver these in person.

It was almost noon, and Doug took another look around his desk and office. A file folder caught his eye: midyear budget review. *Wow,* he thought, *it's a good thing I saw that. It's due Friday morning.* Doug realized that it would take at least a couple of hours to compile the report and that he'd never be able to get it done before leaving for the airport, and began to consider who he could get to do it for him. Just then Don Grey walked by. Don was fifty-three, had been passed up for promotion several times, and worked at a number of odds and ends around the office, killing time until he took early retirement at fifty-five. Doug asked Don to come into his office and was about to begin explaining the budget review project when Marilyn returned his call and asked what sales he needed. Doug said he wanted the Kroger sales for the previous weekend and Marilyn said she'd get them right away.

Doug showed Don the budget review folder and told him what was needed for the report. Don said he didn't know anything about budgets and wanted to go to lunch, but Doug assured him that everything he needed was in the file and that if he had any questions, all he had to do was follow the format from the first quarter review. Meanwhile, Marilyn dropped in with the sales figures and Doug was able to compose the sales report and a cover memo as Don looked through the file.

It was now 12:30 p.m. and time to leave for the airport. Doug thanked Don for his help and promised he'd have no problems with the review. *Man,* thought Doug as he left the office, *it was tough getting out of here on time, but at least everything's all set.*

Analysis

At first blush, it appears that Douglas Furr is not perfect but at least an improvement over Creighton Barrel from Bulldawg Beverage. Creighton may have worked a little harder, but Doug got more done. Or did he?

Doug's clear and overriding number-one priority is to get out of Dodge for the rest of the week. We'll leave unanswered the question of whether a management seminar justifies killing three and a half days of prime time and, even if it were free, whether it would yield more benefits than reading a book on management an hour a night. Unless he's flying in from the West Coast, why would he need to be catching a 1:30 p.m. flight in the first place? He plans a little beach time or some unwinding around the pool or the bar, perhaps. Is it January and is he flying in from north of the 42nd parallel? That would certainly make the seminar of greater value to his company.

Beyond his potentially questionable motives, look at how he uses his people. No minds, only arms and legs. No empowerment, only the assigning of tasks he wants to get out of the way. He walks out of the office believing everything is all set, but just what will await him on his return Monday morning? Don Grey, whose own number-one priority is to go to lunch and tick off one more day before retirement, certainly will never again make the mistake of walking past Doug's door. Do you think that budget review will be buttoned down just right? Jim Schourtz has been assigned to attend a meeting with no idea of what he is to do while there or afterward. Since Jim is Doug's assistant, why hasn't he been empowered to make any and all decisions pertaining to holiday promotions? Had Doug begun this process first thing Monday morning instead of two hours before boarding his flight, he could have held a premeeting briefing with Jim to give him all the needed information, guidelines, and boundaries.

One thing you can say for Doug's secretary: She's learned to keep out of sight. Therefore she gets out of low-priority time-wasting tasks that Doug ends up doing himself. Douglas Furr is neither dedicated nor effective, and watching him operate raises disturbing doubts about the competence of *his* manager.

Assuming that you *are* dedicated, and that after reading this book—not just attending a seminar—you are an effective and competent manager, consider what you need to do to embark on being an empowering delegator. As a starting point, make believe you're leaving, or being run over by a truck on your evening run, or shot by a jealous spouse—yours or someone else's—today. Who would do what? Of course you like to believe you're indispensable, but no one is. The world will go on just fine without you. Then, having surmised who would do what under those conditions, have those people do those respective things anyway. You may have already grasped the fact that you are setting out to eliminate your job. Right! That is exactly your objective, and do not fear this means you will no longer be needed and thus become unemployed. Managers don't get fired for eliminating their own jobs. They get promoted, usually to a position with considerably more responsibility, and attendant compensation, in hope they can eliminate *that* job as well.

To make this process succeed, maintain the perspective of making your employees, not just yourself, look better. Give credit. It's amazing how much you can cause to happen if you never worry about who gets the credit. Your manager, if he or she is competent, is well aware of who's making things happen. On the other side of the same coin, absorb blame. When the inevitable mistakes occur, resist the temptation to blame your employees. Back up their decisions and actions. When asked why things didn't go quite right, your response should be,"No excuse. We'll take care of that."

THE FIVE PRINCIPLES OF DELEGATION

Principle 1: Choose the Right People

Choose those who are capable of handling the task and who will complement one another. Think about how the project might contribute to individual training and development. Then, empower your employees with the authority to do the task and standards of account-ability for getting it done.

Principle 2: Delegate to Challenge

Delegate important and unusual tasks, not just tasks you don't want to do yourself. These fun, interesting, and challenging projects can significantly impact the organization.

Principle 3: Delegate Specific Responsibilities

Avoid gaps, in which no one has been assigned responsibility, and overlays, in which more than one person or team has responsibility for the same task. Provide clear boundaries for the scope of the project and decision-making parameters.

Principle 4: Be Patient and Take Your Time

The team will need time to become oriented and allow its own leadership to evolve. Individuals need time to acquire the expertise to handle the project properly. Provide a realistic time line for accomplishments. Remember the concept of comparative advantage: If certain persons can handle a task at less total cost, it's reasonable to expect them to take a little longer to get it done, especially if they're neophytes.

Principle 5: Involve Them in the Process, Then Leave Them Alone

Involvement leads to ownership and commitment, so communicate with team members to get them on board and up and running. However, once a project has been delegated, let them handle it. They will use their own resourcefulness to work things out and make the day-to-day decisions. Don't bother them.

Chapter 7

The Organization Man Is Exposed

In the first six chapters I've covered the basics of the foundation: what management is all about, and points concerning an effective personal management style. Now, in the next four chapters, I'll put these ideas into perspective and discuss how thinking about management and organizations has evolved in the past half century. To do that, I'll look at the insights of four writers. I've chosen these writers for two reasons. First, at the time they were written, each of their books had a significant impact, affecting how managers viewed themselves and their roles in an organization. This impact was both enlightening and disturbing, shaking up the status quo. Each book made a contribution to the business thinking of its day and provided solid ideas for making individuals and organizations more effective. The second reason for discussing these writers is that their ideas are as valid and applicable today as they were twenty to fifty years ago. Issues they raised remain relevant in twenty-first century organization cultures, and understanding these issues is essential.

CORPORATE LIFE IN THE 1950s

I was a teenaged entrepreneur, mowing lawns and selling everything from candy bars to Christmas wreaths, when William H. Whyte Jr. published *The Organization Man* in 1956. Though I didn't read the book until years later, I can still remember the stir it caused at the time. Remember, now, these were the Eisenhower years, when we all lived in the make-believe world you see in television reruns and old movies. World War II had been over only eleven years, and to adults ages thirty and up the war was a recent, and extraordinarily significant, event. After World War II, veterans had married and moved into the civilian corporate workplace. Most wives stayed home raising the children. Everything was idyllic: the depression was over, the war was over, most had their own homes in Levittown. Americans were ostensibly happy and fulfilled, living on baseball, the Mouseketeers, 6.5-ounce bottles of Coca-Cola, and dreams of a Chevy Bel Air. We never, not once, questioned the notion that ours was a perfect world. Dad went to work and earned the money. Mom stayed home and raised the family. No one doubted that America was, as portrayed on *The Adventures of Ozzie and Harriet* and *Father Knows Best,* exclusively white, Anglo-Saxon, heterosexual, and if not Protestant then at least Christian. The governor of a major state who later became president was once asked why, back in his days as governor, he had not done more to address the needs of African Americans and other minorities. His apologetic answer, "We didn't know they were there," was received with incredulous shock. But it revealed something about the fantasy world the American majority was living in at the time: we *didn't* know they were there. They certainly weren't on prime-time television, living in the suburbs, or employed as managers in corporations.

William Whyte struck the initial blow that shattered the illusion of our "ideal" lives in his pointed description of developing norms in corporate life after World War II. A half century later, *The Organization Man* remains descriptive of many organizations today, especially large, traditional bureaucracies, government, and not-for-profit organizations. Since the vast majority of us must deal with such entities on a regular basis—as an employee, customer, or partner—it's critical to understand, recognize, and deal with Whyte's concepts and suggestions.

The Top-Down Military Model

Today, we would classify Whyte's portrayal of corporate management as a description of the top-down military model. That, of course, is *exactly* what corporate life was in 1956, reflecting the white male veterans who had brought the World War II style of management with them into civilian life. As noted in Chapter 2, that system had been viable in the world economy from 1945 until the mid-1950s. A few years after Whyte's book, American management had begun to accept the possibility that changes might be in order, though in 1956 everything seemed to be working fairly well. Thus, *The Or-*

ganization Man was not received as a solution to a problem or a crisis, but was looking forward in time to what Whyte perceived would be the ultimate failure of the status quo. History proved him right, and his observations gained more and more credibility in succeeding years. The major impact of the book at its time of publication in 1956, therefore, was not an upheaval of organizational thinking but an enlightenment within middle-class America about what was happening to us as individuals.

Whyte's basic concept was that you do not just *work* for the organization but *belong* to it as well, spiritually and physically. Dad's identity *was* the company, just as it *was* the U.S. Army, and his mind and body existed only as extensions of the organization. Whyte described the organization's core premise as "belongingness," the deep emotional security that comes from total integration with the group. This was based on the belief that the group was superior to the individual, attempting to create a harmonious atmosphere in which the group would bring out the best in everyone. Everyone wore the same uniform—suit and tie—at the office, for the absolutely essential company socializing, and also in the ninety-degree heat of an afternoon ball game. No one made waves, questioned authority, or colored outside the lines. You lived in the right neighborhood, had the right friends and affiliations, and joined the right country club. You drank, smoked cigarettes, laughed at the boss's jokes, and hoped your wife created the proper impression on the boss's wife. Your children were perfect in every way. Junior liked to play baseball and looked forward to a business career after fulfilling his military obligation. Little Suzy loved dolls and hoped to attend a college where she could meet a good husband. Drugs were medicines purchased at a pharmacy. Whyte found this proliferation of organization life into the suburbs to be a most interesting phenomenon, observing not merely housing but also a new social institution, noting an unmistakable similarity in the way of life, in essence a communal way of living and a one-class society. With all houses essentially similar, diversity was to be found in possessions and status symbols such as an elaborate television, dishwasher, or pool, though the group determined norms for what was luxury versus necessity, acceptable versus showing off. The group would then ostracize, or otherwise punish, members for buying prematurely or not buying when an item had become a norm. Since the norm was always changing, Mom and Dad had to be on their guard constantly to ensure proper conformity.

Suburbia

Whyte described the predictability of suburban friendships outside the context of company socializing. One key was adjoining driveways. Remember, this was in the days when women stayed at home all day waiting for the kids to come home from school and the major event of the day was the mail delivery. After the mail was delivered, the housewives would walk down their driveways to get the mail and, naturally, linger for a little conversation, and friendships were born. Whyte's theory of adjoining driveways explained why housewives didn't get as well acquainted with the women who lived behind them, though sometimes an intimate circle might expand to include someone across the street or one or two doors down. These opportunities were limited by lines of demarcation imposed by neighborhood "deviants." "Deviants" were those nonconformists who painted their garage doors odd colors, whose lawns were unkempt, or who drove loud, two-seater sports cars (unacceptable showing off). Their driveways were not crossed even for informal socializing, thus defining the territory of housewife enclaves.

ORGANIZATION LIFESTYLE

Whyte was very critical of the organization lifestyle, claiming it was the antithesis of everything that had made America great, the American ideal: the pursuit of *individual* salvation through hard work, thrift, and competitive struggle was the heart of American achievement. The organization was destroying the very essence of individuality and replacing it with conformity. Competitive struggle had been replaced by belongingness and a demand for consensus. To his dismay, in his research between 1949 and 1956, Whyte found that most corporate-bound graduating seniors, children of depression-era parents and many of whom had childhood memories of the depression, were very amenable to the organization's code of conformity. Compromise was a reasonable price to pay to get a depression-proof sanctuary. Whyte (1956) believed, it turned out correctly, that these young men would be a generation of bureaucrats with no adventure or entrepreneurial spirit, saying of them: "Responding to the group is a moral duty, and so they continue, imprisoned in brotherhood" (p. 365).

False Collectivization

Whyte described the central fallacy of the organization and its beliefs as false collectivization: insisting on treating a person, or oneself, as a unit of a group when association with the particular group is not vital to the task in question or may even be repressive. Whyte (1956) emphasized that a group is not a creative vehicle: "People talk together, exchange information, make compromises and agreements, but they do not think, they do not create" (p. 51). Extending that idea, he criticized the entire notion of belongingness and harmoniousness: "Why should there be a consensus? To concentrate on agreement is to intensify that which inhibits creativity" (p. 52). He added, "All creative advances are essentially a departure from agreed-upon ways of looking at things" (p. 59). William Whyte, alone in the wilderness, was crying out for the adoption of a management philosophy based on belief in the individual, not the group, and was frustrated at how willingly young men were selling out: "How far the balance between the group and the individual has shifted. In a word, they *accept*" (p. 394).

Whyte saw the "organization man" syndrome as a threat to the essence of America: "The danger is not man being dominated, but man surrendering. . . . If America ever destroyed its genius, it would be by making the individual come to regard himself as a hostage of prevailing opinion by creating, in sum, a tyranny of the majority" (pp. 32, 396).

Twenty-four years later another creative genius expressed William Whyte's message in a different medium and context:

> The child has grown.
> . . .
> I have become comfortably numb.

You may recognize the preceding from Pink Floyd's 1979 album, *The Wall*. Though this may well be the first time Pink Floyd and William H. Whyte Jr. have ever appeared on the same stage together, they've hit upon the same chord, haven't they? The "organization man" syndrome was rampant when Whyte wrote his book in 1956. It was still a dominant theme when Pink Floyd released their album in 1979. It is still very much with us today. So what does all this mean to you, striving to become a competent twenty-first-century manager? First and foremost, you need to recognize the syndrome, deal with it as a formidable adversary you may just have to coexist with, and not let it destroy or deter you. As Whyte said (1956), "We need to know how to cooperate with the organization, but more than ever, so do we need to know how to resist it. . . . We have choices to make. . . . [We] must fight the organization. Not stupidly or selfishly, but fight [we] must, for . . . the peace of mind offered by the organization remains a surrender" (p. 404).

Fighting the Organization

There are some key words in Whyte's quote: *not stupidly or selfishly.* You must fight the organization, but choose your moments wisely. Don't swing out to the other end of the extreme to become a nonconformist as a pointless way to demonstrate you're not a conformist. Choose the right moment to take a stand on the right issue, assessing the potential gain vis-à-vis its attendant cost. Understand that at times you must just let something go, when it's best to just go along. Your colleagues and higher-ups will be more inclined to accept you as an individual if they're convinced you know how to act properly and are a team player. If, bottom line, you can't get the organization to be flexible and you can't accept its price on you as an individual: go elsewhere. I have known many managers, myself among them, who have bashed their heads against the wall trying to deal with organizations entrenched in conformity and belongingness, unwilling to consider a diversity of ideas and people. You will not change such organizations from the bottom up. Perhaps someday a CEO will appoint you, with all necessary authority and resources, to clean out the executive suite and revamp an organization's normative culture. Maybe you'll buy a company or start one yourself. Or maybe you will finally get to the point where you can begin instituting meaningful changes, assuming you're not assassinated by the managers you threaten on your rise up the ladder. One way or another, though, you need to find a way to affiliate yourself with an organization that treasures the uniqueness of each individual within it.

Once you're part of such an organization, you can incorporate Whyte's points into your management style. Embrace diversity, encourage opinions at odds with your own, and open up channels of communication which challenge all assumptions and methods of doing things. The result will be the development and flourishing of every individual mind. To the outsider, everything will look like chaos, but with you acting as leader and facilitator, productive ideas and results will be forthcoming.

Implicit in your management style is Whyte's point on being unselfish. Don't get me wrong: I would never advocate that you do anything not in your best long-term interest, and you should always expect value for value in every business and personal relationship. That said, you can still find compatibility and accept reasonable compromises to reach a point where your objectives are in the best interest of you *and* the organization, you *and* your people. The higher-ups will be open to giving you more freedom and less oversight if they believe you have the good of the organization at heart. Your people will go the extra mile for you if they believe you really care about them, even when they know that economic realities may compel you to institute job cuts at some time in the future.

Chapter 8

Incompetence in Organizations

When William Whyte wrote *The Organization Man* in 1956, he warned us of troubles ahead. A system established on harmonious conformity was no breeding ground for innovation and productivity, so it was certainly vulnerable to evolving foreign competition. However, even Whyte may not have appreciated how that system would so quickly evolve into stagnation and incompetence, as documented by Dr. Laurence J. Peter in his 1969 classic, *The Peter Principle.*

THE PRINCIPLE DEFINED

Specifically, Peter (1969) proposed that, "In a hierarchy, every employee tends to rise to his level of incompetence" (p. 7). To this day, we routinely hear of people being cited as examples of the Peter Principle, especially in large highly structured organizations, though to be fair we probably should update the wording to say, "In a hierarchy, every employee tends to rise to his *or her* level of incompetence." Back in 1969, incompetence was the exclusive domain of men, whereas today incompetence has embraced diversity.

Peter's hypothesis begins with the logical assumption that employees who excel in their current positions are most likely to be considered for promotion. That's all well and good, but, he notes, competence in your present position does not automatically correlate to competence in the new position. The best salesperson is the one most likely to be promoted to sales manager, but the skills that make someone a good doer are far different from those of a good manager, as we discussed in Chapter 1. The transition may even be more traumatic in a highly technical field. When you promote your best computer programmer to section supervisor, you are assured of losing your best programmer and may very possibly have inherited a supervisor who is inept, frustrated, and unhappy being an administrator. Unfortunately, in many companies, the only way to give salary increases to the best doers is to make them managers.

In Part II of this book, I'll stress the importance of matching the candidate's interests and skills with any proposed position. In the hierarchal belongingness of the Organization Man, though, no one thought much about that. If you fit in and did well, you got promoted. If you continued to fit in and did well in your new position, you got promoted again, and on and on until, Peter proposed, at some point you were finally promoted to a position in which you were incompetent.

INCOMPETENCE

Incompetence could take a variety of forms. The least likely form, strangely enough, was a basic inability to do the work. More common was a situation in which the employee just hated doing the job, such as the example of the computer programmer being made a supervisor. Some individuals display social incompetence. John de Lorean, the architect of the Pontiac Division, did it by getting divorced and showing up at official company functions with a woman less than half his age.

So what happened to employees once they had, inevitably, been promoted to their level of incompetence? Did they get shipped back to their prior positions where they had been competent and productive? No, observed Peter, because that would make the person who had initiated the employee's promotion look bad, if not incompetent. The employee promoted to the level of incompetence was left there to remain for the duration of his or her lifetime employment. The organization had bogged down into a system of incompetent workers at every level of upper management. The chickens had come home to roost.

EXCEPTIONS TO THE PETER PRINCIPLE

Peter cited several examples of apparent exceptions to his principle which, he insisted, were not really exceptions after all. One was the phenomenon of an incompetent worker being "kicked upstairs" to what was purportedly a promotion, accompanied by high-sounding announcements replete with congratulations. However, it was not a true promotion since the person was given a nice title that sounded important with a nice office in some remote part of the building but had absolutely no responsibilities whatsoever. This tactic was merely a way of getting an incompetent out of the way without forcing management to explain how the individual had been assigned there in the first place. It was a handy way of making an incompetent marketing director the chairman of the executive committee, or neutralizing someone who knew too much to let the feds get ahold of him. Many of Peter's examples come from the academic world, in which an incompetent dean can become a university vice president who holds meetings but has no authority and no budget.

Another apparent exception concerned the very rare cases of persons who turned out to be either superincompetent or supercompetent. Generally, a person could be incompetent and remain in place, but every once in a while someone would turn out to be a complete bumbler, so grossly incompetent that management could find no way to put their heads in the sand. This person would just have to go, but more often than not management could escape blame for a bad decision by making this person quit. Some of the tactics of this approach border on the unethical, and you had best be sure you're on solid legal ground. I note several points about disaffiliation in Part II.

On the other side of the ledger were persons supercompetent. What do you suppose would happen to them? Would they get on the fast track with quick promotions and big upward steps? No! Peter suggested that persons who were supercompetent represented a threat to the less competent or incompetents surrounding them and thus were dispatched forthwith. I remember two such supercompetents who were mentors to me in my twenties. Dan Walton was an area sales manager who believed his company's approach to marketing was off target. He defied corporate headquarters and pursued his own strategy, the result of which was the best market share performance and best return on investment in the nation. His reward? He was exiled to the outskirts of Timbuktu. Then there was Rick Harris, who openly proclaimed the need to change his company's corporate culture and eliminate most headquarters staff. The result? He was kicked upstairs but, for an extra level of safety from his influence, to an office in a different building. It was more than twenty years later that someone finally came in and did the job Rick Harris knew had to be done, firing 2,500 people at headquarters, after which more was getting done than before.

Dan Walton and Rick Harris taught me most of what I learned about sales, marketing, and management in my days of puppyhood. However, they also taught me something I alluded to in Chapter 7, namely that if you're truly competent, you must guard against being assassinated on your way up the ladder. Choose your battles carefully, don't be perceived as a threat, be seen as a team player, and be viewed as very competent but not supercompetent. In other words, this is a game you must learn to play and play to win.

CREATIVE INCOMPETENCE

We'll get more into corporate gamesmanship, as the concept evolved in the 1970s, is discussed in Chapter 9. Peter didn't get into the idea of playing business and management as a game, but he sowed the initial seeds by advocating "creative incompetence." His point was that an employee needed to recognize when he or she had reached the highest level of competence, beyond which any promotion would take him or her to incompetence. Then, to prevent a promotion, the employee needed to feign incompetence in the current position so he or she would be left there. An example might be a successful salesperson in a desirable location who wants to avoid being transferred to an executive staff position at the miserable corporate headquarters location. Another could be a professor who wants to avoid being asked to join an exclusive task force that will kill three or four perfectly good weekends thinking about a strategic vision for the year 2135.

Creative incompetence, to be done right, must not be overdone, and it's not in your best interest to appear incompetent on the job itself. Thus, most of Peter's suggestions for creative incompetence address social incompetence rather than professional incompetence. But even with social incompetence, don't appear super socially incompetent or it might just be the end of you. John de Lorean crossed the line showing up with a beautiful young woman. The husbands may have enjoyed the scenery, but the wives made sure de Lorean was history.

Instead, to appear marginally incompetent Peter urges obsessive behavior about good causes, such as economy. Turn out lights in every vacant office you see. While in a meeting with a superior, start rummaging through the wastebasket, pulling out rubber bands and paper clips while commenting on the need for thrift. Peter also suggests standing out from the crowd in subtle ways, such as bringing your lunch when everyone else eats out, or occasionally parking in a vice president's parking place. As a variation of the de Lorean scenario, you might offend the boss's wife by imitating her laugh just within her earshot. That should be just enough to have her sabotage your promotion but not get you fired.

Chapter 9

Let the Games Begin

I expect that the majority of men and women reading this do not have an objective of avoiding promotion. On the contrary, I'll bet that 85 to 90 percent or more of you are interested in moving up in your organization. Moving into management has always been a goal for you, never to be questioned. As we move into the subject of corporate gamesmanship, I'm going to ask you to question the unquestionable. From this point forward, regularly ask yourself, Do I *really* want to go into management after all? Personally, I've been both a manager and a doer, and I'll tell you what: I'd much rather be a high-paid doer. I believe I was an effective manager and appreciate what it takes to be successful in management, but I like to go home at the end of the day and not have to be concerned about anything but what *I* have to get done. I like doing things hands-on. I don't like meetings, paperwork, or elegant dinner and social environments. When accused of preferring the companionship of dogs to people, I thank the person for the compliment. Too often, I've seen people move along a career track because they believe it's the thing to do and it's expected of them. They become managers but they don't love being managers, and thus they burn out or fail. Effective management is challenging and stressful, and it must be what you really want to do if you want to be good at it. If it's not, don't follow the path in the first place. If creative social incompetence is not your forte, be able to take a stand and just say no if that's the right decision for you. Too often, it's assumed that anyone with the ability will, of course, want to rise as high in the organization as fast as possible, and that there's something wrong with anyone who won't play that game. It's an assumption of one of the most interesting books of the 1970s, on gamesmanship, *The Gamesman* by Michael Maccoby (1976). He seemed unaware of the contradictions arising out of his assumptions, reflecting a common view—then and now—that anyone who has what it takes must shoot for the top rung on the ladder.

THE SCIENCE OF GAMESMANSHIP

Peter toyed with the idea of playing business life as a game, but it was *The Gamesman,* in 1976, that made gamesmanship a science. *The Gamesman,* twenty years after *The Organization Man,* was a watershed. It redefined the business environment, traditionally viewed as group conformity, to one in which the individual warrior sought his personal victory.

Although *The Gamesman* had a very significant impact on the thinking of businesspeople, especially young businesspeople, in 1976, its shortcomings dated it and caused it to go out of print within a few years. Most notably, the book's title, *The Gamesman,* was literally that: *The Games*man. Maccoby was a sociologist who did his research for the book by conducting interviews with businessmen and their wives. For William Whyte in 1956, it was appropriate to talk about the Organization *Man,* since at that time, the workplace was almost completely male dominated. By 1976, however, women had begun to assume positions of responsibility that rendered archaic a perspective limited to male principals and their wives. In addition, Maccoby presented a decidedly negative view of the business environment, painting it as devoid of humanness and feelings, leaving the reader somewhat down and depressed about the entire enterprise. I will note some of those points. Despite these limitations, though, *The Gamesman* offered a radically new view of business and a strategy for exploiting personal opportunities, perfect timing for the Baby Boomers as they moved into their thirties.

THE FOUR TYPES
OF BUSINESS ENVIRONMENT PERSONALITIES

Maccoby proposed that the business environment was composed of four different types: Craftsmen, Jungle Fighters, Company Men, and, naturally, Gamesmen. He advocated that one should be a Gamesman, understanding the other three characters and playing them as pieces on a chessboard in a game in which winning wasn't the most important thing—it was the only thing.

The Craftsman

The Craftsman was a person most like a clockmaker or home builder two centuries ago, today holding a position as a computer programmer, accountant, or marketing research analyst. These people were independent perfectionists who strove to build the best, with a passion for quality and doing things better, motivated by the problem to be solved and the challenge of the work itself. Craftsmen are the consummate doers, analytic by nature and fully focused on the task at hand, thus neither competitive nor aggressive. As in the previous example of a great computer programmer being a questionable candidate for section supervisor, one should be wary of promoting a Craftsman to management, since an isolationist attitude may be inappropriate for a position in which a person must motivate and get results through others. Many Craftsmen are naturally socially incompetent—no *creative* social incompetence is required, as you may have observed if you've ever seen a bunch of computer geeks or economists at a cocktail party. Therefore, they are often quickly eliminated from consideration for promotion to management positions that require subtle interests or the need to sell themselves.

Maccoby holds Craftsmen in utter contempt because of their inability to play or disinterest in playing the game and moving up in the hierarchy, but something never dawns on him: The Craftsman is the only one of his four characters who is truly happy, personally open, and approachable, with a satisfying family life. The Craftsman leaves work at the end of the day, carries no troubles home with him, and has open and loving communication with his wife and children. This all seems lost on Maccoby (1976), who within a paragraph says of a Craftsman, "Bill has not developed a deep understanding of himself or others" and then continues on to describe Bill's "priority values of quality, problem-solving, and a satisfying family life" (p.71). It never dawns on Maccoby that, as I will illustrate, the Gamesman is the most unhappy person of all. It's classic denial.

The Jungle Fighter

Maccoby's second character is the Jungle Fighter, a power-hungry predator with a kill-or-be-killed attitude who wants to be feared and believes that fear stimulates better work. These people are not team players and, in fact, will attempt to develop group cohesion by making other parts of the organization appear to be the enemy. Jungle Fighters believe themselves to be good people trying to survive in a dog-eat-dog world, but they will use and exploit other people, keep them dependent, and then cast them off when no longer useful. Jungle Fighters comprise about 1 percent of the population but cause about 98 percent of misery not related to incompetence. They may be found in all types of organizations, from the Fortune 500 to your local PTA. Perhaps you've had the pleasure of dating one. So, why on earth would people knowingly bring a Jungle Fighter into their midst? In crisis situations or roles that don't require trust and interdependency—such as bringing in a hatchet man to lay off 50 percent of the workforce—a Jungle Fighter may be just the ticket, especially if the other managers don't want blood on their hands. Remember, though, that these people are snakes: don't be surprised if their fangs get you when you try to get them out of the tent.

I've had to deal with only four Jungle Fighters—I mean four real, genuine mean Jungle Fighters, not your basic garden variety—in all my years of business, and I was able to handle them all reasonably well. It's not all that different from handling a mean dog: show no fear, but don't get into a down-and-dirty scrap in which their bite is worse than yours. Never show emotion, and respond to their tirade with neutral statements or clarifying questions. After a while, when they discover you won't show submission but won't engage them in a brawl, they'll move on to a more satisfying target.

The Company Man

Maccoby's third personality, the Company Man, describes the gracious, courteous careerist who sticks to the rules, resists change, and won't take risks. These people enjoy serving others and the organization as a way of serving themselves and, although they believe in performance and people, are more concerned with security than anything else. Thus, consistent with the William Whyte prototype, Company Men are more concerned with maintaining the organization rather than setting goals and doing anything creative. They desire approval by authority and overvalue the company in relation to their family life, feeling insignificant and lost when separated from the organization. Their identity is the company and they have few, if any, personal or social interactions outside the context of the company. They live their lives and present themselves not on the basis of any independent judgment but from the perspective of what the company would expect and approve of. Maccoby, and likely most of the Baby Boomers in his audience, consider Company Men boring, irrelevant, and old. They are to be patronized, if it's in your best interest, but not to be considered serious players. Company Men, however, may be impediments to your progress and career, so they must be manipulated as necessary until you pass them going up the ladder. Naturally, it is unthinkable that you will ever go *down* the ladder, and thus you will never see them again.

The Gamesman

As the title would suggest, Maccoby's book, and world, revolves around his fourth and final player, the Gamesman, a highly imaginative gambler who is cool and daring, is fast moving, and loves change, competing for the pleasure of the contest and the sheer exhilaration of victory—a person who wants to influence courses of events by taking calculated risks and utilizing new methods. The Gamesman is Maccoby's Superman, the profile for success. The Gamesman is a winner, classifying others—namely, other Gamesman—as winners or, namely, Craftsmen and Company Men as losers. The Gamesman is the great warrior and leader whose employees love him and would walk through fire for him. The Gamesman is also extraordinarily unhappy, a fact that Maccoby seems not to notice, even as he writes the words. Wives of Gamesmen consistently express surprise at the portrayal of their husbands at work, expressing the fact that they see a different person at home, someone who is distant and uncommunicative, isolated from them and the children, unable to share deep friendship and intimacy. Furthermore, even in the business environment, Gamesmen are condemned by a fatal flaw: Their attitude of win or lose/triumph or humiliation means they must win every game every time or be defeated. Being too proud to accept a secure but humble place and unable to lose with dignity, they are ultimately condemned to a tragic end. Says Maccoby (1976):

> The fatal danger for gamesmen is to be trapped in perpetual adolescence, never outgrowing the self-centered compulsion to score, never confronting their deep boredom with life when it is not a game, never developing a sense of meaning that requires more of them and allows others to trust them. . . . An old and tiring gamesman is a pathetic figure, especially after he has lost a few contests, and with them, his confidence. Once his youth, vigor, and even the thrill of winning are lost, he becomes depressed and goalless, questioning the purpose of his life. (p. 111)

I don't know about you, but personally I find that characterization extremely depressing and not something I'd want for me. It is, nonetheless, his vision of Superman. But if you find that unappealing, his overall view of management and corporate life is bleaker still:

> The process of bending one's will to corporate goals and moving up the hierarchy leads to meanness, emotional stinginess, but not full-blown sadism. Although more than a third of the managers expressed sadistic tendencies, they are controlled and channeled, employed within the game in the form of jokes and put-downs or in the service of the team against opponents. There is just enough fear and humiliation to keep the hierarchy glued together. (p. 200)

He goes on to say:

> Few of the managers we interviewed mentioned helping other people as a goal in their lives. . . . Those who strive for success lose their concern for others. . . . Corporate work does not develop qualities of the heart, such as compassion, generosity, and idealism; to the contrary, it has a negative effect on this development. (pp. 212, 226)

I guess my reaction to *The Gamesman* in 1976 was typical. I was very intrigued by the characterization of the business world as a game. I guess I'd always thought of it that way, and played it pretty well that way, but this book came along and helped me focus and quantify my ideas. I found Maccoby's four characters very enlightening: they helped me better understand many of my colleagues and employees. But I absolutely, positively wanted nothing to do with becoming one of his Gamesmen, and if indeed his description of the business world turned out to be accurate I would plan a life building decks and painting houses. Playing a game was one thing, but living in an atmosphere of despair and evil was something else. Fortunately, Maccoby's description of management and corporate life has proved, at least in my experience, cynical and unrepresentative. Good management will not tolerate such an environment if only out of purely pragmatic reasons. Good people will be driven away, the media will be attracted, and ultimately the organization will suffer. But still, in the 1970s, we all lacked a vision of how to create the kind of organization with which people would love to be affiliated, for which they'd work hard and be rewarded accordingly, and which would stand for and bring out the best. We're finally beginning to understand that now, as we'll see in Part III.

On a more short-term, personal level, I appreciated Maccoby's basic concepts, but didn't particularly care for his approach. Intuitively, I knew there must be a better way to go about playing the corporate game, but just couldn't put my finger on it. Then, along came Mark McCormack.

Chapter 10

Win-Win Gamesmanship

Many excellent business books have been written since the 1950s, but I believe the greatest of all is *What They Don't Teach You at Harvard Business School,* the 1984 classic by Mark McCormack, which is as relevant today as it was the first day it hit the shelves. Everyone was talking about it from the moment it came out, so I eagerly bought a copy and set to reading it. Almost from the beginning, I found myself nodding in agreement as I wound my way through its pages. What made it such a great experience was not that it presented any radically new perspective of the business world, but that it articulated all those things I had sort of learned and sort of knew. I had just never brought all its ideas and concepts together to articulate them as an integrated whole. Mark McCormack gave me a flash of enlightenment about what it took to understand and succeed in business and management. I'm pleased to say that I'd already figured much of it out by the time I read his book, though at many points I couldn't help but wish I'd known some of his concepts ten or fifteen years earlier.

Maccoby's *The Gamesman* had addressed playing the game, but its prototype was an essentially unhappy person who played to his or her own selfish ends in an environment lacking in humanness. Although in my business experiences I had observed Maccoby's characters, and had seen examples of the Organization Man and confirmation of the Peter Principle, I was nonetheless convinced that most people in business were pretty decent folks. I'd seen plenty of people who were Gamesmen, playing the system to their own ends, and though they had their share of triumphs, eventually they seemed to lose and suffer the inevitable humiliation of defeat.

MCCORMACK AND THE GAME OF BUSINESS

McCormack shared my perception of businesspeople generally being reasonable human beings who were working in an organization out of enlightened self-interest. He also saw it as a game, but here was the difference: McCormack saw the game as something you played to be effective, winning on a personal level as you got along well with others and made a positive contribution to the organization. It wasn't so much about playing a game that I can win as it was about playing a game in which I can enhance my career by working with others and making things happen: win-win gamesmanship.

The theme of *What They Don't Teach You at Harvard Business School* is that the college degree only gets you in the door. A university education gives you some knowledge, but more than that it teaches you how to deal with, get along with, and make things happen through other people. It's an endurance test and demonstrates your ability to take on a daunting task and refuse to quit until it's completed. Still, that degree gives you only a chance to get on the playing field for a trial run in which you must demonstrate effectiveness by using your capabilities to achieve certain ends and results. That means doing your homework and knowing how to play the game itself.

Intuitive Management

McCormack's basic premise is that you need to develop and apply "street smarts" to the business environment. Never taught in the traditional business school, this meant intuitive management, an applied people sense or common sense, the ability to make active, positive use of instincts, insights, and perceptions. His focus is on individual impressions and achievements rather than on getting results through others, so you might wonder why I have selected his book to review when it is not specifically about the functions of management. My reasoning is twofold. First, it takes effectiveness, positive achievement, and positive impressions to get the initial foothold into management. After that, once you get in the management game, you must continue to demonstrate effective achievements and impressions or you'll get Peter Principled. That means your career will stagnate and, in today's climate, you're on the way out the door. Worst of all, unless you're perceived as an up-and-coming winner, the people you want to attract won't want to work for you, current employees will be looking to jump ship and tie themselves to a rising star, and, in a self-fulfilling prophecy, down you go. So, bottom line, you need to have your own personal winning strategy to be a successful manager of others.

A major component of McCormack's strategy centers around reading people, observing aggressively, talking less, and listening more. In particular, look to those situations outside the formal business environment in which people are more likely to reveal their innermost selves. Examples might include situations such as dealing with waiters or airline employees. I'll bet you've had experiences like I've had, with a person you thought was a well-mannered business professional, who seemed to feel he or she had the right to yell at or otherwise demean such people. If you spend a lot of time in airports you know that on a regular basis, especially in the winter months, flights will be delayed or canceled. I've watched some of these jerks take it out on the gate agent, demanding action now because they're important people. Their tirades accomplish nothing except to enable everyone to see what they're really like, causing an irretrievable loss of respect. It's a similar situation out on the tennis court or playing cards, in which the individual never admits mistakes and is always blaming his or her partner. People are fairly guarded during formal events such as meetings, but McCormack suggests you pay attention to the fringe times, just before the start time and the first several minutes of the meeting, when their real selves are more likely to show.

You may know of Mark McCormack as one of the pioneer sports agents and a leader in the field of sports marketing. He shares many of the insights one can gain out on the golf course, which makes his book especially enjoyable reading if you like golf. You can learn a lot from the so-called "gimme putt," one of such short length that the player doesn't have to bother to tap it in. Some people refuse all gimmes, even from three inches away, implying that it's hard to do them a favor. Others just *take* a gimme, even if it's six feet away, suggesting that they have big egos and won't *ask* for a favor but *expect* one. Then there are those people who sort of give it a halfhearted try with a one-handed sweep. If it goes in, fine. If not, they propose they weren't really trying in the first place and just take a gimme. McCormack believes such people are hard to pin down, have a capacity for self-deception, and tend to exaggerate.

CREATING IMPRESSIONS
AND GETTING AHEAD

McCormack (1984) has some excellent suggestions for creating impressions and getting ahead; one quote in particular encapsulates what business is all about, even if you're a doer who wants to remain a doer for the rest of your life: "Create an overall, ongoing impression of competence, effectiveness, maturity, and fair-minded toughness: The kind of person people want to do business with" (p. 27).

To create the desired impression, do the little things right: attire, your phone manager, phrases you use, and the way you meet and greet people. He's big on efficiency and so am I. Here's my standard: If I get a request for something and I'm going to do it, I have three action tiers.

> Tier 1. I can knock it out in a couple of minutes. Do it now, with an immediate note or an e-mail reply. At the least, do it today.
> Tier 2. Moderate time requirement, say up to an hour or two. On their desk first thing Monday morning or e-mailed by Sunday night.
> Tier 3. Bigger stuff with a longer time frame. Not only get it done on time but do it before they're even starting to think about looking for it. Consider this: It takes no more time, and probably less, to get something done sooner, not later. All you have to do is get ahead of the curve *one time* and then stay there. And it creates a nice impression. I enjoy getting departmental e-mails reminding the group of deadlines when I know my part of the assignment has already been turned in.

McCormack is big on business gestures, especially doing something for the kids, but notes their effectiveness is lost when presented as "You owe me one." Flatter legitimately. Be careful on that. A while back, a colleague came up to me and said, "Bob, you look great!" I appreciated the compliment, taking it to mean I was as studly as ever and hadn't lost a thing. Then, minutes later, I overheard him say, "Tom, you look great!" to someone forty years my senior, in a wheelchair equipped with an oxygen tank. I realized then he had actually meant, "Gee, Bob, aren't you dead yet?" Similarly, don't ask, "Hey, where did you get that suit?" unless the suit looks especially nice. I wouldn't even think of looking at pictures on someone's desk and saying how lovely his or her children are, but I would say,"Hey, I saw where your kid made the All-Star team."

To get ahead, McCormack says to get the facts. Understand the system—there's always a system—and the rules. Know who's hot and who's not. I realize this may sound inconsiderate, but do not have lunch with the veteran employees who have plateaued or Peter-Principled out. Identify those people who are rising quickly—they're almost certainly at the center of the hot projects. Get to know them. Emulate their performance patterns. Make friends and mentors. Build trust and loyalty.

Learn to say "I don't know" and "I need help." If you make a mistake, be able to say, "I was wrong," but say it only once and put it behind you. You will appear unnecessarily weak by apologizing repeatedly. Move on, having learned from the mistake.

Respect Confidentiality

As noted in his basic premise, McCormack is suggesting you use simple common sense, which would seem easy. Apparently it's not, as so many ostensibly intelligent people seem to lack it. A fundamental: Respect confidentiality and learn to keep a secret. Nothing may be quite as aggravating as having a meeting on something confidential then going back to your desk to find an e-mail waiting from someone who has already learned about what was discussed, especially if it concerns some sensitive personnel matters. Respecting confidentiality means telling no one, not even your spouse or an old friend a thousand miles away. Some managers—you might want to try this one yourself—make a point of testing a person by telling him or her something in confidence and seeing if it ever gets back to them. If it does, it's a sure bet that person will never be told anything in confidence again and will be systematically excluded from sensitive meetings in the future. A career has just run out of track, a high price to pay, but the appropriate price for not knowing how to shut up.

Respecting confidentiality is only one of McCormack's examples of self-discipline. He also counsels people not to act impulsively, to resist the temptation to "tell it like it is" when it is not in your best interest to do so. Recently, I learned of a sales rep who was asked by a senior member of management about his supervisor. The rep answered, accurately, that the supervisor appeared to be at his level of incompetence and was an unpleasant person to work for, plus had been drunk and disorderly in front of customers. Unfortunately for the rep the supervisor quickly learned what was said and turned his wrath upon him. Better to have said nothing at all or damned with faint praise, saying something like, "He seems to be trying his best." I know someone who said of a general manager, "He's an excellent administrator," which, roughly translated, means, "He's a lousy leader." Hedging or declining to answer any follow-up questions should signal to any observant person that something should be looked into; in this way you can be quoted verbatim and not be accused of having said anything that could come back to haunt you.

Personal Beliefs

Along the same lines, don't use the office to make your personal statement about your personal beliefs. Whether you're into women's rights, gay rights, animal rights, or religion, I don't know and I don't care. Furthermore, it has nothing to do with our working relationship in a business organization, so leave it at home. That goes double for the "love-me-for-myself" syndrome, in which people seem to feel a need to flaunt their weaknesses as well as their strengths. I've been in meetings in which people just start babbling about their drunkenness, neuroses, and marital infidelities as if it were incumbent on them to air all their dirty laundry in public. I've said it before. I'll say it again: learn to shut up.

What They Don't Teach You at Harvard Business School is a great book not because of anything it has to say about conducting job functions; it's great because it's so enlightening on how to conduct yourself in a professional business environment and how to think outside the traditional analytical and quantitative business school mind-set. The conformity of the Organization Men was destined to lead to stagnation. The task-focused Craftsmen knew how to do the job but lacked the people skills to motivate employees and sell themselves. The Gamesmen were so focused on selfish triumph that they couldn't build long-term strategic alliances in their professional and personal lives. Mark McCormack turned on a lightbulb and people said, "Yes, that's the way to get things done."

I hope my selective review of business writers from 1956 to 1984 was helpful in providing an explanation about management and the nature of people in organizations. Familiarity with Whyte, Peter, Maccoby, and McCormack is of value not only for an appreciation of what happened in the past and how we got to where we are but also because all of the issues and ideas they raised are still in play today.

Part I is just about finished. In the next two chapters, I'll fine-tune the message and put it all together to summarize what I've done through this, the first third of the journey.

Chapter 11

Managing versus Operating

In the first ten chapters, I explored numerous points about management and reviewed significant writings that portrayed the business environment and profiled its players. Now, in Chapters 11 and 12, I integrate these points and concepts to more clearly articulate what effective management is all about.

FUNCTION CLASSIFICATION: MANAGING AND OPERATING

In this chapter, I look into a very basic classification of a manager's function: Everything a manager does is either managing or operating. Managing, as described, is planning, organizing, staffing, directing, and controlling activities of others to achieve objectives for which you are ultimately responsible. By contrast, operating is the direct conduct of business functions, completing a task yourself. Every manager's job is a combination of managing and operating, though there will be more managing and less operating at each successive step up the ladder. If you reach the top of the mountain, your job will be almost exclusively managing, though some operational tasks will command your personal attention, and some CEOs seem to get a kick out of appearing in the company's commercials. The difference between managing and operating can be subtle—there are many gray areas—so this chapter features twelve examples to help clarify the concept. You can use these examples to create an assessment of activities in your own job. Those tasks classified as managing will generally be activities appropriate to your role as a manager, and you should continue to do them. But activities you classify as operating deserve further scrutiny. Ask yourself, Should I be doing this, or does this task present an opportunity to delegate a task and empower my people? At its worst, an operational activity might qualify as a low-priority time waster. With that in mind, let's go through the twelve examples. As you read through them, first decide whether the activity is managing or operating and then, if it's operating, whether it's something you should be doing at all.

Example 1: Long-Distance Options

Meeting with a telecom service representative to review long-distance service options: All right, I started with an easy one. This is operating, and almost certainly an inappropriate task for a manager. Empower a team, probably a team of one, to make this decision. Make sure the team understands your needs, specify boundaries, and tell the team when you need its final decision.

Example 2: Annual Budget

Determining the annual budget in your area of responsibility: This is managing, making the resource decisions that will profoundly affect the activities and limitations under which all your people will operate. Making the money decisions is one of your most important management functions. However, it does not extend to running off copies and assembling them into three-ring binders.

Example 3: Office Supply Request

Approving a budget request from one of your employees to purchase a clipboard and a dozen felt-tip pens: This is one of those gray areas. Yes, it's a budget issue, but since the request is for such a small amount, it's so trivial as to make it operating. It's micromanaging at its worst. I've known managers who have raised questions about two-dollar expenditures. I've personally been asked about an eleven-cent phone call. Such nitpicking is not only a waste of your time but also downright demoralizing for your people. You may know you will approve some expenses. If that's the case, why on earth are you wasting time subjecting people to the approval process in the first place? Set parameters—some combination of type of purchase and amount—and establish procedures for automatic approval of such expenses. Later, if you find some employees are abusing the system and twentydollaring you to death, you might need to revisit the issue and clarify expectations. Until then, don't sweat the small stuff.

Example 4: Entertaining a Higher-Up

Entertaining someone from chain headquarters to negotiate a promotional program: Though such a program may have a significant impact on your company and its people, you're doing the entertaining and you're doing the negotiating, and thus this is operating. However, some thinking may be in order for this example. The first and most important question is whether your presence is necessary and/or expected. If the person on the other side of the table is a vice president of marketing, he or she may be just a little put out if you send an underling, even if that person has complete authority to initial an agreement. It might be tantamount to the United States sending the deputy assistant secretary of state to the funeral of the prime minister of Great Britain. Having said that, such a situation might still present an opportunity to bring someone along with you, an up-and-coming protégé who could gain valuable experience witnessing the process. This person could be introduced to the vice president as the one assigned to give complete attention to all the day-to-day details of the program, paving the way for him or her to assume responsibility for implementation issues. Involving your subordinate at this early stage would personalize his or her relationship with the vice president, opening the doors for future contacts. As such, it would constitute management, directly contributing to the employee's development and training. In time, that employee might be able to fully handle all aspects of organizing and negotiating promotional programs with the chain, further helping to make you unnecessary and thus promotable.

Example 5: Performance Review

Conducting a weekly performance review to determine progress of a newly hired employee in your training program: This is the essence of managing, assessing performance and coaching the employee to help him or her set and exceed objectives. Doing so right out of the gate helps build the communication and relationships that are so essential to your effectiveness as a manager. Early on, the new employee sees you as someone who knows what's going on, who recognizes what he or she is doing well, and who helps him or her address those things that need to be worked on. Even though you may not be directly involved in the employee training program and are kept fully apprised of the employee's progress, take the time to begin the mentoring process and show the new employee you care. It's time well spent in planting the seeds for a productive long-term relationship.

Example 6: Trade Convention

Attending a trade convention to learn about the latest developments in high-speed production equipment: This is operating. Even if you are the person clearly most knowledgeable about this subject and it represents an important investment decision for your organization, this is a definite candidate for delegation. I've known many managers whose management progress was impeded or ended because of their unwillingness to let go of their area of operational expertise. As such, their reputation was always that of the production equipment person or the advertising creative expert, inconsistent with the status of a manager of people. Organize a team to attend this convention and empower them to come up with a recommendation. Naturally, give them benefit of all your knowledge and expertise. Give them standards and boundaries. But do not permit them to reverse-delegate the final decision back to you. Coach them, give them advice and counsel, but give them ownership. Consider this: How about telling them that you'll send their final recommendation directly to the CEO, or have them personally present their recommendation, and that you'll sign off on it without even looking it over first? Sound scary? Well, think about it. As long as you've set appropriate standards and boundaries and have given them the necessary input and coaching so that they know how to go about assessing alternatives and making a recommendation, you should have a high level of confidence that their recommendation will be a good one. It's not as though they've gone out on an information-gathering expedition and have dropped a bunch of stuff on your desk to help you make a decision. You've empowered *them* to make the decision. You've given them ownership. It's their baby, with their name on it. What do you think the chances are that they'll gladly put in extra time and effort to make sure their recommendation is a good one? I think chances are pretty good. Let them run with it.

Example 7: New Sales Territory

Deciding whether to add a new sales territory: This is management, specifically organizing and staffing. In Part II, I address several of these points in detail, but for now I'll just say this: No matter how good a manager you are, you will fail unless you have the right people, properly trained, in the right positions. Good organizing and staffing decisions are the prerequisite to success.

Example 8: Simulated Sales Call

Conducting a simulation of a sales call in a role-play exercise with one of your sales reps to help him or her prepare for the appointment: This example is probably managing, part of coaching and mentoring. Yes, you want to empower people and make them able to operate independent of you, making those day-to-day decisions on their own, but that doesn't mean handing them a list of prospects and a set of car keys. Work them through a dress rehearsal of the call, with you playing the prospect as realistically as possible, and you will optimize their probability for success. I hedge my classification on this one, though, to consider the situation in which the exercise is nothing more than a canned module out of a standardized package of training materials. An example might be something like rolling off a memorized presentation: "Hi, I'm Fred Frumpp from Amalgamated Bromide. Today, I'm going to tell you about . . ." and on and on for five minutes or so. First of all, I trust you are not training your people to deliver canned monologues. In any case, if the exercise is nothing more than something any staff person in the training department could handle, it doesn't qualify as coaching and thus is operating.

Example 9: Local Business Club Engagement

Speaking to a local business club about your company's plans and objectives: This is also operating. This situation is similar to Example 4, though there is no implicit direct follow-up to this activity. Ask yourself, Is my presence really necessary as a matter of protocol, or will this present opportunities for building relationships which require me, personally, to become involved? If you can't answer with a yes, let someone else handle it.

Example 10: Cross-Functional Team

Discussing with two of your people an idea you have for a project they might initiate with colleagues in another department: This is the consummate role of a manager, facilitating the formation of cross-functional teams. We trust you will have already run this by the other department's manager who has, in turn, spoken with some of his or her people to suggest they get together with some of your people. Doing this, you are providing the opportunity for employees to work cooperatively and independently in an atmosphere likely to bring out their creative best and generate enthusiasm and excitement. Here, you've let go of control of the outcome and let people run with something and see just how excellent they can be. It's a little scary doing this, and you'll be excused for being a bit apprehensive the first time you empower a cross-functional team, but as long as you provide proper guidance, with the attendant standards and boundaries, chances are good you'll be pleased with the results.

Example 11: Hiring Summer Help

Interviewing a friend's son, who is interested in a summer job: At first blush, this sounds like hiring and staffing, and thus managing, but it's another one of those gray areas. This is a kid looking for a summer job, not a member of your core team. Say good morning and introduce him to the person who will take him over to human resources. For you to conduct the interview is operating, and it should be delegated.

Example 12: Attending a Sales Call

Calling on an account with one of your salespeople to show the customer your management cares about his or her business: The key to this one is the stated purpose of the activity. If all you're doing is to show you care, this is operating and a wasted opportunity to turn it into a learning experience for your sales rep, which would constitute managing. Don't just show up. Coach!

I hope these examples have proved useful as thought starters. Take a look at a typical day for yourself, perhaps even maintain a log of all your activities for a week or so. You've already eliminated the ten classic time wasters that were addressed in Chapter 4. Now, take that one step farther to make sure you're concentrating on managing, limiting your operating to those activities in which your personal attention is genuinely required. That alone will make you more effective and ready to enhance the skills which are the subject of Part II and the intangibles of Part III.

Chapter 12

Put It All Together

By now, you should have a solid idea of what management is all about and how to approach the process of being an effective manager. The selected business books I have reviewed gave some insight into the nature of people in organizations and how those perspectives have evolved over time. Now, I bring all those ideas together and build on them.

THE EIGHT POINTS OF MANAGEMENT

Point 1: Your Identity

In Chapter 1 I described the need for you to be identified with management. This requires that you must not *need* to be liked. It's all right to *want* people to like you; that's natural. But *needing* to be liked usually means you're acting in a high school mind-set and to some extent you're being one of the guys. That is guaranteed to undermine your position and cause your employees to lose respect for you. Teamwork is a great concept, but you must still differentiate your status from that of your employees. You must affiliate yourself with management. You cannot and must not socialize with employees as if they are peers. Don't get me wrong: informal social interactions off the job are a great thing, and they help build relationships and teamwork. Just don't delude yourself into thinking that *any* contact with employees is entirely social. It isn't. It's work, and always keep in mind that the employee you socialize with on Saturday may be a person you must command or discipline on Monday. Perhaps one of the most difficult transitions in the business world is to become a manager of a group of people with whom you've had a peer relationship. I caution you against ever allowing yourself to get into that position or to so promote another employee. It is exceedingly difficult to redefine all those relationships, but it must be done or the manager will fail. I worked with one organization, though, in which a newly appointed manager handled it well. In their group, all the employees traditionally left at about 3:00 p.m. on Fridays and descended on a local establishment for socializing and refreshments. They hung out until 6:00 or 7:00 p.m. and, of course, arranged for cabs or designated drivers. I was curious to see how the new manager would handle this situation, and I was impressed with what he did. As always, he headed out with the whole crowd at 3:00 p.m. and, upon arrival at the establishment, bought the first couple of pitchers. About thirty minutes later, the pitchers had been consumed, and it was someone else's turn to buy the next round. At that moment, he said he had to be going and bid the crowd farewell. He had shared socializing and fellowship, appropriate for a manager, but did not remain with his employees as the party began to roll. I'm sure he would have loved to hang out for the duration, as he always had, but he recognized that would have been inconsistent with his new role as manager.

In a more subtle vein, be careful to properly affiliate yourself with management in your day-to-day conversations. Always say, "The reason why *we* have this policy . . ." never "The reason why *they* have this policy . . ." If you refer to upper management or organizational policies and procedures in the third person, you're disaffiliating yourself with management. To put it bluntly, you're copping out.

Point 2: Your Role

You are not "the boss" of the old military model, doing all the thinking, making decisions, giving orders, kicking ass, and taking names. If you utilize employees only as extra arms and legs rather than brains, your focus is on obedience, not development. You will never discover the potential your people have to offer, and the best of them will leave. You are a manager, a coordinator, and facilitator whose job it is to empower individuals and teams. Create an environment of partnership and pride of ownership. Your job is not to do but to delegate.

Point 3: Perspective

You are a coach and leader who creates a long-team vision: where we are going, why we are going there, what this means, and why it is important to employees. Do not delude yourself into thinking that your reasons or the organization's reasons for wanting to do something are sufficient. Employees have a right to know what it means to them and what's in it for them. If they don't buy in, your long-term vision is an illusion.

After establishing a shared vision, help develop a series of short-term goals and objectives, with individual and team roles working synergistically to make that vision a reality. Never forget that your vision and objectives can be achieved in only one way: getting and keeping customers. Having a customer focus is a given for an organization to be viable. That means a commitment to quality, with continuous improvement on an ongoing basis. Ideally, you have the differential advantage of a uniquely superior product and/or service. At the least, you'd better have a cheaper price on a product and/or service comparable to the competition. If you have neither one nor the other, you won't be in business much longer.

Point 4: Standards

Working in teams is a great idea as long as there's no place to hide. Ultimately, you must have individual responsibility and accountability, even as you backstop decisions and assume ultimate responsibility. You cannot condone people who do not pull their weight or who are incompetent. Employees produce or they go—it's as simple as that. As you know, the same goes for you. There should be no uncertainty concerning the boundaries within which employees operate and the standards under which individuals and teams will be evaluated. Ultimately, all results come down to long-term profitability for the organization, meaning revenue, return on investment, and cost control. Every activity, yours and your employees', must ultimately link to profit.

Point 5: Critical Skills

For your employees, that means all necessary resources for training and development. It means letting them think, insisting they think, and influencing their thinking. Empower them to make decisions consistent with quality, customer service, and profitability. Get them to think of themselves as owners and partners, spending the company's money as if it were their own, which, if you think about it, it really is. Let them have an entrepreneurial mind-set, empowered to make decisions at the point of encounter, asking what it's going to take to get a customer or make a customer happy, then deciding whether the decision is a good one.

For you, the most essential critical skills are effective communication and listening. Get out of paralysis by analysis, and enhance your basic street smarts. Get all the facts you can within a reasonable time frame, and then go with your gut. Manage your time. Avoid low-priority time wasters, and delegate operational activities that do not require your personal attention. Hire people smarter than you. If they're not smarter than you, or they always agree with you, you don't need them. But once you empower them with total project management, get out of their way. Keep your manager apprised of what your employees are doing, and give those employees the credit. Document and communicate achievements, noting how they relate to profit. Care, but don't care too much. Remember, it's only a game.

Point 6: Available Information

In this day and age, it is likely impossible to keep information from anyone, but even the attempt to do so implies distrust. Of course you don't want proprietary information to fall into the hands of the competition, and that's a legitimate risk. But even worse is employees not having the knowledge and information necessary to make the best decisions, particularly if they're being held accountable for those decisions. True partners share information.

Today, one of the most sensitive pieces of information centers around prospects of layoffs and firings necessitated by rapidly changing business conditions. Such prospects generate fear and apprehension, which can be devastating to morale and productivity. Here, too, let employees know what's going on. Yes, you run the risk of alarming people and causing them to head for the job market before the ax falls, which may make it even more difficult for you to achieve your results. But sharing the information lets you all be in it together and enhances prospects for getting down to brass tacks to do whatever might be done to save revenue, save jobs, and save the company. Instead of no communication with employees, which means they'll fear the worst, lay it all out on the table. It is likely that everyone will ask, "What can *I* do?"

Point 7: Embrace Diversity

Different keys open different doors. On my key ring, I have a key for the Cutlass and a key for the front door. The front door key isn't much good for trying to crank the Cutlass. That doesn't mean the key isn't any good. All it means is that I should restrict use of the front door key to the front door and not try to extend its application elsewhere. As noted, a wide variety of personalities are at work in the business environment, including Organization Men/Company Men, Craftsmen, Jungle Fighters, and Gamesmen. Beyond that, in any enlightened organization, great diversity exists among employees. They have different backgrounds, different values, different lifestyles, and different attitudes about their jobs, the organization, and you. This diversity is a strength, but it's also a management challenge. A one-size-fits-all approach to management is no longer viable, and it is guaranteed to lead to frustration. Instead of asking, "What is this employee's problem?" ask yourself, "What key will unlock this person's commitment to high performance?" The challenge is to find compatibility between the individual's needs and objectives and the needs and objectives of the organization. Within this context, especially among the most talented people in their twenties, is an essential distrust of you just because you are management, particularly if you're over thirty. At best, you will receive patronizing respect until you engender trust and command real respect. I've gotten so I love it when I get that in-your-face attitude. It demonstrates to me I'm dealing with a person who has his or her own identity and attitudes. Those people make the best employees. It also signals to me that I've got to take a leadership role, illustrate I know what I'm doing, and set the standards of performance by which this person will be evaluated. That makes me more effective, staying focused on what I should be doing. All of which, I guess, is to say that the glass is half full.

Point 8: Be Proactive

Take a proactive role in your employees' career progress. I've purposely saved this one for last. Many managers believe it's in their best interest to retain their top employees and so they do whatever they can to keep them. If that means giving recognition to everyone who contributes, I'm all for it. If that means fighting to get them raises and doing whatever you can to help them make a whole lot of money, then do it. If that means relieving them from unnecessary paperwork and hassles, great, that's part of being a good manager. But beyond that, many shortsighted managers go wrong. They may view a certain employee as indispensable and actively campaign to prevent him or her from being promoted. Absolutely, positively never do that. The short-term benefit you might enjoy by holding on to that employee will be far more than offset by the negatives which will accrue from resentment on the part of the person retained who will believe, rightly, that you are stifling his or her career progress. Furthermore, other employees will perceive, rightly, that you are more concerned about taking care of yourself than taking care of them. Instead, despite any possible short-term challenges, do anything you can to help employees move up and out. That means not trying to hold on to indispensable people and thwarting their progress. But more than that, it means taking a proactive role to help your better people get better jobs, within your company and without. You heard that right: better jobs outside your company as well as within. That may sound as though you're operating at cross purposes with the best interests of yourself and your organization, but not so.

If all your people know that you'll do all you can to help them build their résumé and get a better job somewhere, don't you think they're a whole lot more likely to work extra hard than if the prime beneficiary were you or the organization? Beyond that, don't you think some of them will so appreciate your unselfish attitude that they choose to remain where they are rather than move on to supposedly greener pastures? Sure, you may endure a little chaos when you lose an indispensable employee, but long term, people will want to work for you and they'll be more committed.

There's a great deal of similarity between business and personal relationships. If you have a good one and want to keep it, the worst thing you can do is to try to control that person and prevent him or her from getting away. Instead, provide the individual with freedom and opportunities, and hope he or she will choose to stay. It's unlikely an up-and-coming star employee will stay with your company for life, just as it's unlikely that high school sweethearts will marry and live happily ever after, but it just might happen. Teach them to fly, give them the freedom to fly, and let them elect to stay.

The foundation is complete, and now you have a sense of the management environment in organizations and how to go about being a participant. Part II explains the critical functions you'll need to attend to all day.

PART II:
FUNCTIONS

Chapter 13

Hiring: Before the Interview

"I COULDN'T HAVE DONE IT WITHOUT THE PLAYERS"

Several years ago one team or another—it wasn't the Cubs—had just won the World Series and the media was conducting interviews with the champion team's manager. He was asked to share his secrets of the triumphant season, and one of the things he said was, "I couldn't have done it without the players." That statement must stand as one of the great understatements of all time, though he wasn't saying it to be funny and didn't seem to appreciate the irony in what he said.

Generally, the difference between success and failure in any organization, as in sports, is effective management. Think of your personal experiences in all the jobs you've held in your lifetime. I'll bet in many situations you worked hard, had a winning attitude, and did your utmost to do what had to be done and do it right. By contrast, I suspect that at one time or two you did the absolute very least you could do and get away with it, had a lousy attitude, and looked for opportunities for things to go wrong while ensuring that you would be held blameless. You were the same person in both of these environments, so it's probably fair to say that effective management, or the lack thereof, was a significant cause of your contrasting performances. The same probably holds true in championship sports teams. There's likely not all that much difference in the talent of the club that wins the World Series versus a team that misses the playoffs by a couple of games and goes home at the end of September. Sure, there are injuries and there are breaks, good and bad, but just as in business those things have a way of evening out over an entire season. Having said all that, it is likely that a very great deal of difference exists in the talent of a World Series champion and that of a team which finishes last in its division. All of us long-suffering Cubs fans know that changing the manager and coaching staff won't make all that much difference if you don't have the right players in the first place.

In Part II, I explore actions you must take as a prerequisite to success. First, identify and hire the right people for the jobs that need to be done. Then, determine exactly what it is you expect an employee to do and how it will be evaluated. Monitor his or her performance, coach, and follow up. Finally, reward achievement and take whatever action is necessary to rectify unsatisfactory performance. These are the essential tasks of your job.

PRECAUTIONS REGARDING THE HIRING PROCESS

Hiring used to a simple process, or at least it seemed that way. You didn't have enough people to get all the work done, so you roughed out a description of what you wanted in the form of a new employee, got the word out you were hiring, talked to someone—probably a young white male—who seemed like a really sharp guy, so you took him on. In the interview process, you had a good gut feeling about what a successful employee was like, so you winged it through the interview and made a seat-of-the pants hiring decision. It never dawned on you that this was how things were done by teams that consistently finish last in their division, that such a process is virtually guaranteed to result in bad hiring decisions, and that such an approach might very possibly land you in trouble with the law.

The vast majority of organizations want to hire the person best qualified to do the best job. Their managers would not want to treat anyone inappropriately nor would they wish to discriminate against any qualified candidate. They wish to be completely fair and unbiased, making a hiring decision based exclusively on a person's ability. But, lacking the necessary knowledge and skills, they make a less-than-optimum hiring decision. And though they sincerely believe they are totally innocent of any wrongdoing, they sometimes get sued.

It's unfortunate, but I must begin this segment with a reminder that we live in a litigious society. It was bad enough when that person spilled coffee and then sued the fast-food restaurant because it was too hot. Now, overweight people want to blame restaurants or food and beverage manufacturers for their obesity, breweries are the target of alcoholics, cigarette companies are being sued by people who knew thirty years ago that smoking was bad for them, and gun makers face the wrath of the families of shooting victims. It is probably just a matter of time before a victim of arson sues the manufacturer of matches. I'm not going to digress into a discussion of the merits, or lack thereof, of such legal actions, but only point to them to illustrate the need to understand the potential legal pitfalls at every step of the hiring, retention, and firing processes. If you don't hire a guy because he smells bad and looks like he's slept in his clothes for about four days, you'd best be able to document how you quantify it and how it's relevant to satisfactory job performance. Many people out there would love to sue you just to see what happens. They may not win in court, but they'll be satisfied to see you have to spend countless hours defending yourself and incur five- or six-figure legal bills. The threat of extortion to preclude a wave of bad publicity has proven an effective tactic for numerous individuals and groups. You'd better know the law and be within the lines. And there's actually a benefit to all this: you'll make better hiring decisions, which will help build a championship team.

STEPS IN THE HIRING PROCESS

Step 1: Prepare a Position Description

Prepare a competency-based position description. Remember: A position description includes a job description (what the person does in performing the required duties of the job) and those specific skills and other criteria necessary to do so.

If you're creating a new position, by necessity you'll need to build the position from the ground up and make some adjustment in other positions and perhaps some adjustment in the organizational structure to accommodate the new position. Even if you're merely refilling an existing position, take advantage of this opportunity to consider either eliminating or restructuring the position. This is reorganizing on the go and a form of continuous improvement. Why leave your organizational structure intact for a protracted time, letting it become stagnant and unresponsive to ever-changing business conditions until after two or three years or so it's become completely dysfunctional and requires highly disruptive major surgery? Instead, every time you make a hiring decision, fine-tune your structure and make adjustments in existing position descriptions. For example, say you have two marketing manager positions, each staffed by a competent, experienced person making $60,000 a year. One of them leaves. Your first inclination might be to seek a person to fill the existing position at its current salary. However, you might be able to hire a clerical person who could take over the routine duties of those marketing managers as well as those of an assistant marketing manager who is making $40,000 a year. You can hire that clerical person for $30,000 a year. Relieved of their former routine duties, the remaining marketing manager and the assistant marketing manager can be promoted and take over the other duties of the departed marketing manager. Give each of them a 20 percent raise; it's not really a promotion if you don't give them a meaningful raise. The person who was the remaining marketing manager now gets $72,000 and the person who was the assistant marketing manager now gets $48,000. You will have created three new position descriptions, recognized and promoted two employees, and fine-tuned your organization to fit the ever-evolving business environment. Promoting from within, you've probably done wonders for morale among all your employees, and, in case you didn't notice, you just reduced payroll by $10,000. Nice little contribution to the old bottom line.

As you develop new position descriptions, specify all major responsibilities and determine the relevance of this position in your organization's big picture. Identify all the critical competencies and quantifiable traits that profile a successful person in the position. As you do so, be sure to note certain critical criteria, the two or three "must-have" characteristics to do the job successfully, and other preferred criteria, other "nice-to-have" skills, experience, etc. For those criteria, note what training would be necessary to bring a candidate up to speed. A candidate might be deficient in certain critical criteria but could still be viable for consideration if those skills could be addressed in a short time. As an example, "fluency in Spanish" would be more of a problem than "ability to send e-mail."

Developing a competency-based position description will have benefits down the road. First of all, it will help you develop necessary tools to evaluate the qualifications of potential candidates. In addition, it will help you develop specific performance standards for evaluating employees who are hired for the position.

Keep in mind that all position criteria must be job related and that you may face a legal obligation to demonstrate that criteria are necessary for successful performance. This is particularly true if the criteria have an adverse impact on a class of persons with protected status. One such example was a municipality that required custodial workers to have a high school education. They were sued on a complaint that the degree was not necessary for the specified duties and that its requirement inordinately affected minority candidates, a higher proportion of whom did not have a high school degree.

You must be able to document that any hiring criterion is predictive of successful job performance. Be especially careful if you use any form of testing to evaluate candidates. First of all, you must prove that performance on the test is positively correlated with performance on the job. Furthermore, you may not use a test that has a negative impact on a protected group if another test, equally predictive, has less adverse impact. For instance, if you have a test that is passed by 80 percent of Caucasians but only 50 percent of African Americans, you may not use that test if another test exists, equally predictive of on-the-job performance, which is passed by 70 percent of Caucasians and 55 percent of African Americans.

I'll say this now and remind you again when touching upon other legal issues: This book is intended only to point out areas in which the law applies. My objective is not to present legal advice but to impress upon you the need to utilize your human resources department or an attorney to be sure you are in compliance with all statutes and requirements. With that in mind, let's do a quick overview of some of the more prominent points on which you should seek input and counsel.

Step 2: Make It Legal

Be sure that everything you do is legally nondiscriminatory and provides everyone equal employment opportunity. Let me lead into this segment with an editorial statement: If you do not embrace diversity, you are a fool. I'm not talking about all that touchy-feely peace-and-love stuff, either. I'm talking about cold hard cash. It's in your economic best interest to hire the person best qualified for the job. It's to your economic detriment to hire a less qualified person who's more like you. Diversity brings new and creative thinking to address emerging opportunities, especially in the smaller, more profitable niche markets. You should choose diversity for the good of your organization and it should not be forced upon you. I note this because many people, understandably so, have come to perceive compliance with the law as one great big encumbrance. Once again, there's no need to digress into a discussion of legal complexities or to complain about persons who routinely employ extortion as a tactic to remedy ancient evils. The glass is half full. Let's get on with it and be sure we're in compliance.

As noted, all hiring criteria and all hiring practices must be nondiscriminatory and job related. This does not require preferential treatment for any group of persons, only the same opportunities. Affirmative action aside, though, there's something to be said for the benefits of hiring candidates who help you attain greater diversity in the workplace. For disabled candidates, you are expected to provide "reasonable accommodation" but are not expected to endure "undue hardship," admittedly nebulous terms. You are not expected to fill quotas, but if 199 of 200 employees are white, male, and heterosexual, someone out there may be inspired to start rattling your branches to see what falls out of the tree.

Discrimination *is* permissible if you can demonstrate that there is a bona fide occupational qualification (BFOQ). You may, for instance, specify female custodians for the women's locker room, and persons of Chinese origin for a Chinese restaurant, though on the latter you might be treading on thin ice. A while back, the government threatened action against a leading restaurant chain known for its young, scantily attired, female servers, insisting they offer equal opportunity to men. The chain responded with billboards of hunky, hairy guys dressed in their waitress outfits. The public thought all of this a bit much, and the feds backed off, but it should serve as a good example of how easy it is, even with good intentions, to get into serious and potentially very expensive problems.

I did a considerable amount of work with a company that readily agreed it considered race in placing persons in field marketing positions, but the company insisted that race was tantamount to a BFOQ since their southern distributors were disinclined to do business with African Americans, qualifications notwithstanding. The situation was exacerbated by the fact that most of their strong markets were in the South and field marketing districts in the North were the road to nowhere on this company's career track. I strongly expressed my professional opinion (ignored and resented) that it was incumbent on this company to offer opportunities based on qualifications and without regard to race, and to inform their distributors that the person appointed to their district was the person who had total and sole authority to represent the company. Their unwillingness to take a proactive stance ultimately resulted in a lawsuit on behalf of their employees, recently settled at a cost in the high eight figures.

These few examples and anecdotes should make it abundantly clear that you need to be buttoned down and prepared to demonstrate that all your hiring practices are nondiscriminatory and job related. Since perils exist out there that you've never even thought of, you need professional advice from someone who has all the facts. When you don't hire someone who is physically repulsive, with a face that not even a mother could love, someone you think in no way could ever represent your company, you must be able to cite specific job-related criteria that were the basis of your hiring decision. Just let anyone overhear you say the word "ug-*lee*," and we'll see you in court.

Step 3: Generate a Candidate Pool

How you go about assembling your list of candidates will vary depending on the nature of the position being filled, but always look for qualified candidates inside your organization before looking outside. The key question, of course, is the candidate's potential for success in the new position. Certainly, someone's track record and job history are the best predictors of success in the future, but don't forget the Peter Principle: Success as an outside sales rep or account executive may be a necessary, but not sufficient, indicator that someone will be happy and successful in management. Remember that you are not looking for someone who necessarily has experience in a similar situation. If you're going to insist on experience, you will by necessity tend to go outside the organization for candidates. The result may be frustration on the part of current employees, eager for an opportunity to prove themselves in a new and challenging position. Even more significant, you are attracting people already familiar with a position and thus lacking enthusiasm for an adventure and learning experience. Over time, the combination of those effects may be highly detrimental to morale and lead to a lethargic company culture.

I'm always amazed that some organizations never seem to learn what they get when they hire a veteran with past success at a certain position. The vast preponderance of the time, they get an overpriced person who has nothing to prove and perceives he has nothing to learn. He's comfortable, and comfortable employees invariably underperform.

If you're hiring for a "professional" position, which I define as entry level with college education and up, you should rely more on your personal network and industry contacts and less on advertising, especially in mass-circulation newspapers. Having said that, you may be advised to post a position widely to ensure attaining a "representative" pool of candidates.

If you're an "attractive" company—profitable, well known, with low turnover and good pay—many of the best candidates should seek you out, unsolicited. I routinely advise graduating seniors to identify companies they're interested in and to initiate contact at the point of encounter, whether it's a broker, retailer, or the ultimate point of sale. For pharmaceutical companies, it's doctors and pharmacists. For consumer nondurables, it's the retail store, corporate store headquarters, or the broker who represents the company at outlet and buyer levels. For services outsourcers, go to their customers. For services providers, go see the people at the place where those services are being conducted. A little basic prospecting and networking leads to the person who has the sort of position a candidate is seeking, which readily helps him or her identify the manager who makes such hiring decisions. Candidates who take such initiative say a lot about themselves with those actions and are probably worth the time it takes to give them a thirty-minute screening interview, even if you have no positions open at present. Very possibly a manager in another location might want to talk to this person and, in any case, who knows? Tomorrow you just might need someone.

Especially for positions requiring specialized experience and qualifications, you may find candidates through your network of professional people in your industry and community. Communicate what you're looking for through these colleagues to see if they know of someone, or if they themselves would have an interest in a proposed position. Often you will hear of people working for your competition who would be receptive to a discreet inquiry, if that's an avenue you'd wish to consider.

If you're interested in recruiting new college graduates, go beyond the shotgun approach of merely posting position openings at the career center. Instead, seek out professional organizations on the campus. These organizations are usually looking for speakers and will be receptive as long as you go beyond the job pitch and have something insightful to say about business and your profession. If you're looking for accountants, go talk to the student accounting society. If you want marketing and sales students, see the marketing association. Be a big spender and invest in pizza or subs. Encourage interested people to talk to you afterward, and get them started in the steps of your hiring process.

In some circumstances, you'll want to employ headhunters to identify and screen candidates for you, especially for specialized positions. Or you may want to outsource certain positions entirely. Would it make sense to outsource custodial, landscaping, and security functions instead of hiring employees to do those functions? How about accounting, payroll, and legal? You might well find that outsourcing yields superior performance *and* saves you money. It will most certainly save you time.

Should you elect to advertise a position, do it right. First and foremost, that means selecting the right media. The Internet is not the place to go for unskilled positions in your local market. At the other end of the scale, newspaper classifieds are inappropriate for very highly specialized positions for which there would be few qualified candidates. Wherever you advertise, think about your ad from the candidate's point of view and ask yourself how someone you want to attract would react to the ad. Traditionally, recruiting ads have addressed only areas of content, the qualifications and skills required, and basic duties of the job, something like this:

> Consolidated Peptide, the nation's leading supplier of protein-based industrial lubricants, has an immediate opening for project coordinators. Degree in chemical engineering and minimum three years' experience in lab technology required. Candidates should be well versed in scientific methodology and a collegial working environment. Salary contingent upon experience. Send resumes to Consolidated Peptide, 313 Gulf Breeze Parkway, Gulf Breeze, FL 32999.

Nothing is really all that bad about this ad, but it doesn't exactly jump out at candidates and make them say, "Wow! That's a place I might really like to be." Also consider the action it requests: drop a résumé in the mail, then wait and see what happens.

Instead of the basic traditional ad, think of your ad as the first step in a marketing program designed to attract the right candidates and then sell them on your company and its people. In a potentially serious personal relationship, you probably don't ask for a kiss twenty seconds after being introduced. Similarly, don't ask a candidate to fire off a résumé on the basis of seeing an ad. Use the ad as an opportunity for the candidate to learn more about your company and its people. Describe what the company is all about and what it stands for:

> What is it about Amalgamated Bromide that earned us the honor of "the Most Admired Company in the Metroplex"?

> Learn more about our innovative approach to technology and people, and how our project coordinators help our company serve the region.

> If you have a degree in chemical engineering and experience in lab technology, and want to be part of a team of professionals working together to make a difference, we'd like to meet you. Bring your résumé to our career information program at the Pensacola Marriott Wednesday evening at 7.

Quite a difference, right? Seeing the latter ad from the perspective of the candidate, it's easy to see how it would elicit more interest. Also, the action requested is a chance to get together, consistent with the positioning of this company as one concerned about its employees and customers.

One of the limitations of print ads is that they may not be seen by persons not actively looking for a job—people who might be your best candidates. That's where your network of professionals may be more helpful. I'd also recommend against running blind ads in which your company is not identified. I've heard horror stories from people who responded to blind ads that were being run by their own companies. In any case, the better candidates will usually not respond to them. Finally, specify exactly how you want the candidate to respond. In the second sample ad, that was an in-person get together. For a more traditional response, specify what they should send and where, if they may e-mail in lieu of snail mail, or if they can do it all through your company's Web site.

Do keep in mind that an ad has the potential to generate a monumental number of responses. I've heard of situations in which thousands of job seekers descended on an employer and chaos ensued. If that's a possibility, a minimum of planning will let you pass out employment applications and pencils to all candidates, informing them you'll get back to them to schedule any follow-up. In the "drop by and get acquainted" scenario, you might want to screen visitors to confirm they have the necessary qualifications and experience. For those who do, on to the session. For those who do not, or didn't bother to do as asked and bring along their résumé in the first place, here's an application and pencil. After the session, you can file the applications. They can keep the pencil.

Similarly, get some clerical help to sort out what comes in online or through the mail. There's no need for you to look at the 90 percent of candidates who don't meet the basic requirements.

Finally, it's only common courtesy to give all respondents an immediate acknowledgment that you have heard from them. If they didn't make the initial cut, send them the "Although we were impressed with your background, it is not exactly what we are looking for at this time. However, we will keep your résumé on file and we wish you the best in your job search." If they did make the initial cut, keep them updated and informed every step of the way until they either get a job offer or are deemed out of the running and given the "another candidate more closely matched the needs of this position" response. I've had candidates call me to ask about their status and I knew they'd been excluded, but I wasn't allowed to tell them so until we'd made our final decision on whom to hire. This is hardly fair.

Step 4: Screen Résumés

Everyone looks good on a résumé, even more so when its author is lying. As noted in the prior segment, clerical help should free you of ever having to look at résumés that lack documentation of necessary credentials and experience. You should also eliminate those individuals who submit paperwork containing errors in the résumé or cover letter and/or isn't customized in *some* way. Next let's touch on some of the things to look for to help whittle down the remaining pile to a manageable size.

Most résumés will open with a brief statement of the candidate's career objective. This should be customized to address your company and probably the specific position being sought. At the least I would look for, "Entry-level field sales position in the consumer products industry, with opportunities leading to sales management," but I would like to see it customized to read, "Entry-level field sales position with XYZ Company . . ." With such a stated objective, the candidate is opening the door for you to ask questions about why he or she wants to work in your industry and for your company, providing an opportunity to demonstrate he or she has done the homework. Do not look kindly on sophomoric statements, such as, "To find an environment where I can demonstrate my interpersonal communication skills and attain my potential." You might forgive this from a new graduate who doesn't know any better.

As you review the résumé, look for credentials and specific achievements that match the position requirements. Look for a pattern of career progression and specific documentation of the candidate's impact on sales and profits. You want concrete phrases such as "Managed" and "Responsible for" with achievements such as "Exceeded quota by 20 percent" or "Led region with forty-four new accounts in six months." Be wary of qualifiers, such as, "Assisted in" or "knowledge of." The only item you're concerned about on education is degrees received, though for specific positions you would be interested in certifiable skills. Pay no attention to schools "attended" and be wary of lengthy descriptions of three-day seminars or one-day sales training programs. Always validate education directly from the institution that granted the degree, and confirm that the institution is not merely a degree mill.

Look for relevant affiliations and activities, particularly professional organizations in which the candidate took a leadership role. In addition, involvement in charitable and community organizations may say a lot about a candidate's character and willingness to work hard. By contrast, look askance at notations about recreational interests or affiliations irrelevant to the professional area. I remember interviewing a candidate for an organization in Florida. When I asked the reason for her interest in this organization, she responded, "I love to sail." That was enough for us to find plenty of job-related reasons to eliminate her. Someone else, under professional associations, listed an organization that combined religion and surfing. This was not appropriate, and it was helpful in determining that his field of study did not match position requirements.

Immediately eliminate any candidates who speak ill of former employers, either on their résumés or in person. If they're blunt about spewing negatives about someone else, just think what they'll be saying about you when they leave your organization, which they will. They might not be all that good as team players, either.

I *hate* the phrase "References available on request." What a waste of space! *Of course* they're available on request! However, on that point, I pay no attention to references supplied by a candidate, as I pay no attention to unsolicited letters of recommendation which are always, predictably, laudatory. We'll get into reference checking in Chapter 14.

Step 5: Get the Specifics

"Professional" positions usually start with a résumé. Candidates seeking unskilled positions may not even know what a résumé is, let alone have one, though when I deal with such persons I encourage them to put together a résumé and will help them do so. In any case, all candidates should fill out a formal application before the interviewing process begins. A résumé may have some broad generalities, but the application cuts down to specific, verifiable facts.

If you're hiring for anything beyond the most basic position, you should also go beyond the one-size-fits-all standard company application form. Remember, you want a structured format that addresses all job-related issues and helps you differentiate among those who are qualified, marginally qualified, or not qualified. Early on, the form should address any "deal killers," items that absolutely eliminate a candidate from consideration. For instance, if a job requires overnight travel three days a week, it would be a deal killer if a candidate is unable to be away.

The latter point is an example of why it's absolutely essential to run any application by human resources or an attorney. You are in violation of the law if you ask candidates whether they have small children, believing that would affect their ability to manage overnight travel. You may ask only the job-related question of whether they would be able to accommodate overnight travel. You may not even ask such seemingly innocuous questions as date of birth (potential for age discrimination) or country of citizenship. You may only ask, and must verify, that they have a legal right to work in the United States. The potential pitfalls are endless, so don't go this one alone. Get competent professional input when developing the application.

Fine-tune the application so that it is an easy-to-use screening tool, enabling you to run through it and quickly do a checklist that evaluates key points on qualifications. Keep deal killers near the beginning to spare yourself having to read through anything more than necessary for candidates who will definitely not make the cut.

After these first steps—clerical elimination of résumés clearly unqualified, screening of résumés, and detailed assessment of application forms—you've probably pared the candidate pool down a good bit. Now, further clerical help can verify education and other factual information. False statements on the résumé or application are, of course, automatic deal killers. Don't be surprised, though, to see misrepresentations of material facts. Incredibly, some organizations out there still do not verify all the facts, and thus many candidates will lie. I'm not talking about stretching the truth or creatively interpreting facts. You'll need to get to the interview itself to dig up that sort of thing. You'll discover that candidates are still one course short of receiving their degrees or they misstated dates of employment to fill in awkward gaps. They may try to give you a reason for their "mistake" or explain how it's just a matter of paperwork at the university from which they claimed a degree. Yeah, right.

Before scheduling formal interviews, you might want to take one more step and do a preliminary screening interview by phone. At that time, you can clarify any outstanding questions about the candidate and the position. I witnessed one farce in which three candidates were flown in for interviews over a period of three days each. The winner was subsequently phoned with a job offer that he declined because the salary was inadequate. That never should have happened. Before bringing anyone in for an interview, the candidate should be informed of the proposed salary and benefit package, the job start date, and the deadline for acceptance of the position should an offer be made. Sure, some negotiation can occur, but not if the proposed salary is $80,000 and the candidate wants $150,000, and not if you must have an answer by September 1 and the candidate is unwilling to make a decision before the first of the year.

In addition, the initial telephone screening interview can clarify any factual information that must be validated or would influence a final decision concerning who will be invited to the interviewing process. If you've done the job well at every step of the way, you've identified the best candidates for the position, communicated with them and helped them see they might want to consider being affiliated with your organization, and determined who are the best of the best. Those are the persons to bring in for interviews.

Chapter 14

Interviewing and Hiring

If you've followed procedures as described in Chapter 13, you now have a pool of candidates that represents the best of the best, people you believe are qualified for the position and would be positively predisposed to accept an offer. You're probably down to at least three candidates, at best no more than five or six. But who's going to get the final nod? That's what you'll have to decide in the interviewing process.

If you've screened résumés and verified factual information, you should be reasonably confident that all your finalists have the ability—the "can do" qualifications—to handle the requisite functions of the position. At least, they can be brought up to speed with a reasonable amount of training. Of course, you'll need to clarify and confirm ability in the interview, asking for specific examples of experience. That's the easy part of the assessment. More challenging is to get a handle on the "will do," a candidate's willingness to work hard and endure at least some degree of personal inconvenience to get the job done right. There is also the intangible of manageability by you, whether the candidate's style of operating is compatible with your management style. If you're a by-the-book, by-the-numbers manager, you're probably already difficult enough to work for. Why hire an employee who demands maximum freedom and a minimum of oversight?

Let's look at another case that bridges points raised in the prior chapter and issues on interviewing, which we'll discuss in this chapter. First, consider the candidate's résumé. Look it over and see whether you would have selected this candidate for an interview in the first place. Then read the transcript of an interview conducted by a manager who was doing a get-acquainted screening before sending the candidate to speak with the next person in the process. The transcript is mercifully short, but it should enable you to assess your gut feeling about how well the manager did interviewing the candidate. We'll get into specific points and considerations straightaway.

CASE STUDY: JOHN BURKE

The Résumé

John Burke
7454 Asphalt Trafficway
Kansas City, MO 64141

PERSONAL INFORMATION

Age: 29
Height: 5'11"
Citizenship: United States
Place of Birth: Remington, Indiana
Health: Excellent
Wife: Jane, age 27
Children: Gary, age 2; Wyatt, age 4 months

EDUCATION

MBA (marketing), University of Notre Dame, South Bend, IN, 2003
    GPA 3.2 of 4.0
BA (management), University of Wisconsin, Madison, WI, 1999
    GPA 3.3 of 4.0
High school: Lafayette High School, Lafayette, IN, 1995
    GPA 3.3 of 4.0

EMPLOYMENT EXPERIENCE

2004-present: Midwest Products Co., Kansas City, MO
    Brand Manager, Fabricated Products
        Coordinated reports for top management
        Developed sales forecasts
        Handled budgets under profit center responsibility

2003-2004: Inn-Dee Enterprises, Indianapolis, IN
    Marketing Manager, Consumer Products
        Reviewed sales and profit trends
        Maintained liaison with field sales reps
        Assisted staff in achieving departmental objectives

2001-2003: Green Door Restaurant, South Bend, IN
  Operations Manager, Night Shift
    Managed restaurant staff
    Trained new employees
    Coordinated marketing and advertising programs

1999-2001: Procter & Gamble Co., Cincinnati, OH
  Project Manager, New Products
    Compiled and summarized marketing reports
    Evaluated test market performance
    Assisted in development of recommendations for new product rollouts

1995-1999: University Union, University of Wisconsin, Madison
  Assistant Manager, Food Services
    Planned and prepared menu items
    Interacted with customers
    Assisted in maintenance of physical facilities

1993-1995: Kroger Store #171, Lafayette, IN
  Customer Service Representative
    Provided service to customers
    Helped maintain inventory in various departments
    Responsible for building of marketing and merchandising devices

INTERESTS AND HOBBIES

Golf
Sailing
Baseball (Indiana State Championship semi-finalist team, 1995)

ASSOCIATIONS

American Marketing Association
Young Republicans
St. Luke's Episcopal Church, Lafayette, IN
Delta Tau Fraternity–University of Wisconsin
  Treasurer 1996-1997
  Social Chairman 1997-1999
Jaycees–Kansas City

CAREER INTERESTS

Marketing management position with growth company which offers opportunity for advancement and recognition of performance

The Interview

Jim McGuire is director of brand management for Tri-State Industries. He is interviewing John Burke for the position of marketing manager, grocery products.

MCGUIRE: Good morning, John.

BURKE: Good morning.

MCGUIRE: I trust you managed to find our office without too much trouble.

BURKE: No trouble at all.

MCGUIRE: Care for a cup of coffee before we begin?

BURKE: No, thanks. Just had a cup before coming over.

MCGUIRE: Fine [glances at the résumé]. I see you went to Notre Dame.

BURKE: Yes, sir.

MCGUIRE: [Smiles] Your name sure doesn't sound Irish.

BURKE: Well, actually I'm half Irish. My mother's side of the family.

MCGUIRE: Notre Dame's an excellent school.

BURKE: It sure is.

MCGUIRE: Anyhow, John, the position we're talking about today is marketing manager for grocery products. We need someone with a strong marketing background and trade experience. Do you feel you can bring that to us?

BURKE: Yes, I do.

MCGUIRE: Why do you think we should hire you?

BURKE: Well, Jim, I've had a good education at good schools plus I've had real-world experience. Working at a grocery store in high school was especially valuable.

MCGUIRE: How so?

BURKE: In college and graduate school it really helped me understand what was taught in the classroom. And in the business world it's enabled me to be a more effective marketing manager.

MCGUIRE: Yes, in this position we feel a candidate should appreciate what happens at the store level.

BURKE: I certainly agree.

MCGUIRE: You'll have fifteen people reporting to you. Do you feel you're a good people manager?

BURKE: I believe I am. I'm easy to get along with and enjoy working with people. I was social chairman of my fraternity at the University of Wisconsin.

MCGUIRE: Do you have any weaknesses?

BURKE: I'd have to say I'm a well-organized person and I strive to do the job right. Sometimes I'm disappointed when other people accept lower standards than I do.

MCGUIRE: Fine. Let's go across the hall now so you can meet our director of marketing.

PROBLEMS WITH THE RÉSUMÉ

First of all, let's consider the candidate's résumé. Definitely impressive educational credentials, no doubt about that. As far as employment experience is concerned, it's important to draw a time line to consider all concurrent activities in his life. At first glance, you might look askance at a move from Procter & Gamble to the Green Door Restaurant, until noting that the restaurant job was something he worked at while a student pursuing an MBA.

Personally, I have a problem with any résumé that's more than one page long. As I say to job seekers I've coached, I've been around awhile and I've done a few things, so if I can do my business résumé in one page, you can do yours in one page. For this candidate, there's no need for the first segment on personal information, all of which is irrelevant, and no reason to list high school under education. Someone with a bachelor's degree should not even list an associate's degree unless something about it was truly unique.

John Burke listed six jobs, which is far too many. Generally, the last three, four max, will do it. Yes, there will then be gaps, but those can be addressed in the interview or a prescreening phone call. Certainly there is no need to list part-time jobs in college, unless the candidate is a recent graduate, and—oh, no, not again!—absolutely nothing from high school unless, same deal, the candidate is a recent high school graduate.

His interests and hobbies are irrelevant and inappropriate. Associations should be limited to professional associations and exclude any reference to politics and religion. Leadership roles in college organizations are important, but only for recent graduates. Career interests should probably be at the beginning instead of the end, and in any case it's nebulous and not customized. This résumé can slashed down to one page.

When assessing a résumé, take a step back from it, read between the lines, and try to envision the person, above and beyond the facts on the page. My first impression, as I've described, was a concern about the length of the résumé, due primarily to irrelevant details. I don't know about you, but I'm not that enthusiastic about hiring employees who have a penchant for irrelevant details. Beyond that, I am concerned about a lack of career progress, especially after leaving Procter & Gamble to pursue an MBA. Even the MBA business makes me uncomfortable; couldn't the candidate have worked toward the MBA while still at P&G?

Finally, my worst fears are confirmed when I analyze descriptions of prior positions. No specific responsibilities and achievements are listed, only vague generalities. The college and high school jobs demonstrate exaggeration and embellishment, suggesting that this guy's BS overwhelms his BA. In the trade, this is known as the "Apollo syndrome," so named for a candidate who described providing critical input to NASA scientists, which upon further investigation turned out to be coffee. When this candidate writes, "Handled budgets under profit center responsibility," I suspect he carried them from the copy room to a secretary's desk. This candidate would never have made my final cut, though it looks like he might find a place to hide at Tri-State Industries.

INTERVIEW PITFALLS

We have yet to discuss the fine points of interviewing, but even at first blush it's clear that McGuire is incompetent. Just the statement "Your name sure doesn't sound Irish" is enough to bring on a lawsuit. It sounds friendly and sociable, but in court it's the same as "You sure don't look Jewish" or "You sure don't sweat much for a fat boy." If you didn't hear it the first time: make no reference to religion, ethnic background, or any other personal characteristic that's not job related.

Compounding the serious legal faux pas, McGuire asks trivial questions that obviously call for an affirmative response and fails to follow up on other questions. As I'll describe momentarily, candidates are expecting "What are your strengths/weaknesses?" and "Why should we hire you?" That's not to say you shouldn't ask those questions, but they won't be all that useful without a couple of follow-ups to help you ascertain whether the candidate has something to say or has merely prepped responses to some of the more common questions.

CONDUCTING A SUCCESSFUL INTERVIEW

Now that we've touched upon what not to do in the interview, let's get on to what you *should* do. For starters, don't forget to go beyond having candidates sell themselves to you. It's of equal importance that you sell the candidate on the position and, especially, on your organization. It's no secret that in the past few years management in numerous high-profile companies has been guilty of egregious conduct affecting employees, stockholders, and the general public. Some of these people have lined their pockets with tens of millions of dollars, using creative accounting and out-and-out fraud, which has brought their companies and employees to financial ruin. Understandably, many employees and most prospective employees are wary or downright distrustful of management. I will spend a lot of time on this in Part III, but for now let's just say that it's incumbent on you to satisfy any prospective employee that your company and all its associates manage themselves by the highest ethical standards. Unless you do that, the best people won't come to work for you. And unless all your associates, starting with management, actually do live by such standards, those remaining are condemned to failure. In Chapter 13, I described having a get-acquainted session for certain positions, an informal environment in which people could get to know something about your organization and its people. Whether or not you hold such an activity in the recruiting phase, be sure that in the interviewing process you paint a picture of your company, its vision, its culture, and its values. Put yourself in the candidates' shoes and help them appreciate all the intangibles that will make them choose to affiliate with you.

Ask the Right Questions

When the interview begins, make the candidate comfortable, perhaps with some small talk or something describing the aforementioned nature of your organization and its values. Then, as you get down to business, don't wing it. Have a plan. Ask the right questions and ask them right. Start with closed-ended questions to fill in any gaps or supply missing information. Confirm specific competencies and experience:

"Did you report directly to the vice president of sales?"
"Are you certified to do tune-ups on a VTEC engine?"
"How would you go about establishing a sales force compensation system?"

In a similar vein, you want to get an idea of whether a candidate has experience dealing with issues likely to be faced on the job:

"Have you ever managed an employee whose performance was short of standards?"

A "No" to that question suggests little management experience or, more unlikely, experience managing nothing but good employees. In either case, follow up. To a "Yes" ask, "What did you do?" To a "No," "How were you able to keep all your employees at or above standard?"
Don't ask:

"What would you do if you had an employee whose performance was short of standards?"

A response to this question is theoretical and does not address the critical point of whether the candidate has any real-world experience dealing with inadequate performance. Theory is all well and good, but it's no substitute for a proven capability. Ask direct questions to determine what the candidates know about your company, its products, and your industry. It is inexcusable if they not have done their homework. Simple questions such as "Why do you want to work in this industry?" and "Why do you want to work for this company?" are good openers. Then take it from there to see just how much preparation they've done.

Two contrasting examples demonstrate how revealing this can be. Both involved final-semester college seniors. In the first case, a sales manager from M&M/Mars asked a candidate to name two of their products. The candidate couldn't even come up with "M&M's and Mars." The interview was terminated on the spot. The other example was a vice president of a pharmaceutical company who was visiting the regional office where a candidate was having an initial screening interview. This company generally did not hire people without outside sales experience, so this person was considered an unlikely hire. The vice president, who later admitted he wanted to have a little fun making this kid feel foolish, asked if he could sit in on the interview and ask a few questions. He opened by asking the kid to talk about the company's products and the standing of each in the marketplace. The kid responded, without notes, by describing each product, its competitive advantage, and its approximate sales relative to the nearest competitor. He went on to describe new products in the pipeline and their status in Phase 1, Phase 2, and Phase 3 trials. That kid got hired at a $70,000-a-year job, fresh out of college. When he recounted the story to me and I asked him why he had learned all that for the interview, he just looked at me and said, "How could you *not* know all that if you were interviewing with a company for a job?" Well, as the prior example illustrates, many don't, and that says a lot about them.

As alluded to early in the chapter, skills, abilities, competencies, and knowledge are the easy part. Willingness, intangibles, and basic horse sense can be a little tougher to pin down, but are at least as important as tangible skills. If a candidate is currently employed, or at least ostensibly so, you might ask:

"Why are you considering leaving your current position?"
"What's it like working for XYZ?"

In this day and age, the primary reason for looking elsewhere is because the present employer is going belly up or is "rightsizing" and facing a few thousand lost jobs. There's nothing wrong with that, though if the company is flourishing you might seek to reassure yourself that the candidate is not about to be fired for cause. What you're hoping for with these questions is an insight into what motivates this candidate: Is it freedom, money, future prospects for a career, or something else? This also gives the candidate the opportunity to speak ill of his or her present employer, which should be a red flag. Sour grapes are not predictors of happy team players.

What you want to hear from those prior questions is that the candidate likes working for the present employer but is looking for more opportunities and challenges. This is a good chance for him or her to demonstrate knowledge about your company and industry, and ways in which the candidate would contribute to your success.

As noted, there's not much point to asking obvious yes/no questions and moving right along, but they can be useful as a setup for a follow-up question. For example, similar to the case study, you might ask, "Do you think you have what it takes to be an effective manager?" This is guaranteed to get a "Yes, I do" response. Follow up with, "What does it take to be an effective manager?" to see whether the candidate can properly describe the characteristics of an effective manager.

Use more open-ended questions to evaluate willingness and manageability. Try to get a sense of how the candidate thinks and acts in a professional setting.

> "Tell me about an important goal you've set for yourself in the past three years."
> "What was this goal?"
> "How did you go about quantifying it?"
> "What outside inputs did you use in setting this goal?"
> "What kinds of obstacles did you face? How did you deal with them?"
> "What were the results?"

You're looking for an indication that the candidate can set quantifiable goals and see them through to fulfillment, dealing with obstacles and demonstrating flexibility to handle unforeseen circumstances. Also, be alert for cues that indicate the candidate works well in a team environment. A goal to run 2,000 miles this year, including a marathon, may be admirable but suggests the candidate is more a loner than team oriented.

In a similar vein and directly related to the professional environment, proceed along related lines:

> "What do you do when you encounter difficulty working through something on your job? Give me an example."
> "Tell me about something you've accomplished as a member of a group."
> "What kinds of new ideas and approaches did you come up with?"
> "How did you persuade others to support these? What kinds of objections did you encounter? How did you deal with them? What was the outcome?"

To gain further insight to the candidates' ability to set priorities with the attendant steps of execution, ask the candidates to describe their greatest achievements. This will give you a more specific response than the nebulous "greatest strength" question. Again, follow up to get the details in a manner similar to that of the "important goal" question. Just as important, have them describe their greatest failure. Look for indications that the candidate accepts accountability for results, good and bad, rather than passing the buck when things don't go as planned. Were the candidates able to make their failures learning experiences, enabling them to take different and more appropriate steps in future situations?

To get a sense of their motivational fit and manageability, ask them to describe the best job, then the most monotonous or worst job they've ever had. Similarly, ask about the best boss and the worst boss. Their "best job" should be a close match to the position you're filling, and their "best boss" should profile you or, abilities and competencies notwithstanding, prospects for a long and happy relationship are marginal.

Take Notes

Throughout the interviewing process, it is absolutely essential that you take notes and specifically quantify your assessment. To the extent it's possible, utilize a form to score responses on a scale from superlative to gruesome. Tell the candidate in advance that you'll be taking notes and, if you want to make it a bit more challenging for the candidate to see your scoring, use a code. I've always used the acronym "MAKE PROFIT," an old standby from the retail trade, ten letters that do not repeat. Thus, "M" is a ten on a ten-point scale, "A" is a nine, and so forth. Then, after assigning a score on an item, jot down some notes about reasons for evaluating an item as you did. After the interview, while facts are still fresh in your mind, look over your notes and fill in details. This is especially important for documenting intangibles that are not part of the structured interview format, such as persons who are condescending or rude to the office staff, or who indicate a willingness to provide proprietary information from their current employer.

Assessing Behavioral Cues

Formally assess nonverbal communication and other behavioral cues. Look for good eye contact, the ability to listen, and some indication they're alive, involved, and interested. Good candidates will interview you as much as you interview them, and they will demonstrate interest and enthusiasm in the position and your organization. You want them to appear observant, noting things in and around your office which give an indication of your interests and personality, providing an opportunity to establish common ground. They should boast, modestly, about some significant achievement, but stated in terms of "We did this" rather than "I did this." The "we" statement indicates a cooperative team player rather than someone more focused on individual recognition.

In most cases, the candidate should demonstrate a command of proper business English. Do not for one moment assume that a college degree implies that a candidate can read or write at or above a fourth-grade level. Be wary of candidates who consistently respond with "Right! or "Exactly!" or who use nonfluencies such as "You know." As you learned in Chapter 13, it is incumbent on you to demonstrate that communication skills are job related. If they are, quantify and document them in the interview.

Give consideration to candidates who ask about opportunities to make a contribution to your organization and its bottom-line objectives. Conversely, be wary of candidates who inquire about perks, fringes, and vacation policies early in the process. Finally, insist that a candidate ask for the job. If not a direct request, at least expect a candidate to state unequivocally that he or she wants the job and ask about the next step in the process and its timetable.

Background and Reference Checks

With a structured planned interview format and a quantitative assessment of job-related criteria, you've been able to rank order your candidate pool and determine which individual gets an offer. Before you do, though, do the next level of background checks and reference checking to confirm your decision. Before interviewing, you verified education and other specific credentials. You confirmed that the candidate worked at the places indicated on the résumé and application. If the position offered a company car or otherwise required operation of a vehicle, you procured driving records. Now, before making the hiring decision, you need to go a little deeper. Depending on what happened in the interview process, you may well have two or three closely qualified candidates who performed equally well through their interviews, and your final hiring decision may hinge on this last step.

Consult your human resources person or attorney before going deeper into background checks. At one end of the scale, you already know it's illegal to verify marital status or political affiliation and that you can be headed for trouble by asking about such items. At the other end of the scale is negligent hiring, *failing* to dig up facts you should have had to make a hiring decision.

Here are some interesting examples. Company A hired a clean-cut young gentleman who proceeded to stalk and assault another employee. He had done the same thing to a colleague at his previous place of employment. The assaulted employee at Company A sued Company A and won on the basis of negligent hiring; the courts ruled that the company should have uncovered facts about the man's prior conviction and never should have hired him in the first place.

Consider Company B, which hired a woman who stated that her five-year hiatus from the workforce was taken so that she could stay at home and care for her children. Actually, she was serving five years in prison after being convicted of embezzling from her company's clients. When, naturally, she repeated those actions as a representative of Company B, the clients of Company B didn't go after her but went straight to the deeper pockets of Company B.

Then there's Organization C, a youth sports organization. Concerned about potential liability, Organization C requested that all twelve of its coaches in one local market agree to a police background check. No problem, said eleven of the twelve, who were promptly confirmed with unblemished backgrounds. Big problem, said Coach 12, on the basis of his constitutional right to privacy. This guy was their best coach, highly dedicated, and was happily married and had two beautiful children, so, decided the board of Organization C, he must be all right. Who can argue against constitutional rights? You know where this is going. Guess which coach decided to engage in a little postgame extracurricular activity with one of the kids. And guess whether he'd been previously convicted for the same thing, which would have come to light with a background check. Right! And guess who the parents went after in the lawsuit. Right again!

Closely related to negligent hiring is the issue of negligent referral, which is the failure to provide critical information a hiring company needs to know. So, if one of your former employees had stalked and assaulted a colleague, and you fail to disclose this when a potential new employer contacts you for a referral, you can be held liable if that person stalks and assaults someone on the new job. Just to complicate matters further, the former employees may turn around and sue you when your negative referrals knock them out of the running. Thus, it's no surprise that many companies have a policy of verifying dates of employment and nothing more. To return to a point raised a few chapters back, it's no surprise that many employees elect a career path as a high-paid doer to avoid such lose-lose scenarios.

Still, if you've decided to be an effective manager, you've got to find a way to obtain reliable references. As noted, pay little or no attention to references supplied by the candidate, all of which are guaranteed to be glowing. Instead, perhaps through your professional network, identify someone in the candidate's former company who knows of the candidate or can steer you to someone who does. The referral chain from your network into and through the former company is far more likely to yield candid responses than if you just contact someone as a cold call.

I'm a strong believer in pretending that everything I say or do is being videotaped 24/7. That way, although anyone who wishes to can be displeased with my words or actions, I never have to worry about being confronted by something I didn't want known or acknowledged. Also, I can readily defend, which I may have to in court, the transcript of anything I say at any time. Earlier, I cited examples of statements that needed to be read between the lines, such as damning with faint praise. This is the way to communicate when soliciting a referral from a former employer as you seek out valuable information without saying anything you wouldn't want read back in court. For instance, you could ask, "What kind of information do you think it's important to obtain when making a hiring decision in your company?" This is innocent enough. If the other person responds, "It's important to know whether someone has ever been convicted of a felony (a fact, by the way, that a potential employer has a right to know), not just locally but anywhere in all fifty states," unless you are really dumb you would be alerted to the message that you need to thoroughly explore the candidate's record. It's a subtle shade of difference, but all the referrer has done is help you discover a relevant fact on your own rather than directly stating that the candidate had a felony conviction in Alaska. Similarly, I like to conclude the referral interview with "Hiring is an important decision, so you always want to consider as many candidates as possible. If you were considering Shauna today, would you make her an offer or continue to interview others in the pool of candidates?" There is only one acceptable response to that, which is an unequivocal endorsement: "Make her an offer. Don't let her get away." If the referrer is disinclined to make an unqualified positive recommendation, all he or she has to say is, "You're right. Hiring is an important decision." That means, as I write on the bottom of my notes, she's a no.

Making the Offer

In the interviewing process, be sure to specify, and reiterate when making an offer, that the position is "at-will employment." That is, the employer is free to terminate the employee at any time for any reason or for no reason at all. Such a designation will not spare you from all potential suits over unlawful termination, especially for protected classifications of persons, but it helps. As soon as you make a hiring decision, call the candidate in person plus, simultaneously, put the offer in writing via e-mail and/or letter. Understand that a good candidate will usually have multiple employment prospects. If you're his or her number one choice, you might get an affirmative response on the spot. Should the candidate need some time to make up his or her mind, assuming you've properly communicated the parameters of the position and its compensation, it probably means he or she is considering alternatives. That's all right, but you should then give a firm deadline for accepting your offer, perhaps five business days. The candidate can then contact the other prospects, or the current employer, and employ the "impending event" negotiation tactic to compel them to come to the table with a specific offer in a limited time frame.

Do whatever you think best about matching a competitive offer. You may believe a particular candidate is worth a better offer, but give consideration to the impact on current employees when they find out—which they will—how much you paid that new hire. However, under no circumstances respond to a counteroffer from the candidate's present employer. In all likelihood, such a candidate is more interested in playing both ends against the middle than in becoming a contributor to your team. Should the present employer make him or her a counteroffer, all well and good. The candidate chooses between the two alternatives and gives you a yes or a no. If the candidate comes to you with the counteroffer, asking you to up the ante, take your offer off the table on the spot and feel lucky for having avoided a bad hiring decision.

Chapter 15

Conducting Performance Reviews

Who knows why, but annual performance reviews have always been the redheaded stepchild of management. Managers hate them because they're a hassle, so they put them off or do them informally or haphazardly. Employees dread them because they expect a dressing-down for all that hasn't gotten done, through no fault of their own, of course, but due to management ineptitude. Essentially, it's like a parent reviewing a kid's report card in a situation in which it's impossible to make all A's. The parent is uncomfortable, the kid is uncomfortable, and bad feelings and confrontation are inevitable. At best, both parties get through the encounter with a minimum of discomfort. At worst, their relationship is damaged or at least bruised. It just shouldn't be this way.

Properly handled, the annual performance review is the primary vehicle for you to coach and mentor employees, guiding them toward achievements and rewards. Properly handled, it should be looked forward to by both you and your employees. Properly handled, it generates an environment of continuous improvement for your employees and your organization. So handle it properly.

THE PERSONAL REVIEW

As with most things in life, effective performance reviews depend upon advance preparation and adequate planning. The manager has the plan for the event and acts as conductor, but both parties need to prepare in advance. Give the employee about a week to do a personal review, and have him or her come to the meeting with specifics for four major topics of discussion:

1. What do you consider your most significant achievement in the past year? Why? Describe the impact it had. (Closely related question: What I like most about my job is _____ _____.)

2. Of goals you wanted to accomplish this year, what one are you least satisfied about? What happened and why did it happen? (Closely related question: What I like least about my job is _____.)

3. Where do you want to be and what do you want to be doing in this organization in three years?

4. Name three or four important goals you would like to achieve in the next year, and for each describe:

   • Standards for evaluating its achievement
   • Resources and/or training needed
   • What help you need from your manager
   • What impediments you anticipate and suggestions for dealing with them

CONDUCTING A SUCCESSFUL PERFORMANCE REVIEW

Your objective in the performance review is to have a relaxed two-way dialogue, going back and forth in a collegial professional manner. You don't want to control the conversation with an employee unprepared to adequately respond to your questions. By doing the self review, the employee will be ready to discuss specifics of what happened in the past and will have some idea of where he or she wants to go in the future.

Consider these preliminary points. First, what happens in the performance review should come as no surprise to an employee. The position description should have clearly articulated duties and standards, and it serves as the foundation for the review. Day-to-day or week-to-week follow-up and coaching should provide the employee a good sense of how he or she is doing throughout the year. Whether he or she has exceeded expectations or just barely met the standards, the employee should know it and be ready to talk about what happened in the past and why, what he or she wants to achieve in the short term, and where he or she wants to be in the intermediate term. If the employee hasn't met standards, he or she should know that, too, but instead of a performance review you're addressing a performance problem, as I'll discuss in Chapter 16.

In addition, be sure to conduct the review in a quiet place where no interruptions can occur. It is unconscionable that the phone ring or that someone tap on the door, as happened in the Consolidated Cupcake case study. Have a plan for the structure and format of the review. Do it in writing, with quantifiable scales that rate the employee followed by notes on the specific details. Be consistent, especially when reviewing employees with the same position description. Remember that you're doing an objective measure of performance against observable and measurable standards.

FIVE PHASES OF AN EMPLOYEE PERFORMANCE REVIEW

Phase 1: The Social Phase

Phase 1 of the performance review is the social phase, which should be relatively brief, perhaps a minute or two. Make the employee feel at ease with a little small talk on a positive focus. Be careful here. A bit of small talk is all well and good for an employee who's had a great year and is looking forward to doing a little feedback on the past and planning for the future. By contrast, employees who haven't done as well as hoped may be downright uncomfortable with you going on about the weather or the Bulldawgs crushing the Gators, waiting for the other shoe to drop and the ax to fall. In such a situation, minimize the small talk and cut right into outlining the meeting format and the reasons for it. In doing this, phrase your message from the employees' perspectives and what's in it for them: "What we're going to do here today is to help you set goals and determine what you want to achieve in the next year, what you need to get that done, and how I can be of help." You should not convey, "What I'm going to do today is see how you measure up and assign your duties for the next year."

Phase 2: The Information Phase

Phase 2 of the performance review is the information phase, or feedback on the past. Here, you'll be doing an objective evaluation of the employee's performance vis-à-vis the goals and standards agreed upon at the last review. Naturally, part of your preparation will be to look over those goals and compare them with actual performance. Sometimes this is fairly straightforward; at other times it is more difficult to define. For instance, for a sales rep in an assigned geographic territory, you have numbers on sales, new accounts, and all the other relevant accomplishments. For a staff person who works with colleagues in a team environment, procuring one individual's data may be more of a challenge, but it must be done. Ultimately, everything comes down to individual performance measured against objective standards, since every employee is compensated and rewarded individually on payday. At times you may have to reward employees, to some extent, as a team. But to spread out all the rewards, and all the praise, equally is to ignore the fact that in all groups, some individuals make more of a contribution than others. Ignore that fact at your peril. It amounts to false collectivization and will demotivate your best employees.

It's said that the devil is in the details. You may have all the "big picture" numbers in front of you, but it's the little things, day in and day out, that differentiate good employees from very good employees, very good employees from stellar employees. No matter how much time you allow for preparation, there's no way you'll ever recall all those little things that happened over the past year—little things which, in their aggregate, become very significant. Therefore, throughout the year, maintain an incident file on all your employees in which you document all those details day by day. When Employee A contributes a little extra, document it. When Employee B is an hour late on a request, document it. When Employee C yells at a colleague, document it. Incident files are readily updated and maintained electronically. Just be sure they can't be accessed by others. Having detailed incident files pays off in two ways. As noted, they'll help you do a more effective job in the performance review, but also they'll be the documentation you'll need if you face the necessity of disciplining or firing an employee. By the time you begin to perceive that a certain employee is a problem, wouldn't it be nice to already have three or four specific documentations of the issues of concern?

A key question to ask yourself in the information phase is whether performance was within control of the employee. Did inadequacies in training or supervision negatively affect performance through no fault of the employee? Were there extraordinary events, from floods to terrorism, that totally altered the playing field? I was working with a company that managed a number of distribution centers in the Midwest. One of its clients demanded a more lucrative arrangement, threatening to market its products through an alternative distributor otherwise. The company declined to alter the arrangement, and the business was lost, resulting in a ten percent loss in total sales. Then the company withheld bonuses from their distribution center managers for failing to achieve their sales goals. The distribution center managers had nothing to do with losing the client, and they had no input or influence on the company's decision. They believed, rightly so, that the company was punishing them for something over which they had no control. Their best managers quit shortly thereafter, though they were able to retain their least competent managers.

I feel very strongly that tangible rewards should be provided for good performance and a lack thereof for unsatisfactory performance. Though money, in and of itself, is not a motivator, it's a great way of keeping score. It's necessary, albeit not sufficient, for building morale within a highly motivated workforce. Because monetary rewards must be tied to performance, what better time to put it on the table than at the performance review? Verbal praise is nice, but praise with a few bucks attached is even nicer. As you move into the last three phases of the performance review, making modifications in the position description and planning for the future, take the opportunity to reward the past as you chart the path toward the future.

Phase 3: The Position Description Revision Phase

Remember how I described continuous improvement as one factor to consider before interviewing potential candidates? Make minor modifications on an ongoing basis rather than maintaining a rigid organization structure until facing a major reorganization after two or three years or so. This same concept is at work in Phase 3. Take a look at the employee's position description from a year ago and contrast it with what he or she is doing now. For a variety of reasons, from changes in your company and its needs to an employee's willingness to take on additional challenges and responsibilities, that old position description may be a bit dated. Compound that with new goals and objectives for the future, and it's apparent that the old position description needs an overhaul. As you revise and update the position description, be sure to consider implications for training and resource needs, and plan and budget for them accordingly. Finally, implement and communicate any organizational changes that have taken place.

Phase 4: The Planning Phase

Phase 4 of the performance review is the planning phase, in which you and your employee agree on specific goals and standards and set dates for completion. It is absolutely imperative that you involve the employee and solicit his or her input. Adopt the perspective of, "What can you do next year?" instead of, "This is what you need to do next year." Employees will surprise you. Given the opportunity to set their own goals and objectives, they will generally choose to be excellent and go for the gold. More important, you'll elicit better performance because the employees are shooting for their own goals, not yours. They've taken ownership of their objectives, which will result in better performance.

Recently, a sales rep told me of his experience in a performance review. His manager asked him what he felt he could do the next year, and he replied, "I can get a sales increase of 5 percent." "Not good enough," the manager replied, "you've got to do ten percent." A year later, when the rep had attained a 6 percent increase in sales, the manager brought him in and said, "You didn't meet your sales objective." "I made *my* sales objective," responded the rep. "I just didn't meet *your* objective." Don't let something like this happen to you. Unless the employee buys in and signs off on the objective, he or she simply isn't committed to attaining it.

Phase 5: The Closing Phase

Finally, in Phase 5, you summarize and confirm all the goals, standards, and dates that have been established. Then, consistent with your role as a coach and leader, you must have an ongoing system to help the employee meet those goals, meeting regularly between formal reviews. Later in this chapter, a case study will describe such a weekly coaching session.

You'll make some modifications in the performance review for a brand-new employee. Generally, in such a situation, you'll hold the initial review after the first ninety days of employment and thus you will not be able to assess achievements vis-à-vis objectives in the information phase to the same extent as with a veteran employee. In the first ninety days, the new employee is just getting oriented, but after that amount of time he or she should be ready to engage in a two-way dialogue to agree upon future goals and objectives. Until that time, let's face it, brand-new employees are pretty much incompetent and need to have someone show them how to walk into a room without the door hitting them in the behind. Having said that, within ninety days, perhaps even thirty or less, you should be able to identify employees who are having problems or who are just not going to cut it. If they need extra help, coach them and conduct a formal performance review within thirty days, providing specific guidance for goals and standards, with an attendant action plan, to get them through the orientation period.

Within ninety days, you will be aware of those who just won't make the grade. When that happens, which it will, take a step back and see what might have gone wrong with the hiring process in the first place, so you can learn from this mistake. But rather than prolonging the problem, do what must be done and cut the employee loose by the ninety-day mark. Although it's hoped that this will not happen very often, you can prepare yourself and the employee for such an eventuality by explaining at the time of a job offer that employment is probationary during the first ninety days. This is particularly critical if you hired someone through an agency, where their fee may be contingent on a new hire remaining on the job for a minimum period. You may save that fee, but don't stop there. If a new hire didn't work out, it might be a good idea to meet with the agency to see whether it needs modified guidelines concerning candidates to send over. That doesn't alleviate you of ultimate responsibility for the hiring mistake, but it might help them screen out people with characteristics similar to those of the person who failed. In any case, if after ninety days it's apparent that the new hire isn't going to work out, do everyone a favor and let him or her go. Accept the fact that everyone will know that, in essence, you've acknowledged making a mistake in the hiring process. Take solace in the fact that most managers make such a mistake and, like all mistakes, it provides you the opportunity to critique your process and get better at it.

Previously, I noted the importance of ongoing coaching between reviews as a vehicle to help employees reach their longer-term goals. Take a look at a case study that addresses this.

CASE STUDY: ARKLATEX INDUSTRIES

Rosetta Stone is a sales manager for Arklatex Industries; Ida Druther is one of her sales reps. It's first thing Monday morning, and they are holding their weekly meeting to review the previous week and to make plans for the coming week.

ROSETTA: Your sales were pretty good last week—twelve percent over quota.

IDA: Thanks. Yeah, things stayed pretty busy. We moved some merchandise.

ROSETTA: This new marketing program is really beginning to take off. Life's got to be getting pretty miserable for those bozos at Delmarva who call themselves our competition.

IDA: I'm not so sure. They're not exactly sitting back. They've been stepping up their activity in a lot of my accounts.

ROSETTA: Well, big number one isn't afraid of them. Okay, Ida, let's go through our checklist of priorities for last week. First of all, new package feature in Wal-Mart. Did we get floor displays, with point-of-purchase material to communicate the feature price?

IDA: Pretty much, I guess. In most stores, anyhow.

ROSETTA: Meaning . . .?

IDA: Delmarva has a promotion with Gillette. They've tied up floor space near the checkout through this weekend, and there just wasn't any way we could get a good location.

ROSETTA: But you did get an extra display . . .

IDA: Yeah, but in about half the stores we had to put it way in the back.

ROSETTA: Well, at least we got the display. That's better than nothing at all. Next, rollout of the new season's line at JCPenney.

IDA: No problem.

ROSETTA: Way to go. Let's see. Availability of men's accessories in the Duvon Boutiques.

IDA: No sale. Mr. Duvon hasn't authorized it.

ROSETTA: But it's one of our hottest growth lines. Didn't you tell that to the store managers?

IDA: Sure, but they can't take it without Mr. Duvon's approval.

ROSETTA: Hmm. Last item. Did you deliver the new display cases to Kay Jewelers?

IDA: Thursday. But some of the store managers are just leaving them out back to stock up extra inventory.

ROSETTA: Well, that's three out of four and a score of seventy-five percent. Now, for this week, three promotional features, and we'll want the usual extra displays with point of purchase.

IDA: All right.

ROSETTA: And those display cases at Kay: Got to get them on the floor in all stores.

IDA: Their floor space is pretty well tied up with Delmarva and Arrow.

ROSETTA: Put 'em someplace—just get the best location possible. And finally, we've got stock rotation and shelf resets at Gayfers tomorrow morning at six a.m.

IDA: Six a.m? Can't the two merchandisers handle that?

ROSETTA: They're handling their own stores. You and I will do Gayfers.

IDA: Damn. That's a lot of work.

ROSETTA: I know, and that's why I'll give you a hand. It's good to get your hands dirty every once in a while. You don't mind, do you?

IDA: I guess not.

ROSETTA: That's the spirit. It'll help raise your score for the week, too. We're a team here, Ida, the big Arklatex team. Those bozos at Delmarva haven't got a chance against number one.

Analysis

One thing you can say for Rosetta: she has a great attitude, replete with enthusiasm. That's an important part of managing and coaching, but it's only the frosting on the cake. Unfortunately for Rosetta, she's all frosting and no cake, which, as you may have discovered, can make your hands a bit messy.

For starters, Rosetta totally fails to establish a two-way dialogue with Ida. She just rolls through her prepared list, checking off, "Did you do this, yes or no?" She's getting little feedback from Ida about the state of her territory, and what input she does get is ignored. As a manager, you cannot personally learn everything you need to know about your area of responsibility, particularly if your employees are field sales reps. You can't get face to face with all the customers and prospects on any kind of a regular basis. There's no way you can know what's happening in every outlet or other point of encounter. Even in the office, you can't learn about all those things you need to know about without having that two-way dialogue and feedback from all your employees. Ida brings up several points on which she needs advice and coaching, and she identifies areas demanding the attention of management, but her voice is not heard.

Rosetta's system for evaluating performance is woefully inadequate. It's qualitative, with no consideration for the specifics of the achievement. Her standards are not founded upon sales and profitability. Each activity, however complex or trivial, is weighted equally.

In sum, although I believe Rosetta is dedicated to her company and her job, she fails as a manager. In most performance reviews, you're working with your employees as a colleague and partner, guiding them toward excellence. Sometimes, though, employee performance is not up to standards, and your meeting will take on a different tone. This is not something to look forward to, but it's something that must be done. Like everything else about management, it must be done right.

Chapter 16

Handling Performance Problems

Basic to your job as a manager is getting results through your people and holding them accountable. Sure, everyone is different and, as I've said, the same key will not open every door. Employees all face their own personal challenges, professional challenges, and demons. But as a manager, you must uphold standards and accountability or your employees will lose respect for you and you will fail. No, you don't have to treat everyone alike as long as you treat everyone fairly. But when it comes down to standards, never forget that you are doing an objective measure of performance without consideration, except in severe short-term situations, of personal issues. It's reasonable to make an allowance for the effects of loss of a loved one ninety days ago, but the same cannot be a valid excuse for unacceptable performance a year from now. You cannot ask about dependent children in the interview, so those dependent children are no excuse for unsatisfactory performance on the job. You cannot set lower standards for certain people because you like them or feel sorry for them. All employees must meet the standards and pull their weight or they go. Your job as a manager is to evaluate your employees based upon a quantitative assessment of their contributions.

You may have reason to believe an employee's performance is being affected by alcohol, drugs, or other personal problems, but tread softly on that turf. Be certain that you're in compliance with the law and acting in a manner consistent with company policy. What is the basis for determining probable cause? What rights do you have in demanding an employee submit to a sobriety test or a psychological evaluation? An individual staggering around the office with a bottle in his or her hand is a far cry from perceiving him or her to be a little sleepy and sluggish from being out too late. Lighting up a joint in a meeting is quite different from the person seeming to forget something occasionally. It's one thing to bring a machine gun to the office and murder the copy machine but quite another to be a bit on edge and irritable.

Generally, you're on thin ice legally if you accuse an employee of alcohol, drug, or other personal problems without clear and compelling observable facts. Even then, keep your conversation focused on performance and encourage the employee to volunteer reasons for his or her poor performance. Many companies have explicit policies for dealing with these issues, and you should elicit the help of your human resources person or other expert to fully apprise you and help you deal with the situation.

I see more and more companies that, due to restructuring and layoffs, have fewer and fewer employees facing more and more responsibilities. Men and women with spouses and/or children are putting in sixty, seventy, eighty hours a week just to keep their jobs and make ends meet. Consistently, such employees are running into performance problems due to sheer burnout. They're working so hard and facing such horrors of commuting that they have no time for families, no time for fun, and no time to do the creative thinking you're paying them for. They feel like gerbils running on a wheel all day, getting nowhere. They're stressed out and frustrated. If this sounds like your company, it's time to rethink your assumptions. Your very expensive engines, which you need to drive you to your future, are losing their efficiency and are about to blow the head gasket.

Take a look at a case study in which a manager deals with a performance problem. As you read through the transcript, you'll note that the conversation quickly deteriorates, resulting in termination of the employee. Consider how well the manager, Harry, handles the situation and ways in which he could have been more effective. Then ask yourself whether this company is better off to be rid of Steve, the employee, and whether his firing serves as an effective warning to other employees.

CASE STUDY: THE FUBAR COMPANY

Harry is the sales manager for the Fubar Company; Steve is one of his salespeople. Late one afternoon, Steve is having coffee in the break room, talking with two of his co-workers, when Harry approaches.

HARRY: Steve, how 'bout stepping into my office for a moment? There's something I need to talk to you about.

STEVE: Can't it wait, Harry? We're working out our plans for going up to the Auburn game next weekend.

HARRY: No, it can't wait. You're in hot water with personnel and we're going to deal with this right now! [Harry turns away and heads for his office. Steve and his co-workers exchange concerned glances.]

STEVE [to his co-workers]: I'll talk to y'all later. [Harry is already seated at his desk when Steve arrives at his office and sits down in a chair.]

STEVE: What's the problem, Harry?

HARRY: You know what the problem is: your absenteeism. You're missing too much time on the job.

STEVE: What the hell are you talking about, Harry? I've missed two days' work all year, and that was back in January when I had my wisdom teeth removed.

HARRY: Well, then, it must be because you've been clocking in late. You're supposed to be here thirty minutes before we open.

STEVE: My job's getting done. I'm on the floor by the time the doors open.

HARRY: That's not the point. You're expected to be at work by the designated time.

STEVE: Anybody say I'm not getting my job done, Harry?

HARRY: Listen, you don't make the rules around here. You're expected to clock in on time, and if you're late too often you're subject to discipline.

STEVE: I haven't been late too often.

HARRY: Well, if you hadn't been late more than allowed by company policy, I wouldn't have gotten this notice from personnel.

STEVE: What exactly is the company policy?

HARRY: That's something you can get up in personnel. I'm pretty sure it says no more than two days a month.

STEVE: You're pretty sure. How many days was I late last month?

HARRY: I'm not sure exactly how many, but it was far more than two. I can think of several mornings when I was trying to find you and you hadn't come in yet. Anyhow, I'm writing up a disciplinary report for your file.

STEVE: This is a crock, Harry. You've never talked to me about this before. I've been here five years and I've never had a disciplinary report.

HARRY: Steve, I don't like this any more than you do. Look, if I had my way I wouldn't care when you clock in just so long as you're getting your job done. But you know how personnel is. They've got their rules and we're all stuck with them.

STEVE: You're coppin' out, man. I haven't missed any time without a good reason, and you're writin' me up.

HARRY: It might do you some good. Maybe you'll be a little more careful about getting here on time from now on.

STEVE: You're a real SOB, Harry.

HARRY: You think so, hey? And you're insubordinate. You may be interested to know that along with this disciplinary report, I'm going to include a formal reprimand and I'm taking it up to personnel this afternoon. What do you think of that?

STEVE: You know what I think, Harry? I think that instead of taking it up to personnel you ought to take it up where the sun don't shine.

HARRY: All right, mister, have it your way. Okay, I won't give you a formal reprimand. Instead, you can clock out and get the hell out of here right now, because you are fired.

Analysis

I believe most would agree that this was a bad situation badly handled. Steve's first statement was clearly disrespectful and inexcusable, but Harry's response was worse. Instead of taking command of the situation with a neutral statement expressing the need to address a matter expeditiously, he responded emotionally in front of Steve's co-workers. So much for praising in public and reprimanding in private. Then, when they begin their discussion in earnest, Harry knows neither the facts of the case nor the standards of policy. Worst of all, he tries to be a buddy with his "I don't like this any more than you do" line and totally abdicates his management role, referring to personnel and their policies in the third person. Steve will have none of it, lets Harry know what he thinks, and is outta there. Yes, I believe his firing serves as an effective warning to other employees—warning them that Harry is not just incompetent but dangerously incompetent. They have learned to respond to Harry in one of four ways: yes, sir; no, sir; no excuse, sir; and sir, I do not understand. If they are not idiots, they will most effectively deal with Harry by pretending that they are.

SIX STEPS FOR ANALYZING
PERFORMANCE PROBLEMS

Let's consider how this or any performance problem might be handled more effectively with the six steps for analyzing performance problems.

Step 1: State the problem situation. Identify the difference between what is happening and what should be happening. Here is an illustration of the importance of specific standards and quantifiable measurements of performance. In this case, the standard is no more than two tardies in a calendar month. Steve has exceeded that.

Step 2: Define the problem, the who/when/where/how/why. This is when you bring in all the facts, an example of the value of maintaining detailed incident files: "During the past three months, you've been late four, three, and four times respectively. These are the dates and the times you clocked in."

Step 3: Identify causes. All Harry did was react to bad behavior with punishment, an approach I've noticed many parents take with their children. It's akin to beating a dog until he finally stops doing something wrong. But unless you figure out *why* something is happening, chances are you won't be successful in modifying a person's behavior. Is it due to a lack of specific standards, or lack of an awareness of the standards? Does it reflect a lack of skills or training? Or does the employee just not care? As described in Chapter 15, circumstances or barriers may be beyond the employee's control. In a caring but not patronizing or condescending manner, the manager should ask the employee if he or she can think of any reason why the problem is occurring. If the employee can't or won't come up with a reason, all the manager can do is reiterate the standard. If the employee volunteers a possible cause, the manager can try to help him or her work out a solution. Just remember that managers are not social workers and it's their job to enforce standards. For Steve, it might be as simple as personal distractions at home which prevent him from leaving on time in the morning. Persuading him to rearrange his activities or just set the alarm fifteen minutes earlier may be all the manager needs to do.

Step 4: List the possible solutions. Help the employee think through any number of alternatives which will bring performance up to standard.

Step 5: Choose one solution from the list created in Step 4. It does little good to merely present three or four alternatives and hope the employee will select one. Get the employee to make the commitment: "Here's what I'm going to do differently, which will resolve the problem."

Step 6: Develop an action plan. Here's where you, in your role of a manager, take command and say, "Okay, this is what we're going to do." In Chapter 17, I discuss the steps for firing an employee. In this case, the first time the problem has been discussed, neither firing nor even a formal written warning would seem justified. A verbal warning, with an understanding that a written warning will follow in the event of excessive tardiness in the next six months, would seem sufficient.

Some managers have told me they believe there is a need to build in flexibility for enforcing rules and standards to make allowances for extenuating circumstances. For instance, say Steve has been late the permissible two times going into the last day of next month. Then, that day, he has a dead battery or a flat tire. Would you write him up? How about if a plane crashed on the freeway, blocking all lanes? What if, as he walked out the door, the little old lady next door fell down the stairs and broke her hip? Would you really expect him to tell her, "I'll call nine-one-one on my cell phone on my way to work, but I can't be late. Try to keep warm. See ya!"

I believe it's absolutely essential that you enforce standards and do what you said you'd do in Step 6: Late three times, get written up. Write him up. There's no reason to doubt that managers who bend the rules due to extenuating circumstances have good intentions, and there may be, as described, events beyond an employee's control which deserve consideration. But bend the rules at your peril. In essence, you haven't bent a rule but created a new rule. Furthermore, you have opened Pandora's box, subjecting yourself to a never-ending process of having to decide which excuses are valid and which are not. If Steve can be late three times because his next-door neighbor got hurt, why can't I be late three times because my kid was sick? Or my dog was sick? Or the goldfish died and we had to hold a memorial service before flushing it?

In your written warning, you can note those special circumstances, such as, "Loss of loved one." For Steve, you can note it was just three tardies and the last one happened on the last day of the month due to a neighbor's accident. But then, again, note standards and one solution. For Steve, excessive tardies in the next six months will result in a one-week suspension without pay. For the person who lost a loved one ninety days ago, think it through very carefully and decide what is fair and consistent with the best interests of the organization. The needs and convenience of any one individual can never supersede the needs and best interests of the organization.

Chapter 17

Sayonara:
Firing an Employee

In Chapter 16, I discussed steps for handling performance problems. You hope, just as every manager hopes, that those steps will restore the employee to meeting and exceeding standards. However, you know and we all know that sometimes it won't work out that way and you will have to face one of the toughest jobs for a manager: firing an employee. Even if you have specified "at-will" employment at the outset, you may still face legal repercussions from terminating someone, so, as always, handle it properly.

The discussion in Chapter 16 addressed escalating stages for dealing with performance problems, stages that constitute the first steps in firing an employee. I noted then the importance of having standards and documented facts, specifying expectations for future performance and spelling out the consequences for failure to meet standards. This approach is absolutely essential in firing an employee for cause and the best way to avoid potential legal problems.

In the cases of certain egregious behavior, you should skip all these steps and fire the employee on the spot. Your company should designate certain actions as cause for immediate termination and clearly communicate this to all employees. Certain offenses concerning the use of alcohol or drugs on the job would result in immediate termination. So might flagrant sexual harassment, even as a one-time event. Cheating or other forms of stealing, and blatant or overt violence are reasons for immediate dismissal.

When I explore normative cultures in Part III, I note that you may inherit a team in which certain inappropriate behaviors have previously been tolerated or even encouraged, notwithstanding that they were a clear violation of existing policies. In such a situation, you need to clarify future expectations and consequences rather than suddenly enforce rules which have become irrelevant.

THE FORMAL STEPS
FOR TERMINATING AN EMPLOYEE

Step 1: Verbal Warning

Step 1 in the firing process is a verbal warning. Here, as noted, you must be specific in quantifying present behavior or performance in contrast to standards. Give the employee specifics about future expectations and, for performance, a time frame for meeting standards. In the case of inappropriate behavior, the time horizon may be open-ended. Clearly articulate the consequences for failing to fulfill expectations, and follow through with appropriate action. Do not make exceptions or renegotiate conditions at some point in the future lest you risk losing credibility and respect from *all* employees. If you say to an employee, "You must achieve ninety percent of quota within six months or X will happen," X *will* happen if the employee hits eighty-nine percent every month. After your meeting, then, write a detailed summary for your incident file.

Some managers like to write up a meeting summary and then sign the summary and ask the employee to sign it as well, as an acknowledgment of what was agreed upon. Other managers find this somewhat awkward and confrontational, especially with a verbal warning, and prefer just to send the employee a memo of understanding, concluding it by requesting that the employee communicate with them if anything in the memo is inconsistent with the employee's understanding of the agreement.

Step 2: Disciplinary Interview and Written Warning

Should the employee fail to perform or behave as expected, you move past informally dealing with a performance problem and on to Step 2 in the firing process: a formal disciplinary interview and written warning. At this stage, you would do well to consider including another manager, a human resources person, or someone else to be a witness to the proceedings. As in Step 1, the written warning will specify expectations and time frame with explicit standards, but now the consequences will have escalated. No longer will the employee merely face talk and memos. At this point real actions will be taken if expectations are not met. Now, you will write a detailed summary of your meeting and all understandings, which will become part of the employee's permanent file. Again, you may or may not ask the employee to sign such a document, though it is more likely you would wish to do so in this situation than with a verbal warning.

If expectations have still not been met, you must do what you said you would do. This will be unpleasant for both you and the employee. Hoping to avoid the negative event, I have read of managers—though I have never actually met anyone who does this—who advocate giving the employee a day off with pay to think things over, perhaps to compose a top ten list of things he or she needs to do to improve performance. These managers, whoever they are, wistfully hope the employee will take the day off and achieve enlightenment that they should resign. To me, such an idea sounds like indecisive and inept management. These employees have already had plenty of time to think it over. Through your coaching, they've had the opportunity to see everything—a top ten or a top twenty—they need to do to improve. A day off with pay is a joke, and if they return with a top-ten list instead of a resignation, implicitly you're granting them an extension for its implementation. I have no problem with having an employee create such a top-ten list at Step 2, when they first get a written warning, or even at Step 1, at the verbal warning. However, at either step, what you must do is straightforward: if the employee has not met expectations, he or she faces the specified consequences at the specified time.

Step 3: Formal Probation/Suspension Without Pay

Before the ax falls and before saying sayonara, some companies employ a Step 3: Formal probation and/or suspension without pay. Others, who may derive some masochistic pleasure out of prolonging pain, use formal probation as Step 3 and then use suspension without pay as Step 4, postponing the final act until Step 5. Do whatever makes you feel good, but ask yourself: If the employee has still failed to meet standards after the formal written warning of Step 2, do you *really* think that person will ever turn out to be viable? As Harvey

Mackay (1988) says, "It isn't the people you fire who make your life miserable, it's the people you don't" (p. 167).

Step 4: The Termination Meeting

You told the employee what had to be done or he or she would be terminated. The employee didn't cut it. Now it's time for the termination meeting.

In Part III, I describe a situation you may very well face as a manager: terminating good employees who, through no fault of their own, have fallen victim to restructuring. For them, as with an employee fired for cause, you will follow the same procedures for the termination meeting, though of course in such a situation you will not address any performance issues.

At the time the employee is contacted to schedule the termination meeting, he or she should have a pretty good idea what the meeting is all about. You will not say, "Could you please drop by my office tomorrow morning at ten so I can fire you? Shouldn't take more than fifteen or twenty minutes." Instead, ask, "Could you please drop by for fifteen or twenty minutes so I can go over some things?" This is sufficient. Nevertheless, since the employee is likely to surmise that the end is near, take a couple of basic steps before making the phone call. Deactivate all of his or her computer, phone, and pager codes, company credit cards, and anything else with which the employee might exact revenge.

Before getting into the termination meeting, you need to think about something. Ask yourself, Why does my company hire all these security people, anyhow? Is it because we're afraid of being attacked by the competition? No . . . Are there legions of the poor and homeless who want to barge in and steal our BMWs and Rolexes? No . . . Do anarchists and terrorists want to destroy us and our way of life? Well, maybe. But for most organizations, security exists for one primary purpose: protection from disgruntled former employees. In a nutshell, you would prefer that someone you fire not return to murder you or, if he or she is particularly inventive, invade your home and take it out on your family. Keep that objective in clear focus from the very first moment of the termination interview. Take command of the situation. Do not let it become an issue of feelings and personalities. Allow the employee to save face.

Be thoroughly prepared for this meeting. Have all records, forms, evaluations, or other germane information at your fingertips. Do all necessary human resources paperwork in advance. Button down all the facts and specifics you'll address in the meeting. Nothing should be left for a follow-up meeting to finalize arrangements or post-employment conditions. Everything should be handled now because, to put it bluntly, the employee will never again set foot in your place of business after the termination meeting. Almost certainly, you will want a witness present, probably including a human resources person if he or she might need to address questions. Having a witness or two will also reduce the likelihood of emotions getting out of hand.

Be firm and tactful, and get straight to the point. Provide no small talk, no buffer, such as, "All of us are aware of the severe economic challenges faced by our industry. Pressures on sales and profits have forced us to examine everything about the way we do business. We've come to realize that there is no alternative to making difficult choices." This type of introduction only makes a bad situation worse. Come out and say it: "Fred, we're going to have to let you go." Follow up with a face-saving statement, even if the employee has been fired for incompetence. You can still tell the worst performer about the strengths and qualities that would help him or her be successful in another company. To the victim of restructuring, make only a simple statement that the way business is, you have to make layoffs.

Be prepared for a negative reaction, especially from persons for whom their job is their identity. Employees may cry and beg for one more chance, grope for any point on which the decision might be re-opened for negotiation, but it cannot be. The decision is final. Do not discuss performance except perhaps to say, "You had to do X." No need for accusations, no comments about the employee or his or her shortcomings. Nothing further should be discussed about the past. End it with a simple statement: "The decision has been made." This opening phase of the termination meeting should be very brief, perhaps only a minute or two, since there is no longer any point in talking about it. Then, assume command of the meeting by leading the discussion toward what will happen from this point forward. Start by handing the employee his or her final paycheck, adding, if appropriate, details about when any other monies owed will be sent. Even if an employee has been fired for incompetence, the sight of a paycheck covering the next two weeks can do a lot to ease the tension. Many financially sound companies undergoing restructuring make very generous settlements, especially for long-term employees. It's a terrible shock for a fifty-year-old, twenty-year veteran to see it all end, but a severance check of a year's pay will help him or her walk out the door feeling all right, looking forward to finally being able to pursue a path he or she always wanted to take. The whole business might even provide an opportunity to update his or her skills, the lack of which was a likely contributor to termination in the first place.

At this time, also inform him or her of any continuing benefits, particularly family health care. Often, employees not fired for cause may also be provided outplacement services to help them put together a good résumé and assist them in the job search process. Consistent with this, to enable them to appear currently employed, you might permit them to retain their telephone extension and have the receptionist convey an impression that they are still gainfully employed, forwarding outside messages to their voice mail. That privilege might be further extended to include secretarial services on company letterhead. All of this is designed to be as fair as possible to terminated employees while you smoothly ease them out the door. Unfortunately for persons considering them for future employment, it may also be somewhat difficult to determine whether a candidate is currently employed or has recently been fired.

Postmeeting Action

After the meeting, security will help the employee remove personal items from the office, then escort him or her out of the building. Because of all your conscientious advance preparation, all details have been handled, so there will be no need for the employee to see human resources or payroll now or later. Most important, the terminated employee will not be strolling around the office, socializing with and disrupting current employees. Anything he or she needs to drop off or pick up in the future can be done at the desk of the receptionist. Within thirty minutes of the termination meeting, he or she is out the door. Sayonara.

This section addressed the steps of terminating employees "by the book." Unfortunately, as with everything else in the real world, "the book" doesn't cover everything. Firing an employee for cause is neither pleasant nor easy, but it's straightforward, dealing with performance vis-à-vis standards in escalating steps. However, you will encounter other circumstances, such as marginal-to-poor employees with a history of "okay" evaluations because their old bosses didn't want the hassle of firing them and a bad evaluation would have made it more difficult to ship them out to another unsuspecting manager. Even worse, you may be dealing with an employee whose performance meets or exceeds standards but who is not trustworthy or who is a backstabber or a complainer.

CONSTRUCTIVE TERMINATION

For individual cases in which managers want to get rid of an employee but can't do so for cause in a reasonable time frame, a tactic occasionally utilized is constructive termination. However, I must urge you to listen to me very carefully: be *extremely* cautious in applying this tactic. If you are perceived as harassing an employee, it can land you in big trouble and cost you big bucks, particularly if the employee can make a case that he or she was harassed for refusing to grant sexual favors, was a whistleblower, or was a labor organizer. Nasty lawsuits have been filed by employees in protected classifications, and juries have no sympathy for companies who harass older employees to get them to quit in order to escape obligations for retirement benefits. Similarly, they don't much care for companies who try to get rid of employees whose families have health care problems that cause insurance premiums to rise. That said, take a look at how constructive termination can be used to get an employee to tell you to take the job and shove it.

Think back to Chapter 8 and the discussion of the Peter Principle. You'll see examples of constructive termination in what happened to my supercompetent mentors, Dan Walton and Rick Harris. I remember visiting Harris in exile, in his plush corporate suite where he had nothing to do all day, and saying to him—remember, please, that this was my puppyhood when I didn't know any better—what a sweet deal he had, dropping by the office for two or three hours, two or three days a week, and making big bucks in the process. Party heaven. I was surprised when he told me, "No, Bob, I'm only fifty-one years old. I'm still a young man. There are many more things I want to do." That was interesting to me, though I couldn't understand the part about fifty-one being young. Walton, I'm sorry to say, was diagnosed with cancer soon after his exile, and left this world at forty-six. But Harris did exactly what the company expected him to do: he moved on to newer and greater things.

Lee Iacocca relates a similar story in his autobiography. As an executive at Ford, he was always seated at the number-one table, with all the other heavy breathers, at corporate dinner functions. As his relationship with Henry Ford began to deteriorate, Iacocca suddenly found himself assigned to the number-three table, something he described as humiliating, and it was a loud and clear signal to him to start looking for other work.

Relocate the Position

Another common form of constructive termination is to relocate the position or offer the employee a transfer to an unacceptable location. An employee who is happy as a clam in corporate headquarters might quit when faced with his or her functions being decentralized to an obscure regional office. I know of one person whose company first transferred him to a desirable location, where he was delighted to go, and soon thereafter closed that location and presented him with a choice of two undesirable locations or a one-way ticket to the city of his choice. Another colleague, in Chicago, was definitely competent but dressed in thousand-dollar suits and was perceived to be a playboy, which he was. His incompetent managers, out of sheer envy and jealousy, sent him off to Sioux Falls, assuming he'd quit. To everyone's surprise, he went to Sioux Falls, continued to perform well, and shocked management by finding a whole new set of friends, with whom he had a great time.

Reduce Status

Often, constructive termination takes the form of excluding a person from key memos, meetings, and trips, or, as in the example of Lee Iacocca, reducing his or her status within them. A related approach is to reduce in-office status. Move an executive from a four-window corner office with a private secretary to a three-window office with a view of the parking garage, where he or she shares a secretary, and the message is unambiguous. I've seen such office musical chairs go to the extreme of placing the person in a windowless office facing the copy room and providing no secretarial support. That failing, bring in the painters: Move the employee's desk and chair into the hallway, cover everything else with drop cloths, and start painting his or her office. After about two hours, have the painters stop painting and depart, leaving everything as it is. In response to inquiries, the painters will return to finish the job "when they can," which is never.

If you've been reading between the lines, you've gathered that constructive termination is most effective, and least likely to get you in trouble, when applied to higher-level employees. You hope they'll figure out they're not on your team, will be good sports, and will take the opportunity to enter the job market. It would be nice if the world was a place where we all got along and managers could and would do their job of making objective measurements of performance against standards. But in the real world, it's often not that simple. As Henry Ford said to Lee Iacocca, "It's personal and I can't tell you anymore. It's just one of those things" (Iacocca, 1984, p. 134). If you're a management veteran, you've likely encountered "one of those things" from one side of the table or the other.

Chapter 18

Setting Up Sales Territories and Managing Your Own Territory

As you've probably surmised, I'm big on doing marketing and management from the bottom up. Start with a speciality you do well, or some other differential advantage, and build your strategy up from there. That's the diametric opposite of what you learn in most business schools, where they teach you to start with some ivory tower objective and then work your way down to the nitty-gritty details of implementation and execution, which may or may not be feasible or attainable.

The bottom-up approach applies to setting up sales territories as well. Even if you're not in field sales management, don't just skip over this chapter, as its principles have applications to any management environment.

To me, the benefits of the bottom-up approach to marketing strategies are persuasive. That said, many organizations have been successful doing things top down, especially if they are confident in their power and competence throughout the channels of distribution. By contrast, a top-down approach to setting up sales territories is manifestly flawed unless your points of encounter, customer profiles, and relative market dominance are uniformly spread across every portion of your market area. Thus, I've found it interesting to see companies begin with a top-down perspective, only to end up overhauling their territories soon thereafter because they were unworkable. After months or years of modifications, they arrive at something fairly close to what they would have had if they done it right with a bottom-up approach in the first place. I found it difficult to believe that managers had failed to grasp the simplicity and efficacy of organizing territories bottom up until one day in the office I was perusing one of those examination copies of sales management textbooks I regularly receive. I was glancing through and, son of a gun, there, in the chapter on sales territories, was a presentation of the top-down approach. How could that be? I began thrashing around through one of the many piles of rubble in my office and finally located another sales management text I'd recently received. Goodness gracious! Again—the top-down approach! So, I finally understood why so many companies have screwed up instead of set up their sales territories. Their managers apparently graduated from a business school where they use leading textbooks in the sales management class.

Let's go over the top-down approach. I do so not in the spirit of counseling you to avoid sin by providing a lurid description of it, but to challenge you to spot the fundamental flaws in this approach. On the surface, it sounds reasonable, which helps us understand how academics put it in their textbooks.

THE TOP-DOWN APPROACH

Step 1 in the top-down approach is to estimate your total sales potential and determine the number of territories you need. To do so, you start by identifying all the final target consumers, retailers, manufacturers, or whatever in your total market area. Let's say, for example, that would be small businesses with fifteen to ninety-nine employees located in fourteen southeastern states. Summarize the total potential sales for your product or service category, also known as the total market potential. For our example, let's say you're in the business of providing long-distance telephone service. If you prefer, imagine you're selling paper clips. Or toilet paper. Or whatever. You determine that the grand total possible sales potential for your product or service within the target market is, say, $100 million. That's all the business available for you and all your competitors combined. Multiply that by your market share to calculate your sales potential. If, for instance, you command a 30 percent share of the category, you figure you should be able to garner 30 percent of the $100 million market potential, or $30 million. Finally, determine the sales volume appropriate for each territory to calculate the number of territories you need. Let's say you figure each sales rep should manage $2.5 million in sales. Take your sales potential of $30 million divided by $2.5 million per territory. You need twelve sales territories.

Step 2 in the top-down approach is to select your basic geographical control unit; that is, your basis for defining territories. You can break them up any way you want—by state, county, or city—but zip codes are best. Smaller-sized units are much easier for making assignments and adjustments. By contrast, larger-sized units, especially states, would probably need to be broken down further.

Step 3 is to combine control units into territories of approximately equal potential, optimizing territory coverage and minimizing expenses. For example, it would make sense to have the same rep cover Kansas City, Missouri, and Kansas City, Kansas, a good example of why defining territories by states would present a problem. In addition, it would make sense to have territories correspond with media coverage, buying offices, or ownership groups.

With the territory defined, Step 4 is to determine the individual sales rep's activity agenda. This begins with generating a list of customers and prospects in each territory, breaking them down by location and size. Then, for each customer or prospect, specify the number of sales calls to be made each year, how long each call will take, and the travel time between calls. Add it all up, and then break it down to calculate the number of calls to be made each business day and the time required.

How's that sound? No cheating, now. Go back and thoroughly digest the traditional top-down approach and see if you can figure out why it might be a source of problems.

Let's start with the small stuff. Although you might hold a certain market share position within your industry, it's unlikely that your share would be uniform throughout your entire marketing area. A 30 percent share overall might range from a 15 percent share in Territory A to a 45 percent share in Territory B. Or what if you're expanding into new markets in which you do not currently do business or you're an innovative start-up company? By definition, you're walking onto the playing field with a zero share. What makes you think you can instantly rev up to your market share in established markets? For innovative products and services, not only is your market share hard to guess but you have an even greater challenge estimating the size of the total market pie. It's one thing to estimate the total market potential for laundry detergent, quite something else to estimate the total market potential for outsourcing a professional service no one is even aware of yet. Worst of all—and this is where the top-down approach really begins to collapse—it assumes you maintain the specified share of market *for every customer.* That's all well and good if you're Procter & Gamble and your universe is supermarkets, which is probably the basis for the top-down approach in the first place, but it's not realistic for a service company or business-to-business channels in which your share of an individual customer's business is most likely either 100 percent or zero.

It gets worse. The top-down approach implies you will call on everyone, and has no provision for qualifying accounts on the basis of whether they're even worth pursuing in the first place. This is not a problem for P&G—their products will be in every supermarket in the country. It's a big problem for you if it means going four hours out of your way to call on an account which will be good for twenty dollars in sales a year. Sooner or later, you or your sales reps will need to eliminate prospects who may be qualified to buy in the sense that they can pay their bills but are not qualified from a perspective of ever being able to become profitable accounts. This can only be done by canning top down entirely and starting all over again from the bottom up.

But I've saved the best for last. The top-down approach is built on a foundation in which a given amount of sales must be generated. It then goes on to figure out the number of calls that will take and the time required. Big problem. *Big* problem. That could turn out to be two calls, taking a total of three hours a day, or just as easily could be six calls, necessitating a twenty-two-hour working day. The limitation for a sales rep, and the foundation on which a territory must be set up, is not a level of sales but the number of hours available to the rep. The key question is, If my reps are going to be working fifty or sixty hours a week, what should they be doing with their time and how large a territory can they cover? Time available determines the territory. The territory does not determine time required. And the only way of getting this done is with a bottom-up approach.

THE BOTTOM-UP APPROACH

There are six steps to the bottom-up approach to setting up sales territories, many of which are the same, albeit in a different order, as the top-down approach. Step 1 is to select the basic geographical control unit. For the reasons previously noted, let's go with the smallest, more manageable unit, the zip code. Here's where to start and build up, whereas the top-down approach didn't get down to this micro level until after the parameters of the territory had already been defined.

In Step 2, generate a list of all customers and prospects in each control unit (zip code) and break them down by location and size. This is what you were doing in the fourth and final step of the top-down approach, though in that approach you were generating a list for the entire territory you'd already laid out. As before, for each customer or prospect, specify the number of sales calls to be made each year, how long each call will take, and the travel time between calls. Add up the total time required for each individual customer or prospect. Let's say that, for example, if you work Prospect 32534-013, it will take ten hours a year total. In essence, this is exactly what you did in the top-down approach, the fallacy of which, because it was done last and not first, is that the territory could have turned out to require 300 hours a year to work or 6,000.

Now here's where things get different. In the bottom-up approach, you qualify each customer or prospect to determine whether you want to go after them in the first place. Think about that: Every customer and every prospect in every zip code gets a yes or a no. What was that I just heard? Were you screaming? *What a monumental task,* you're thinking, *to qualify every customer and every prospect in every zip code!* I concur with your assessment of the magnitude of this task, but consider this: Such an assessment has to be done, doesn't it? I raised the point before: It's not economically viable to call on every possible person or business who might be a candidate for your products and services. Someone has to decide whom to pursue and whom to skip. If you don't do it, or find a way to get it done, your sales reps are going to have to do it on their own, probably haphazardly and with less-than-ideal results. And isn't it your job as a manager to provide them a way to focus their activities and set priorities? Beyond that, and you may have already figured this out, by pinpointing exactly which ones to go for, and which ones to let ride, you're going to be able to build up a territory the perfect size to keep that rep busy for those fifty or sixty hours.

Step 3 of the bottom-up approach is to determine the account's potential profitability. Note that I said profits, not just gross sales. An account with $100,000 in gross sales with a profit margin of 40 percent is likely to yield more net than a million-dollar account with a

2 percent margin. This step is not easy. It requires some educated guesses. You might think that a certain prospect, if you got its business, would generate profits of $2,000 in Year 1 but would have the potential for $15,000 in Year 2. Consider that as you run your numbers. In addition, as discussed in the next chapter, you might wish to do something with your compensation system to encourage reps to go after business which has good long-term prospects but not much of a payout in the short run. To keep it simple, let's say that Prospect 32534-013, if you get it, will generate profits of $4,000 a year.

The next item on this step is to estimate the probability of succeeding in attaining this prospect if you decide to go for it. Again, this takes an educated guess; you don't need to come up with an exact number. Something in the ballpark is all you need. An easy way to estimate is to categorize the likelihood of success as very unlikely/ somewhat unlikely/a toss-up/somewhat likely/very likely, and assign a probability of success as 10 percent/30 percent/50 percent/70 percent/90 percent respectively. For the example, let's say you feel it's a toss-up that you'd get Prospect 32534-013, a 50 percent probability of success. Now you can calculate the expected profit for this account by multiplying the profits which would be generated ($4,000) times the probability of success (50 percent), or $2,000. Now, as you know, Prospect 32534-013 will not yield a gross profit of $2,000: It will be either $4,000 or zero. But what you're doing, of course, is building, from the bottom up, a list of customers and prospects who, in their aggregate, will earn something close to your estimate.

The final part of Step 3 is to subtract the cost of pursuing and servicing the account, all expenses and other direct costs. It's reasonable to expect that these might vary for a given account between the time during which they are a prospect being pursued and the time during which they are a customer being serviced, just as their profit potential could vary between Year 1 and Year 2, Year 2 and forward. Once again, you can't be precise, but you can come up with a reasonable estimate. Let's say, for our simple example, that the direct costs of pursuing Prospect 32534-013 are $500. Subtract that from the expected gross profit ($2,000), and you have the expected net profit, $1,500.

Step 4 is a simple calculation. Take the expected net profit from Step 3 ($1,500) divided by the time required to pursue and service the account, from Step 2 (ten hours), to calculate the estimated payout per hour invested: $150 per hour. That number tells you whether it's worthwhile to pursue or service that account at all. Chances are that $150 per hour is sufficiently lucrative to pay the rep's commission and your salary, and to make the necessary contribution to fixed costs, with enough left over to put something on the bottom line. If so, Prospect 32534-013 is a "go" and represents ten hours' work that needs to get done.

Part of your job in setting up sales territories is to establish a cutoff point for a prospect or customer to be considered qualified. I readily agree this is not easy, especially when you look at an account which doesn't generate sufficient profits in Year 1 but has the potential to do so at some time in the future. This does not have the precision of a fine watch, but it has to be done! Someone, and it must start with you, the manager, needs to make an assessment of the prospects and customers to determine whether they should be designated as targets. Absolutely get input from the field, other managers, any source you can find. But for every prospect or customer, give it a thumbs up or a thumbs down: we're going for it, or, at least for now, we're letting it ride.

You probably have a pretty good idea where this goes from here for Step 5: Add up all the time required for all the targeted prospects and customers in all your zip codes, and see what you've got. Say, for example, that it will take 24,000 hours to get the job done. How many hours a year does each rep have? If it's 2,000 hours, *that* tells you the number of territories you need: twelve.

Step 6 of the bottom-up approach is the same as Step 3 of the top-down: Combine control units into territories of approximately equal potential, optimizing territory coverage and minimizing expenses. There's a good chance you might not be able to do that precisely. Due to significant travel times between calls, a rep in western Nebraska might not be able to earn as much as someone in suburban Atlanta. But that's all right. Western Nebraska, where someone could earn $50,000 a year, might be a good place to assign an entry-level rep. If he or she did well, a promotion might be in order to suburban Atlanta, where that person could earn $80,000 a year.

Properly setting up sales territories bottom-up is a formidable task, but well worth doing. The territories are going to be far closer in representing a designated workload than would have been possible with a top-down approach, and it's performed the necessary exercise of identifying targets and enabling the sales rep to more readily set priorities. However, what you have created is not set in stone. You could see, walking through the examples, that the market is dynamic. Individual customers will require more or less time year to year. New players will come in, old ones will fade away. And *your* company will change along with inevitable changes in the products and services you offer and changes in the competitive environment. Thus, you will need to build in flexibility to your definitions of sales territories and make provisions for ongoing modifications. Think of it as another form of continuous improvement.

Chapter 13 discussed some of the things you needed to do before interviewing potential candidates. One of the points was to use the hiring situation as an opportunity to rewrite the position description and alter other position descriptions, perhaps promoting other employees. Consider a similar approach in making alterations to sales territories. A rep may have done a good job but, due to a variety of changing circumstances, may no longer be able to cover a territory's potential. The time of moving the rep to a new assignment or his or her decision to leave the company might be an opportune time to create a new territory and perhaps also to modify adjacent territories. Break up a territory *only* if the market potential can't be covered, *never* because you think the rep is making too much money. I know of one rep who, because of a whole lot of working smart, achieved an earnings level of $247,000 a year selling commodity flavors and spices in the food manufacturing industry. Her company decided she was making too much, a strange attitude inasmuch as she was contributing three dollars in profits to the company for every one dollar they were paying her. Anyhow, they pulled in some of her customers to become house accounts, paying her a radically reduced compensation to service them, and lopped off part of her territory and assigned it to a new hire. Predictably, she quit the company, joined the competition, and, I'm happy to report, took practically all of her old accounts with her.

As promised at the beginning of this chapter, the principles of the bottom-up approach to setting up sales territories have broad applications. Let's first consider how they apply to managing your staff.

In traditional top-down management, you have a staff of, say, forty people you try to keep busy all day. If you're part of an Organization Man culture, you take on as much work as possible in hopes of justifying an increase in the number of employees you manage. If you now have a staff of fifty, you automatically have more status than you did with forty, and increase by increase, the perception is that you're moving up the organization.

AN ALTERNATIVE APPROACH

I'm going to suggest an alternative approach: Start with every task or project that is proposed, and figure out what it's going to take to get it done. Remember how we calculated the cost of a meeting? Same idea. Budget out employee costs as salary times two. Thus, a person earning $40,000 a year divided by 2,000 hours a year equals twenty dollars an hour. Charge his or her time at twice that, which reflects what the employee really costs the company. So, at forty dollars an hour plus direct expenses, cost out the task or project. As an example, if it will take twenty-five hours' time ($40/hour × 25 hours = $1,000) plus direct expenses of $200, its cost is $1,200. Ask yourself a couple of questions. First, ask whether the task or project could be outsourced at a lower cost. If it can be done by an outsourcer for $900, it makes no sense for you to do it internally at a cost of $1,200. Next and most important, ask yourself whether the task or project will return its investment in a bottom-line contribution to the company. If the return on investment is less than its cost, the task or project should be deleted.

I'm going to dabble in economics for a moment, but just enough to lay the foundation for the next point. Remember the concept of fixed costs versus variable costs? To refresh you, fixed costs are those expenses incurred whether you produce one widget or 1,000: plant and equipment, management salaries, the company condo in Hawaii. By contrast, variable costs are the expenses incurred for producing one more unit. A quick and simple example: you build a factory to manufacture motorcycles at a cost of $10 million. You must invest the $10 million, a fixed cost, to produce Motorcycle #1. But no further investment is required to produce Motorcycle #2, Motorcycle #3, etc. The factory will be good for producing 100,000 motorcycles over its lifetime, so your accountants amortize the cost of the factory at $100 per motorcycle ($100/motorcycle times 100,000 motorcycles equals $10 million). In the real world, of course, if your accountants are properly creative, they'll expense more of those fixed costs in early years, to minimize tax liability, but let's not go off on that tangent.

If the variable cost of producing one more motorcycle is $3,000, your books will reflect a cost of goods sold as the fixed cost ($100) plus variable cost ($3,000), or $3,100. Now, here's the question: If you can sell one more motorcycle, at a price of $3,050, did you make money or lose money? Based on a cost of goods sold of $3,100, you lost fifty dollars. But in reality, some say you covered all your variable costs plus contributed fifty dollars to fixed costs, so you made money. The argument goes that if you cover variable costs and contribute *something* toward fixed costs, you're making money. I'll return to this momentarily.

Along the same lines, let's go back to the example of a project which would cost $900 to outsource but $1,200 internally. The first reaction is to outsource it. But if, for example, the $1,200 cost of doing it internally represented $800 in direct (variable) costs and allocated $400 in fixed costs (equipment, management salaries, rent for office space), many say you should do it internally. Direct (variable) costs are lower ($800 versus $900) and you allocated $400 toward fixed costs that would have had to be charged elsewhere if not absorbed in this project. Because the fixed costs were a given, focus on direct (variable) costs. The argument proposes you save $100 by doing the project internally. At least that's what it says in my principles of marketing textbook, but I disagree.

Please pay close attention to what I say next, as it may give you an extremely valuable insight for managing expenses, particularly as you move closer to top management: to the largest extent possible, treat all expenses as variable costs. Not only that, make a concerted effect to reallocate fixed costs so that they are treated as variable costs.

Going back to the motorcycle example, it's not as though the $10 million fixed cost of the factory was a one-time investment, because after 100,000 motorcycles you're going to have to tear down the old factory and build another one. And I'm willing to bet the new factory will run a whole lot more than $10 million. You had better be salting away at least $100 per motorcycle toward the day you'll need a new factory or you are, in essence, liquidating the business as you milk the cow dry. In the short term, you're creating a little cash flow selling at $3,050, but it's a mirage.

Taking this back to managing a task or project, do not be deceived by looking only at direct (variable) costs. That hides the fact that the best management solution might be to totally eliminate many of the "fixed" costs in the first place. The example I noted, $800 in direct (variable) costs + $400 allocated to cover fixed costs (total $1,200), versus outsourced for $900, could be an example of a project dealing with information technology, marketing research, accounting, anything. Instead of allocating all those fixed costs across a number of projects, consider what would happen if you outsourced the entire function. You would need fewer people, less equipment, and fewer services, and might even be able to get along with less office space. In other words, many of those so-called fixed costs would disappear. In fact, over the long term *all* costs are variable costs. The answer is to outsource the project for $900 and refuse to participate in the shell game of moving around fixed costs.

Finally, find a way to charge off as many costs as possible, fixed and variable, to specific projects and accounts. You may at first be reluctant to do this for fear of creating a bureaucratic nightmare, but it's good cost management and you can keep it simple. A project manager might think twice about an information technology analysis that had to be outsourced, with the attendant costs charged to his or her budget, whereas he or she wouldn't think twice about having it done internally at no cost. So, instead of having any form of staff support available for the asking, charge off all the costs of those services to the requester. All of a sudden, those persons asking for support and services will have to start weighing costs versus benefits, and that's good management. In essence, you manage staff service and support as an outsourcer and profit center.

I dealt with a Fortune 500 company that had a thirty-person marketing research department providing all support requested by brand managers and field sales personnel, with all its cost absorbed by the company. A new manager came in and converted the department to a profit center, with its entire budget reallocated to the brand and field sales groups after a sizeable proportion was retained as a contribution to bottom-line profitability. In turn, all parties requesting marketing research support were to be charged the full costs of rendering those services. The result was that costs for marking research declined over 60 percent once the requesters had responsibility for weighing cost versus benefit. Brand and field sales groups had more money than before for other expenses, and the company enhanced its profitability.

Take a good look at all your "fixed" costs and challenge all your assumptions. You'll make better financial decisions and enhance your company's profitability by treating more costs as variable costs and charging costs to those parties who are utilizing your staff support and other services.

Chapter 19

Establishing and Managing
an Employee Compensation System

"You mean I get paid for this, too?" These words are most often spoken by new employees selling hot dogs in the Wrigley Field bleachers or new hosts from the Gulf Breeze Escort Service. It's the same attitude you wish to create in the organization you manage. In Part III, I will look at how good managers create an environment in which employees love what they're doing so much that there's nothing they'd rather be doing, whether or not they're being paid for it. They could hit the lottery this afternoon and they'd still want to be back on the job tomorrow. However, most employees do need the money, and, at the least, how much you make is a measure of how much someone thinks you're worth. So if you're pulling down pretty big bucks it can't hurt your status among others and how you feel about yourself. After all I've said about money not being a motivator, certainly people are going to be inclined to do things which make them more money and disinclined to do things which make them less. There's not enough money in the world to get me to spend a year in Antarctica, and I would be disinterested in doubling my teaching load for twice the salary. But if I were going to do a little consulting work on the side, I might be more inclined to put up with the hassle of traveling to a less-than-desirable location for $3,000 a day than do something convenient and local for $500. The bottom line is although you won't want to rely on money alone to motivate people and make them love their jobs, it will influence their behavior, and you should utilize your compensation system to encourage employees to do what you want them to do, and reward them accordingly.

You need to take care to avoid two potential problems when dealing with performance appraisal and compensation systems. One is role ambiguity, in which the employee does not know what specifically he or she is supposed to be doing or how it will be evaluated. You took care of that by establishing observable and measurable standards. The other problem, at issue in the upcoming case study, is role conflict, a disconnect about what is in the best interest of the company versus the employee versus the customer. You may wish to circle my next statement in red pen: *At no time should any employee be expected to do something which is not in the best interest of the customer.* Hopefully, you have inculcated your employees with an appreciation of the fact that it's in their long-term best interest to always be focusing on what's in the best interest of the customer. That's the whole basis for repeat business and referrals. Absolutely unacceptable is a situation in which management implicitly or explicitly rewards employees for doing things not in the customer's best interest and punishes them for doing what's best for the customer. I've seen numerous compensation systems in which sales reps were implicitly punished for providing promised service after the sale. They were given no compensation for providing the service, and there were no consequences for not providing it. Management was telling them, in effect, "You got that sale. Now forget about that one and go out and get another one."

A less serious form of role conflict is a disconnect between the best interests of the employee versus the company. In that case, naturally, employees will do what's best for them. Sure, that's a problem, but not as bad as a conflict in what is in the best interest of a customer. Also, role conflicts between employees and the company can be addressed by management's building a partnership relationship with its employees. Often, such a partnership can be founded upon the compensation system.

To get started, let's take a look at another case study. You'll see that it has a few numbers in it, but don't let that scare you. I've rounded them off to keep everything nice and simple. Look it over and see how well you think the employee, Grace Garland, is doing. Put yourself in the shoes of her manager, Georgiana Starlington, and consider how you would evaluate Grace's performance and how you would address issues about her performance and compensation.

CASE STUDY:
METROPOLIS MANUFACTURING COMPANY

Georgiana Starlington is the newly appointed sales manager for Metropolis Manufacturing Company. She is preparing to review the performance of Grace Garland, a veteran salesperson who has been assigned to the same territory for twenty-one years.

Metropolis Manufacturing Company sells three product lines: Product A, a commodity sold on price in a highly competitive market; Product B, a specialty good with limited applications; and Product C, a revolutionary new product with great growth potential and for which Metropolis holds a patent.

The sales force for Metropolis has been directed to give emphasis to gaining sales and distribution for Product C, and the incentive bonus for sales mangers will be significantly affected by the sales performance of Product C.

Salespeople are paid a commission of 5 percent of gross sales. Median income of Metropolis sales reps is $60,000. Sales for Metropolis Manufacturing Company last year are shown in Table 19.1. Grace Garland's sales for last year are shown in Table 19.2.

CASE STUDY ANALYSIS AND RECOMMENDATIONS

So, how do you think Grace is doing? From her perspective, Grace feels she is doing pretty well. She's pulling down $80,000 a year, well ahead of the average rep. After twenty-one years in the same territory, she's probably just about paid off the mortgage and is likely quite content to continue selling Product A to her long-term customers. She's what we call a "coaster," someone who meets standards but has no desire to do more or progress further. There's nothing wrong with that, by the way. Those long-term, steady, established employees can often be relied upon to get the job done with minimum management oversight. But in this case, Grace's manager, Georgiana Starlington, has a problem because Grace is paying insufficient attention to the innovative and profitable Product C. Since this is affecting the incentive bonus for managers, Georgiana might thus be inclined to rate Grace's performance as less than satisfactory.

But the issue is not Grace's performance. It's the role conflict caused by the compensation system which is rewarding gross sales. Grace has no incentive to push Product C and no disincentive to continue to focus on Product A. Furthermore, she has no incentive to hold the line on prices. In fact, it's just the opposite. On the price-

TABLE 19.1. Metropolis Manufacturing Company's Annual Sales, 2004

Product	Unit Sales	Change vs. Year Ago (%)	Price per Unit ($)	Gross Sales ($)	Gross Profit (%)	Gross Profit ($)
A	10,000,000	−1	1	10,000,000	6	600,000
B	1,000,000	+10	10	10,000,000	9	900,000
C	100,000	+1	100	10,000,000	15	1,500,000
Total	**11,100,000**			**30,000,000**		**3,000,000**
−5% commission						−150,000
Net profit						**2,850,000**

TABLE 19.2. Grace Garland's Annual Sales, 2004

Product	Unit Sales	Change vs. Year Ago (%)	Price per Unit ($)	Gross Sales ($)	Commission (%)	Commission ($)
A	1,000,000	+1	1	1,000,000	5	50,000
B	50,000	+1	10	500,000	5	25,000
C	1,000	+1	100	100,000	5	5,000
Total	1,051,000			1,600,000		80,000

sensitive commodity Product A, she might close a lot more sales by giving a one-half percentage point price concession. Her commission would be virtually unaffected, but it would cut her company's profits by 50 percent.

Generally, most companies are more concerned about profits than gross sales. The bottom line *is* the bottom line, after all. Thus, it makes no sense to compensate employees based on gross sales. Create a partnership by paying them a percentage of the profits. This removes the role conflict and it gives them an incentive to hold the line on price concessions. Now, the one-half percentage point price reduction in Product A, which cuts the company profit by 50 percent, also reduces the rep's commission by 50 percent.

Be very careful about messing with the compensation system, lest employees perceive you as doing this to screw them over one more time. It's essential that any changes you make be seen as fair. In the case study, you'll note that in its entire product line, Metropolis has gross profits of $3 million, of which $1.5 million is paid in commissions, an even 50 percent. A simple solution for them would be to restructure the compensation system to pay 50 percent of profits across all products. Thus, Product A, with a 6 percent margin, would pay a 3 percent commission; Product B, with a 9 percent margin, would pay 4.5 percent; and Product C, with a 15 percent margin, would pay 7.5 percent. With these modifications, Grace's income would fall from $80,000 a year to $60,000, but reps whose sales were more oriented to the most profitable lines would earn more than before and overall compensation for the sales force would be the same—simple and fair.

If, by chance, your company is one of those still compensating employees on the basis of gross sales, you probably should consider implementing a similar change. Calculate what percentage of gross profits is being paid in commissions, and pay out that same percentage across everything. At least that's a good starting point. Let's explore a few more ideas for fine-tuning the compensation system.

If you'll recall some of the points raised in Chapter 18 about allocating costs to specific projects and organizational entities, you may see a similar theme in this discussion about compensation. You want to assign responsibility for costs and charge them off accordingly. Along the same lines, you want to give credit for profits and *pay* them off accordingly. To the greatest extent possible, eliminate salaries and pay employees for achieving the shared objectives of your partnership. Then, your management perspective is unambiguous: You act as a facilitator for helping them make as much money as possible, since every dollar they make for themselves represents proportional profits for the organization. Every day, you should talk to those employees and ask them, "What can I do to help you make more money today?" I doubt many managers are out there doing that, but with a partnership of shared objectives, they should be, and so should you.

As alluded to in Chapter 18, the worst thing you can do is penalize employees because you think they're making too much money (probably a good deal more than you). But you knew, when you elected to go into management, that the best sales reps consistently earn more than the best sales managers. Think of it as the price you pay for the prestige of that title on the door.

Now you see another reason why it's essential to have specific standards that measure the quantity and quality of every *individual's* work, even in a team environment which encourages people to engage one another cooperatively. Since every employee is paid as an individual, you must assess his or her unique contribution to the attainment of the organization's objectives. By marrying performance appraisal with the compensation system, you are sending loud and clear signals about what employees should be doing and how well they're accomplishing their goals. Begin the process by stating quantifiable and measurable marketing objectives. Proceed from there to give individual employees specific quantifiable and measurable goals, with commensurate rewards, for achievements which lead to the attainment of those marketing objectives.

In the case study, employees were encouraged to go for gross dollar sales, which was inconsistent with company objectives. Revising the compensation system to pay as a percentage of profit removes the role conflict but still encourages reps to go for the big guys. As noted in Chapter 18, some accounts may have limited short-term potential, but they may also have substantial potential for the future. You'd like to believe your reps would want to plant a few seeds in those accounts, planning the future payoff, but that might not happen. Many reps, understandably, may focus on what will pay off today. They might need money right now or believe that by the time such accounts become lucrative, they'll be in a new territory or with a new company. Don't expect those employees to take a long-term perspective and look to future rewards. Figure out what you want them to be doing now and pay them for doing that. Chances are you'll want to consider variables other than sales in establishing your compensation system. One based solely on sales might inadvertently encourage a "dump and run" attitude among reps and a focus only on large prospects with significant short-term sales potential. I noted a couple examples of this. For instance, if one of your marketing objectives is to provide service and follow-up, reward it. An employee might earn 80 percent of the commission for making the sale and another 10 percent each for two specified follow-up calls. Or consider the situation in which you want to establish new accounts, even though they might not do substantial business for a while. Establish a special bonus, differentiated by size and type of account, that provides a one-time payoff for opening new accounts.

Along the same lines, consistent with the objective of a broad, diversified customer base, you might wish to consider differential commissions. Going back to the case study, recall that, based on profits, commissions would have been 3 percent for Product A and 4.5 percent for Product B, and 7.5 percent for Product C. That modification alone would have encouraged attention to highly profitable Product C. But you might want reps to give attention to the entire line. For example, at the beginning of the year, you might start commissions a half point lower: 2.5 percent for Product A, 4 percent for Product B, and 7 percent for Product C. Whenever the rep hits quota for two of the products, the commission ticks up a half point for both products. So, when Grace Garland hits her quota on Product A, nothing changes: she's still getting 2.5 percent for Product A, 4 percent for Product B, and 7 percent for Product C. But, when she subsequently hits her quota on Product B, commissions change to 3 percent for Product A and 4.5 percent for Product B, though remaining at 7 percent for Product C. Essential to the concept of differential commissions is that the new rates are not merely paid from this point forward but will be paid on everything sold from the time of the base point. Thus, Grace suddenly has an extra half point commission on everything sold for Products A and B since the beginning of the period, likely the first day of the calendar year or the first day of the fiscal year. Nice kick.

Take it to the next step: If Grace makes quota on all three products, there's another half point on everything. Now she's making 3.5 percent on Product A, 5 percent on Product B, and 8 percent on Product C. You can see the implications. It's November 1, sixty days to go in the accounting year, and Grace realizes that if she can make quota on all three products she will receive a significant increase on commissions for everything sold in the past ten months. Nice incentive to hunker down for November and December rather than slack off and enjoy the holidays. This is, of course, a very simple example of a compensation system based solely on profits for a company with only three products, but you get the idea. Look at your own unique situation and needs, and apply the concepts accordingly.

You should feel no reluctance about explaining your compensation system to customers and prospects. Naturally, that does not oblige you to share proprietary information about your costs and margins. But if you're promising service and support after the sale, it's reassuring to customers and prospects to see that sales force compensation is tied to fulfillment of those promises.

Repeating a theme you've heard before: When you implement a compensation system, Keep it Simple, Stupid (the KISS acronym). That is, simple and clearly understandable, as in, "If I do this, I get that." Nothing defeats the motivational value of a compensation system more than by creating one in which reps aren't exactly sure what's going on and how they stand. Instead of all-out sales blitzing for the last three weeks of a period, they go along as usual, and only ten days too late, when they get their commission check, do they realize what might have been if only they'd done this, only done that.

In all my years of following baseball, I've seen only one player who went 100 percent all out on every play, and that was Pete Rose. Just last night I was watching a game in which an outfielder dropped a fly ball at the warning track. The runner, loafing it because there wasn't one chance in 1,000 the ball would be muffed, wound up on first. Had Rose hit the ball and the outfielder dropped it, he'd have been standing on third. Hell, he might have scored, bowling over the catcher with a shoulder to the face mask jarring the ball free. My point is that you don't have too many employees with the intensity of Pete Rose. They aren't going 100 percent all out every minute of every day. So, what you need to do with the compensation is to create a "game situation" to get bursts of high energy over a limited time frame.

A good example of a game situation occurs when a professional athlete knows the score, sees the clock, and knows exactly what must be done within a specified, limited, time frame. There's an increase in focus and intensity which, for most of us, can be maintained only for limited periods. But just like Chipper Jones, Joe Montana, or John Elway, for your sales reps those game situations add up to a significant enhancement in aggregate performance over the long haul. It's a game situation in which Grace Garland goes into high gear to hit her quota on Product B by December 5 and goes over the top on Product C on December 29. But only if she clearly knows: "If I do this, I will get that."

Some compensation systems tell your people, at a certain point, that it is now in their best interest to stop working. Maybe they achieve a specified increase over last year, get a one-time bonus, and know that any additional sales will only increase the base for next year's bonus. I know one rep who, several years ago, got to the point he felt he couldn't afford to work anymore by November 15 because every additional dollar he made that year would be taken away from him in the next two years. Now he stops working by Labor Day. A bad compensation system, and an egregious example of role conflict. Remember not to punish people for making too much. Limit any amount by which compensation thresholds are raised. Let them go 40 percent over quota this year, and don't penalize them by raising quota and bonus levels by 40 percent next year. Make it, say, half that—20 percent—or, even better, a fixed percentage. Tell your reps they can go 40, 60, 80 percent or more over quota, and the base for next year will never be increased by more than 10 percent. See if anybody still elects to quit at Labor Day.

Well, we're two-thirds of the way there. We've laid the foundation and addressed job functions. With all that in hand, now you're ready for what really makes the difference for success as manager: intangibles.

PART III:
INTANGIBLES

Chapter 20

Leadership in Organizations

By now, you should have a pretty good idea of what management is all about. You should feel reasonably confident in your competence at carrying out the functions of your job, but that's not enough. At this point, you have the skills to be an effective administrator, a person identified with management who can perform the necessary tasks required. It's another major step forward to become an effective manager, the key to which is the intangibles I will deal with next.

Effective management is largely leadership, the specific subject of this chapter but implicit to everything I touch on in Part III. Generally, we think of leadership as an intangible: what a person is and how that person deals with others in getting things done. Still, many elements of leadership have to do with what a person does and how he or she manages specific policies and procedures, functions of the job.

To bridge between "functions," which was just completed, and "intangibles," where I'm going next, let's first examine leadership from a traditional, functional perspective. By the way, nothing is wrong with this traditional perspective. By itself, however, it will not make you a great manager. Leadership functions are necessary but not sufficient for good leadership.

Among the many excellent books on leadership functions, in this chapter I discuss *Leadership and Exchange in Formal Organizations,* by T. O. Jacobs (1971). He discusses fourteen major points about traditional leadership functions, many of which touch on points discussed already. His first four major points deal with the general nature of leadership.

JACOB'S LEADERSHIP FUNCTIONS

Point 1: Nature of the Organization

Leader effectiveness is affected by the nature of the organization: its size, organizational structure, history, present climate, etc. It is also affected by the nature of the members of the groups: their maturity, cohesiveness, skills, etc. Be flexible.

There is no one-size-fits-all for leadership. A style that would be perfect at IBM could crash and burn at Microsoft. Managing a group of senior colleagues at a major accounting firm is a whole different ball game from managing high-tech twenty-somethings.

Whenever you move into a new management assignment, take a moment to step back and survey the territory. Don't assume that what the new team needs is the same recipe that worked so well in your last assignment, especially if significant differences exist in the new organization. I often deal with military veterans who regularly tell me about the challenges of moving into the civilian workplace. No longer can they issue orders and expect them to be obeyed. Instead, they're compelled to identify the unique conditions that affect each individual's performance, and then do a selling job to convince them to perform.

When you first take over, assess whether what should be getting done is getting done. If not, some changes will probably be in order, involving both people and procedures. But take your time. Don't start Week 1 with a whole new style of management before you even know who's who and who's doing what. By contrast, if you discover that the job that needs to be done *is* getting done, be careful about overhauling the system. You may be a by-the-book manager who believes in adherence to the letter of the law on policies and procedures, but if your predecessor was pretty laid-back on rules and regulations while achieving incredibly high quantity and quality of performance, you might just want to leave well enough alone and continue as before. Think of it as a learning experience for you.

Point 2: Guide Them Toward Goals

Help the group accomplish its goals and provide the structure needed for goal accomplishment. This reiterates your role as a facilitator, causing objective results to happen. Note that Jacobs uses the word *group,* whereas today we more often say *team.* There is no difference. Implicit in all this, of course, is that the group/team is not merely carrying out your orders and executing them to the letter. Since you're paying them for their brains, you're going to let them use those brains, empowered to act within the defined boundaries.

Point 3: Balance Task Orientation with Concerns for Personal Feelings

Naturally, specific standards for the task are a given, and although I'm not too big on all this touchy-feely stuff, I readily agree that a positive interpersonal environment is bound to be more productive. You should insist that all colleagues treat one another with professionalism and respect, and you should be close enough to the front lines to quickly spot and correct any aberrations. You should be courteous and pleasant to everyone, not just because it enhances productivity but because it's the proper way to manage.

Having said that, personal feelings and interactions can go too far or become a hindrance to productivity. I know of one manager who is reluctant to criticize the work of a certain employee who becomes emotionally upset at the merest hint that her performance is anything short of the pinnacle of perfection. I know of others who will not confront certain prima donnas disinterested in doing their fair share of trivial and unpleasant tasks. Of course, no manager should accept an inordinate period of nonperformance because of personal issues or because the employee doesn't feel inspired.

Worst of all, interactions can go too far when they start to infringe on employees' personal time. When the picnic every Sunday afternoon has become a de facto mandatory meeting, it's doing more harm than good. I had one boss who believed that a three-day rafting trip through the wilderness would be a great team-building activity. I looked him square in the eye and told him that three days on a raft wasn't my idea of a good time and I wasn't going. The majority of my colleagues who would have been affected by this subsequently came to me and said they felt the same way but were afraid to speak up. The idea was killed, but I've often wondered how many other organizations send their people out on similar excursions and how many employees hate it but feel compelled to go and act gung ho. Recently, one such participant suffered a fatal heart attack on one of these adventures. Predictably, his grieving widow is suing the company and the manager. If nothing else does it, that should give you pause for reflection.

Point 4: Keep Communication Flowing

Open up channels of communication so that members are clear about organization goals, methods used in accomplishing those goals, and standards of performance expected of them.

I would add to this only that, as described in delegation, I'm more concerned with the ultimate result and less concerned about method, as long as everything is within the boundaries of propriety, policies, and procedures. Naturally, those channels of communication are two-way, with communication upward encouraged, especially when it's something you don't want to hear. Unfortunately, many managers respond to bad news by yelling at or shooting the messenger. In the short run, that will ensure you of much more pleasant days, since you'll never get any bad news. In the long run, of course, that guarantees you will fail.

Jacobs's next four points address leader behavior and characteristics.

Point 5: Leaders Must Earn Respect

Group members need to respect their leader. Emotional reactions and behavior cause them to lose respect.

Earlier I noted that a key element to effective management was commanding respect. But you must earn it, it can't be demanded.

Leaders bring a level of emotional intensity to their role, but this should not be confused with emotional outbursts, especially of a negative nature. Under no circumstances should a manager blow up or lose his or her cool, even under the most stressful situations. Don't think you can go back to your employees later and apologize for your behavior and beg forgiveness. Sure, they'll say it's all right and tell you to forget about it, but it's not all right, and *they* sure *won't* forget about it. Once emotions have broken out and words have been spoken, they can never be erased. Damage has been done that can never be fully repaired.

Point 6: Learn to Tolerate Pressure and Uncertainty

Protect other group members from pressure and uncertainty. This is a very narrow line to follow, especially in today's business environment. Back in the days of big old corporate America, with its implicit bond of lifetime employment, there wasn't much pressure or uncertainty about the company or people's jobs being there tomorrow and the day after. Today, with big-name companies falling like flies and taking their employees' jobs with them, it's a different story. I have noted the need to share information with employees, especially when their livelihoods are at stake. You do them no favor by withholding such knowledge under the guise of protecting them from pressure and uncertainty. They have a right to know and to proceed from there in their own best interests.

That said, there's no reason to burden employees with pressure and uncertainty you can carry on your own shoulders. Don't ask them to sympathize or to share your pain if they can do nothing about it and can take no direct action. Protect them from pressure and uncertainty if it helps them be productive and have a happier day. Share the pressure and uncertainty of a probability of job cuts in the next sixty days even though you know that means your best employees may head for the lifeboats and leave you to go down with a sinking ship. Come to think of it, if the ship is going down, you might even need to have those employees on your side, leading you toward a lifeboat.

Point 7: Facilitate Group Goals

Facilitate group goal achievement through problem solving, troubleshooting, and representing the group successfully to management.

Do this within the context of Point 2, in your role as facilitator. Representing your employees to management is giving credit and doing anything you can do to enhance their career progress.

Point 8: Don't Obsess over Policy

Preoccupation with control through rules and authority leads to decreased efficiency and reduced satisfaction—and can lead to resistance and resentment as well.

Generally, an obsession with policies, procedures, and rules leads not to control but to the illusion of control, with obedience limited to whatever the manager can personally observe and enforce. That's usually not much. Employees who are evaluated on obedience to rules do not tend to remain focused on meaningful accomplishments. The good employees simply won't put up with such a system and will go elsewhere. Some of the more creative employees will make a game of it, challenging themselves to achieve high performance evaluations for obeying every letter of every law while purposely doing as little work as possible. The bad employees, of course, will be relieved at having found a place to hide.

Having said all that, there's a point to be made about rules and authority if you inherit a team in a state of anarchy which has no standards and is getting nothing done. In this case, there's a call for a new manager to come in and take charge.

I deal closely with one manager who was appointed to just such a situation. She took over a sales force that was retaining employees with sales as low as 28 percent of quota and no activity standards. She immediately laid down the law, insisting on documented minimums for telephone solicitations and cold calls leading to a required number of appointments and specified numbers of closed sales. Good sales reps found it a refreshing change and welcomed the new authority and standards, which helped them do what was necessary to be successful. Most of the bad sales reps quit upon discovering they had to do something besides sit around all day. One rep, the guy at 28 percent of quota, was shocked when she fired him. She said, "I told you I was going to fire you if you didn't do what you had to do." He responded, "Yeah, but they told me that before and they never meant it."

Jacob's final six points deal with leader-follower relationships.

Point 9: A Good Leader Is Not a Buddy

The effective leader is endorsed by the group but maintains some distance from them. In other words, as I've said, your role is management and you are their boss, not their buddy.

Point 10: Distinguish Employees Through Their Contributions

Make valid distinctions among members based on an accurate as-sessment of their contributions. Making such distinctions means that the most effective leader will not always be the best-liked member of the group. Use standards and accountability as your measures. You stopped worrying about being well liked when you joined manage-ment and focused on commanding respect instead.

Point 11: A Good Leader Listens to the Group

An effective leader is open to influence from the group but does not necessarily involve them in the decision-making process, only giving them the chance to be heard. This is an extremely important point. Good leaders and good managers avail themselves of the op-portunity to get all the input they can get from any reliable source. Followers and employees will be more inclined to support a decision different from their wishes if the leader/manager showed them the consideration of hearing what they had to say. So listen; it can't do any harm, and it will probably do at least a little good.

The preceding, however, does not suggest you practice democratic management or lead through opinion polls. Harry Truman is gener-ally regarded as a good president and leader despite making decisions at odds with prevailing public opinion. More recent presidents, who moved in whatever direction the polls pointed them, are not as highly regarded. As a manager and leader, you are not running a democracy, and if you're making the tough decisions and the right ones, occa-sionally you'll choose a direction different from that advocated by the majority. If it doesn't work out as hoped, you can always say, "I was wrong." People will respect that.

Point 12: Pick Your Battles Wisely

Give in on irrelevant and trivial matters, thus permitting followers to save face, without compromising on important task-related mat-ters. Bear Bryant used to say: "You gotta let a guy win once in a while." There's almost never a reason to totally impose your will on someone to the point you humiliate that individual, even as you fire him or her for never rising above 28 percent of quota. Even a whipped dog can be given a dish of water and tied up in the shade.

Point 13: Empower Your Followers

Be concerned with your employees as persons, train them to accomplish their tasks, and arouse confidence within the group that they can accomplish their goals. In other words, give them the resources they need, then be their coach.

Point 14: Encourage Group Friendships

Most groups are effective when they contain friendship groups. An effective leader will not discourage the formation of such groups, even though they may slightly diminish the leader's influence. The leader should be concerned about isolates within the group.

Jacobs hits on a couple of good points here. Initially, even effective managers and leaders may be concerned about the existence of certain cliques within their ranks, fearing potential for a palace revolt. Almost any group of any size, however, will have friendship groups. It's just not realistic to expect a team of more than three or four members to all want to hang around with everyone an equal amount of time and to all feel the same level of comfort and closeness for every single individual. Let these friendship groups form and flourish, being concerned only if you perceive that the basis for their common ground is potentially detrimental.

Do not automatically be concerned about isolates in a group. Some people simply prefer to get the job done and go home to friends and family. Others are just lone wolves or prefer silicon-based life-forms. You should be concerned, however, and get to the bottom of it, if certain individuals are being shunned or systematically discriminated against. Is there a problem with their actions or is it only who and what they are? Find out and deal with it accordingly.

In sum, Jacobs presents a concise and organized picture of leadership from the traditional functional perspective. No doubt you noticed that many of his points concerning effective leadership closely paralleled points I made about effective management. That's only logical, since managers must, almost by definition, lead. Still, as you were reviewing his fourteen points in detail, I suspect you were thinking that leadership cannot be defined solely in terms of what one does. Indeed, leadership is a complex combination of what one does, what one is, and how one operates. Functions, the subject of Part II and the primary emphasis of Jacobs are essential parts of the foundation. So are appreciation of the management identity and role, as well as the nature of relationships Jacobs touched upon. But inherently, it is suspected there's more to it than that, and it's there I will go next.

CHARACTERISTICS OF GREAT LEADERS

Take a few moments and think: Considering all the people you know of throughout recorded history, who makes your top ten list of the greatest leaders of all time? This could include political or religious leaders, sports personalities, military officers, or business-persons, etc.

When this exercise is conducted, certain persons are consistently cited. Religious leaders include Gandhi, Mother Teresa, and Jesus. Sports personalities include: Vince Lombardi, Tom Landry, Joe Montana, and John Elway, as well as Phil Jackson and Joe Torre. Military leaders most often cited are George Patton and Douglas MacArthur. The wide array of political leaders includes: Julius Caesar, Margaret Thatcher, George Washington, Abraham Lincoln, Franklin D. Roosevelt, Vladimir Lenin, Karl Marx. Among the many business leaders, I often hear Lee Iacocca from the old-timers and Bill Gates, Michael Dell, and Jeff Bezos among the younger set. My list is not intended to be comprehensive but demonstrates that among persons acknowledged to be leaders an incredible diversity exists. So, the question is this: Can we identify certain characteristics generally common to all these leaders—characteristics you can adopt to enhance your own personal leadership qualities? I think we can.

By definition, leadership requires two essential ingredients: (1) followers and (2) somewhere to lead them. You can't be a great leader if there isn't a place you want to go. Thus, there may be leadership failure manifested in a person we categorize as an efficient administrator. Employees can perceive you as a competent and fair manager if you properly implement policies and procedures, and they may consider you a decent person to work for, but that alone will not excite or motivate them. They can be led to a place: the promised land or the enemy capital. In the field of sports, a leader can promote a specific team objective (win the World Series or the Super Bowl) and/or a personal objective (take the home run crown or lead the league in rushing). For the world of business, leadership can encompass a comparable organizational strategic objective (launch a new product which takes the number-one category sales position) and/or a personal objective (sales rep of the year, with gross income of $500,000).

The leader needs a vision: where are we going, what are our goals, our plans, our specific objectives? To be effective, the vision must be built on emotion and feelings rather than solely on facts and content. Thus, Martin Luther King Jr. said, "I have a dream," rather than, "These are my legislative objectives." During World War II the troops responded to "Remember Pearl Harbor," and today employees chant, "We're number one" more readily than "We exceeded quota by fourteen percent!"

Shared Objectives

All of this leads us directly to the next critical point: Effective leadership requires shared objectives. The leader must integrate and unify his or her own goals with those of the followers and those of the organization. In Chapter 19 on compensation systems, I stressed the point that employees will act in their own best interests. That's natural, and as it should be. As Ayn Rand taught us, we should never expect to act against our own self-interest for the sake of another, or expect others to act in opposition to their self-interest for us, at least not within the context of a business and professional relationship. No one cares if you'll look good to the captain if your platoon takes that hill. All that counts is why the troops want to do it. Your people don't care whether you get a promotion and raise. All they want to know is what's in it for them. You are not a leader because you set specific goals and standards for your people and have the authority to enforce compliance or else. You do not become a leader by shouting, "Sergeant, take that hill or I'll shoot you," though such a tactic might well succeed as an attention getter.

Having vision and focusing on shared objectives constitute the foundation of leadership, but there's more, and, in particular, the prerequisite of professional competence. A naval officer is doomed to failure without a thorough understanding of ship operations. I would not fare too well as a basketball coach since all I know about the game is that you can't take more than two—or is it three?—steps without dribbling. You will fail as a manager if you have less-than-complete knowledge about your products, customers, industry, and competition.

I've heard it said—and I tend to agree—that a good manager can manage anywhere. But let's add a caveat: If you're embarking upon unfamiliar territory, tread softly for a while as you take the crash course in gaining basic competence and knowledge. It's no big deal if you move from one consumer nondurables company to another if each has its own sales force calling on the retail trade. It's another story if you're going into a company which manufactures computers and sells them direct to the consumer.

Over the years, I've seen several managers successfully transition back and forth between the beverage and snack food industries, each of which employs direct store delivery. By contrast, more often than not, I've watched managers fail when they were brought into these industries from the big soap companies who distribute through the chains' warehouses. I encourage these people to spend one week riding with the advance salesperson and another week working with the delivery person/merchandiser. Those who do come back enlightened. Those who don't are never perceived as understanding the nature of the business. They never get off the ground, and are generally gone in less than a year.

It's not a negative reflection on you to admit you don't know everything. Go where the action is and become fully competent before trying to lead anyone anywhere. In the words of Lao Tzu, the founder of Taoism, "To lead the people, walk behind them."

Trust and Integrity

I have already noted how essential it is to command respect. Let's expand on that within the context of leadership to include trust and integrity. Employees must be able to trust you implicitly. They must feel fully confident that you will do what you say you will do and that you will not violate their trust. Betray that trust and you will never be able to lead them again, plus they'll warn all their colleagues never to turn their backs on you.

I know of one situation in which a manager and employee were having a private conversation that the manager assured the employee was strictly between the two of them. In this conversation, however, the employee revealed facts that the manager felt compelled to report to his supervisor, who in turn conveyed them to company security, who in turn confronted the employee, who felt angry and betrayed. The manager claimed he had no choice; the information was of such a nature that it had to be reported. I considered his answer simplistic and a cop-out. Although I concurred with the need to forward the sensitive information, it was inexcusable to let the employee leave the room believing that what he had said would remain confidential. At the least, the manager should have impressed upon the employee the need to convey the information, and should have provided the employee the opportunity to have input on how the matter would be handled. The manager should have made the decision about what was to be done and so told the employee before he left the room. A good leader can say to a follower, "I know I told you this, but now I find I have to do that. Let's talk about it." Just don't ever tell them "this" when you know good and well that you're going to do "that." Your followers aren't stupid. Sooner rather than later they'll figure out you're a manipulator, and you'll get what you deserve.

Integrity is closely related to trust. Since there is no honor among thieves, if you cheat, lie, and steal when dealing with others, your employees will perceive, correctly, that you'll do the same to them whenever you feel it's to your advantage or think you can get away with it. You must demonstrate the highest standards of integrity if you want good people to work with and for you and to accept you as a leader. You cannot tell employees to do as you say and not as you do. I find it most interesting to hear parents telling their children not to smoke when they themselves do or lecturing them on the sancitity of marriage as they openly conduct a relationship on the outside. Similarly, you will never lead your employees toward fiscal responsibility once they discover you're padding your expense account. They will never open up fully and honestly with you if they know you lied to a colleague. You and your integrity must remain the ideal your followers look up to.

Confidence

Consistent with what I've noted so far, leaders have a strong sense of self. Certainly, even the greatest leaders can feel apprehension about whether they're up to the challenge or if they will prevail. They may wonder whether their company will survive a competitive onslaught or whether the enemy has set up an ambush around the bend. They may lay awake nights under the weight of knowing that a decision could be the end of a person's livelihood. But that's not what I mean. By sense of self I mean a confidence that they have done everything possible to enable them to make the right decision. They've availed themselves of all possible input from every possible source. They believe, without arrogance, that no one is better equipped to make those decisions than they are. Most of all, they believe they're decent people, developed in all three areas of life: mental, physical, and spiritual. Therefore, in spite of all the inevitable apprehensions, leaders are willing to act, to take risks, and to pursue a different path. Their followers, perceiving that sense of self, see in the leader that person most able to take them to where it is that they themselves want to go.

Self-Discipline

Leaders exhibit discipline, their self-discipline being the prerequisite to gaining authority and discipline within the organization and with their followers. Leaders make themselves take action, and they make no excuses. Using this as a model of personal management, followers may be inspired to impose a regimen of self-discipline upon themselves, achieving more in positive results than would have been possible from discipline imposed upon them from above.

Empathy

Leaders feel empathy, a sense of personal concern and caring, even as they appreciate that at all times the best interest of the organization is paramount. You're probably aware of how Winston Churchill had to sacrifice the lives of many civilians in Coventry lest the Germans discover their codes had been broken. It bothered him greatly, but it had to be done. Unless you're a Jungle Fighter, it's going to hurt you to make job cuts, but you'll do what you must do. It is not insignificant that you see people as human beings and not entries on a ledger. Those remaining will sense it, too. Empathy can't be faked.

Charisma

I often hear it said that leaders have charisma, and I'm a bit uncomfortable with that term because it seems to reek of Hollywood. It's said that President Kennedy had charisma, which, roughly translated, meant more effective nonverbal communication as illustrated in the videotapes of his debates with Nixon. Of course, the wife, the kids, the sailboats, the family, and the marketing of the war record didn't hurt.

Many people are slaves to television and thirty-second sound bites. As Howard Beale said in *Network,* the tube can "make or break presidents, popes, and prime ministers." We have begun to think like the tube and act like the tube. To some extent, we're all caught up in superficial appearances. Peripherals will get you only so far, however. Leadership is substantive; that's the good news. Here's the bad news: you can't, in today's world, just ignore the charisma factor and get in the game. But here's some more good news: it's manageable.

Let's face it: You and I do not equal JFK or Jackie O. in the charisma department. We're too old and/or too ugly. But if JFK was 100 on the charisma meter, there was no excuse for Nixon to get a 20, except that until 1960 no one knew any better. With a little work, Nixon could have kicked up the meter to a respectable 80, enough to get people to listen to his words and consider his positions rather than look at his sweaty brow, five o'clock shadow, ill-fitting clothes, and lousy posture.

You can do the same with a conscious control of your impression formation and management. You don't have to be a prime physical specimen, but it helps to get into decent shape. Invest in flattering clothes, particularly if you tend to the portly side. Be well groomed, and be aware of your gestures and posture. Remember that many people think in thirty-second sound bites, so don't belabor a point for two minutes. Watch your eye behavior and vocal characteristics, whether you're speaking to one person or twenty.

Until they start considering charisma, most managers believe they have what it takes to be an effective leader and can do what must be done. Until they get to charisma, they correctly perceive that leadership is a learned skill which, combined with hard work, will lead to success. Then they get to charisma and all of a sudden feel they don't have what it takes. I couldn't disagree more.

Anyone can enhance nonverbal and verbal communication skills and manage his or her impression to the extent necessary to be perceived as a good leader. Remember that you don't need a 100 on the charisma meter unless you're shooting for a feature article about yourself in the entertainment tabloids. All you need to do is avoid making mistakes and creating a negative impression, unless, of course, you're doing it on purpose to avoid a promotion to headquarters. Work on your impression skills and communication skills and get the charisma meter up to 70. In leadership, where substance really does count, the charisma component is a pass/fail grade, and 70 is passing.

To sum it up and be sure you have no doubts, leadership, as management, is a combination of hard work and skills. Anyone can do it if he or she really wants to do it and is willing to pay the price.

Chapter 21

A Model for Motivation

A short while back, I was listening to the manager of a struggling baseball team plead that it was not his job to motivate the players. I was astonished, since the very essence of effective management and leadership is motivation. Sure, it's nice to delude oneself into believing that employees are all self-motivated and will attain the pinnacle of success on their own, but if that were the case there would be no need for managers and leaders. All we'd need would be administrators, and that organizational style went out with the Organization Man.

Motivation is fundamental to management success, and in this chapter I will construct a model for motivation. To do this, I integrate the ideas of three well-known management and motivational experts. Taken separately, their ideas have been recognized and utilized for decades. Combining them, I find a synergy in which their usefulness and applicability far exceeds the sum of the individual parts.

MASLOW'S HIERARCHY OF NEEDS

You've likely heard of Maslow's Hierarchy of Needs, which has been around for sixty years. As noted in Figure 21.1, it consists of five levels: physiological, safety, social, esteem, and personal fulfillment. Maslow's theory was that before a person could move on to a higher-level need, all respective lower-level needs had to be satisfied. The most basic needs were physiological: food, water, shelter. If these were not satisfied, a person could not move on to safety or social needs, let alone esteem or personal fulfillment. Thus, a person starving to death will risk injury or punishment to procure food. Someone out on the streets with no place to go on a cold rainy night will do whatever is necessary to have a warm dry place to spend the night.

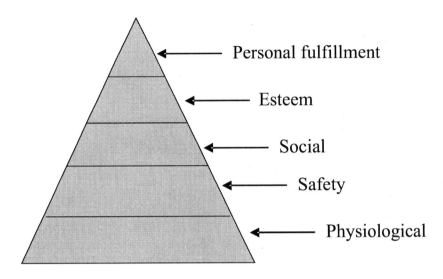

FIGURE 21.1 Maslow's Hierarchy of Needs

Once the fundamental physiological needs are met a person can move on to consider safety needs: freedom from danger and threats, on and off the job. Go from basic shelter to a place in a nice neighborhood. Have a job without risk of injury or death. Eat a decent meal instead of scrounging through the trash.

With both physiological and safety needs satisfied, Maslow theorized that people could move on to satisfying social needs: associating and interacting with others, being accepted and loved. Most, but not all, people will attain this level, generally by junior high or high school. Some don't, though. Even within skilled and professional ranks, a few people never move on to social needs, never have any interest in dealing with their fellow humans. As long as these people don't exhibit antisocial behavior, they may prove to be good employees who simply perform a function for a fair wage and go home at the end of the day.

Most, but not all, people who satisfy their social needs will move on to needs for esteem: one's reputation, having respect, recognition, and status, being needed, and attaining a sense of self-esteem. However, although the majority of people will move on to address esteem needs, a significant minority doesn't even grasp the meaning of the concept. All they want in life is a cold six-pack, a TV dinner while they watch network television, and a heater in the outhouse. Oh, yes—and a date on Saturday night.

Finally, Maslow proposed that people move on to personal fulfill-ment, realizing their individual potential. One cannot have a sense of such fulfillment until late in life, though some people might sense their lives moving toward such a culmination while still in their fifties or early sixties. Again we must ask the question: How many people truly fulfill life's potential or even reach the point where they per-ceive the meaning of fulfillment?

APPLYING MASLOW'S HIERARCHY IN MANAGEMENT

Consider for a moment those questions about what proportion of people move beyond the lower levels of Maslow's hierarchy and, of those still at a lower level, what proportion would move higher if they could. There is no definitive answer—it's a rhetorical question—but how you answer will profoundly affect your attitude toward employ-ees, as I discuss shortly. For instance, when you meet people who are satisfying only their physiological needs, is it your belief that all they care about are those physiological needs and will never go higher, or do you perceive them as having the ultimate potential to reach per-sonal fulfillment? Some people will never go beyond the physiologi-cal no matter what anyone does for them and no matter what sorts of opportunities are provided for them, but the key question is whether you believe most people have the potential, and the desire, to go higher.

Some question every step of the hierarchy. Of those people at a given level, what proportion do you believe have the potential to get to the next level and would be willing to make the necessary sacri-fices to get there ? I believe those proportions are extraordinarily high and that a manager who appreciates that fact will be able to become a motivator of employees. Let me share some anecdotes to illustrate what I mean.

One of my colleagues is a manager of a fast-food restaurant in an urban area. By necessity, he must hire employees from the lower ech-elons of the workforce, many on work release, few with a stable his-tory of employment. Traditionally, managers have viewed such employees with an attitude bordering on contempt. He took a different tack, starting with establishing standards in an environment of mutual courtesy and respect. He facilitates and coordinates their work schedules with their other commitments and helps them access education and training opportunities in the community. The result is that he gets far better than normal job performance with significantly less turnover. Consistently, when employees do leave, it's for a better job, not to revert to unemployment.

One of my first and most vivid memories of the real world was as a seventeen-year-old working in a Chicago factory packing valves. A colleague in the packing department had had the same job for twenty-three years: wiping the dirt off the tops of acetylene torch tips as they came off the line. He explained to me that you had to clean the tip properly or it would burn out prematurely, and that in twenty-three years never had a failure been caused by dirt on a tip he'd cleaned. At least twice a day, the foreman would come by his station and compliment him on how nice the torch tips looked. The employee would beam with pride. This man, though limited in skills and intelligence, most certainly had a sense of esteem and, I suspect, retired from his job having attained personal fulfillment. Had he been treated as a person capable only of lower-level needs, I doubt he would have stayed those twenty-three years and more, and I'll bet there would have been a whole bunch of expensive warranty claims on those torch tips.

THEORY X AND THEORY Y MANAGEMENT

The issue of your perception of employees leads us directly to our second management and motivational expert, Douglas McGregor, who coined the terms "Theory X" and "Theory Y" to describe management's attitudes and assumptions about employees. Note that McGregor's perspective did not deal with different types of *employees,* but the different ways in which *management* viewed and dealt with their employees.

You are classified as a Theory X manager, and a collection of like-thinking colleagues is classified as a Theory X company, if you believe that employees dislike work, will do only as much as they have to and are not looking for responsibility, that employees must be watched continuously to ensure they will do even that, and that employees have little ambition or interest beyond wages and security.

Operating under such a belief system, management attempts to motivate performance through pay, fringe benefits, and good working conditions. This is the model of the old traditional union-management relationship of distrust and poor interpersonal communication.

By contrast, Theory Y managers and Theory Y companies see things through different eyes. They believe that work is part of personal identity, which can be as natural and enjoyable as play and recreation if employees are given the latitude to achieve their personal and creative potential. Managers and companies with a Theory Y perspective seek to create an environment that integrates the employees' goals with those of the organization so that, simultaneously, the individual satisfies personal needs and desires as the organization achieves its strategic objectives. Theory Y managers and companies believe that such a culture will unlock each person's untapped potential and that such employees will be both happier and more productive.

Motivators and Maintainers

Our third and final management and motivational expert, Frederick Herzberg, identified workplace conditions which he classified as either motivators or maintainers. (Specifically, he used the term *hygiene factors* to describe what are now more generally categorized as *maintainers.*) Motivators, most successful in spurring employees on to superior performance, were interesting and challenging work that provided a sense of achievement and personal growth. Recognition of those achievements was then seen to be a further motivator for a desire to accomplish even more in the future. By contrast, maintainers, those factors that kept a person in place on the job but did not motivate him or her on to superior achievements, included pay, fringe benefits, good working conditions, job security, and fair and equitable policies and procedures. Integrating Maslow, McGregor, and Herzberg is the model for motivation as shown in Figure 21.2.

Maintainers address only physiological and safety needs, whereas people are truly motivated by social needs, esteem, and personal fulfillment. Theory X managers and companies are incapable of significantly motivating employees because they address only maintainers and lower-level needs. Theory Y managers and companies recognize that maintainers are necessary. After all, employees do need to pay the rent, buy groceries, and fill up the gas tank. But they go beyond main-

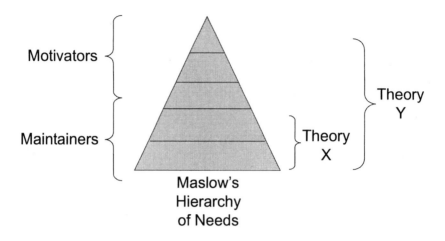

FIGURE 21.2. A Model for Motivation

tainers and lower-level needs to truly motivate people through upper-level needs.

To motivate anyone, you must have a Theory Y perspective and address your employees' social needs, esteem, and personal fulfillment. If you adhere to Theory X assumptions, you will never motivate employees and you will fail as a manager. If you are part of an organization entrenched in a Theory X culture and don't envision it turning around anytime soon, get out now while the getting's good.

CREATING A MOTIVATIONAL ATMOSPHERE

Hopefully, at this point you've begun to appreciate how management is "being" as well as "doing." How you perceive others is absolutely critical to the "being" part of management, and it can't be faked. My colleague who runs the fast-food restaurant and the foreman in the factory share an essential prerequisite to management success: They believe that most people want to move up the hierarchy toward esteem and personal fulfillment, and they create an atmosphere in which people can strive toward their upper-level needs while helping the organization make its bottom line. But certainly they are not so naive as to believe those assumptions apply to *all* people. In the hiring process you hope to gain a sense of a candidate's personal characteristics as well as the basic skills and qualifications for job tasks. Of course, once on the job, employees must meet the standards or they go.

Consider these "being" skills whenever you hire a person who will manage others or is on a career track leading toward a management position. Get them to talk. If you sense a Theory X attitude, a red flag should go up.

If you're in management or considering pursuing it, take a moment to do a little self-assessment. If you're harboring Theory X assumptions, they're likely to prove a severe detriment to your management success. I'm not suggesting you attend sensitivity training; it's much simpler than that. Get out there on the front lines with those people about whom you hold those attitudes—and I don't mean a fifteen-minute visit to the job site, either. Get out there, get to know who's who and what they do at the point of encounter. Make it an objective to command the respect of people who are earning one-tenth as much as you. Based on my own personal experiences and the experiences of numerous colleagues, I'm confident you'll come out of that adventure with a refreshing new attitude and a Theory Y perspective, one which will be reinforced and strengthened every year. You'll break out of the cynicism of the ivory tower, better appreciate your employees, and become a more effective manager.

Be brutally honest with yourself. If, after all is said and done, you still have a Theory X perspective, you're unlikely to be successful in management. If you have a Theory X perspective, you probably won't be very happy in management, either. But as noted, there's something to be said about being a high-paid doer.

Chapter 22

A Perspective on Power

In the previous two chapters, I addressed the first two intangibles of effective management: leadership and motivation. This chapter takes a look at a third intangible, power, and how it ties those other intangibles together.

In this chapter, I first note traditional definitions of power, authority, and leadership and then consider an alternative perspective on power, which has very significant implications for managers. For the traditional view, I refer to Glatthorn and Adams' (1983) *Listening Your Way to Management Success*. Their components of power are not unique, and in fact are the same as you'll find in numerous academic and professional sources. I've elected to cite them because they define the components of power with quick one-line examples that are easy to understand and apply.

THE FIVE COMPONENTS OF POWER

Just to get started on a firm footing, let's look at their definitions of power, authority, and leadership. In other sources, you may find these terms defined somewhat differently, but the essence is similar. Glatthorn and Adams define power as the ability to get others to do what they ordinarily would not do. This broad definition will lead us momentarily to power's five traditional forms used by managers to get employees to do what they want them to do. They define authority as power derived from an organizational relationship, a basic element of management.

I've seen numerous, somewhat varied, definitions of leadership. Glatthorn and Adams define leadership as the ability to influence people to work willingly to achieve group goals. I like this definition because it specifically relates to a team-oriented organizational environment.

Coercive Power

The first, and least sophisticated, of the five components of power is coercive power: "Do this because I will punish you if you don't." To a parent, that translates as "Pick up your room or you can't watch *The Powerpuff Girls.*" On an old Roman ship, it gave a galley slave the choice of rowing the boat or being thrown overboard. In our community, numerous prominent citizens would like nothing better than to go out to the beach for a cold twenty-four-pack, then zip across the US 98 bridge at ninety-eight miles an hour before hitting Interstate 110 and kicking it up to 110 miles an hour. Why don't they do it? Coercive power. Do that, and you'll spend the next several months in jail. For you as a manager, it's, "Be here when you're supposed to be here, and do what you're supposed to do, or you're fired."

Reward Power

The second component of power is reward power: "Do this because I will reward you if you do." This is the essence of working for pay or other tangible rewards. People won't flip burgers or dig ditches for the fun of it—you must pay them. If you're a parent, you've probably discovered it's more effective to give the kid an allowance for taking out the trash or mowing the lawn than merely threatening punishment for not doing so. Similarly, focus on the positive and phrase demands in terms of rewards rather than coercion: "Clean up your room and you *can* watch *The Powerpuff Girls.*" Same deal in the management environment.

Referent Power

Coercive power and reward power deal with content, policies, and procedures. The other three components of power are relationship based, the third being referent power: "Do this because you think well of me," which reflects respect and personal attributes. You've probably discovered that it's more effective to develop a positive relationship with a person and then ask, "Could you do this for me, please?" than it is to have no relationship or have to ask, "Do this and I'll give you an extra ten bucks."

Legitimate Power

The fourth power component is legitimate power: "Do this because I hold a position of authority," which, as noted, means you hold power as a function of your position within the organization. Implicit to legitimate power are coercive power and reward power: the organization has provided you the weapons of enforcement and the resources to reward.

Expert Power

The fifth and final component of power is expert power: "Do this because I know more about the subject," reflecting credentials and professional competence. Thus, neophyte employees will be receptive to suggestions from a manager with experience and expertise in the field. You will seek out a doctor who is a specialist in a particular area. First-semester college freshmen believe that having a PhD means a professor knows what he or she is talking about.

So there you have the basic definitions of power, authority, and leadership, and a recitation of the five traditional components of power. If you're like most managers, you read through all that with the reaction of "Gee, that's nice," but didn't find it particularly enlightening, nor did it provide you with a sudden illumination of some great truth about management, leadership, and motivation. I'd had the same reaction to the traditional terms and perspectives, feeling that something critical was missing, though I never could put my finger on it. All that changed one evening at the Motel 6 in Grants Pass, Oregon, when I was reading *The Anatomy of Power,* by John Kenneth Galbraith (1983).

GALBRAITH ON POWER

Galbraith is best known as an economist, so I was surprised and pleased to see him produce a work on the subject of power which holds extraordinarily significant implications in the field of management. In fact, I consider *The Anatomy of Power* to be *the* most important contribution to our understanding of getting results through others in an organization. It unites, into a brilliantly simple paradigm, the concepts of management, leadership, motivation, and power.

Condign Power

Galbraith (1983, p. 4) begins by identifying three instruments for wielding and enforcing power. The first of these is condign power, which "wins submission by the ability to impose an alternative to the preferences of the individual or group that is sufficiently unpleasant or painful so that these preferences are abandoned." That is to say, your preference would be to kill a case of longnecks and cruise across the US 98 bridge at ninety-eight miles on hour. The alternative—jail and all the attendant costs—is sufficiently painful to make you give up the idea. Your kid would prefer to play with his toys all afternoon and live in sloth, but the alternative of missing *The Powerpuff Girls* is sufficiently unpleasant that he or she completes the designated chores. Sound familiar? Of course! Condign power is another word for coercive power.

Compensatory Power

Galbraith's second instrument for wielding and enforcing power is familiar as well. Compensatory power "wins submission by the offer of an affirmative reward" (p. 5). That is to say, compensatory power is the same as reward power; this is nothing new so far. Galbraith adds an important point here, though, noting that with both condign and compensatory power, the individual is aware of submission. It is visible and objective, attained from being compelled by threat with condign power and by positive reward with compensatory power.

From here forward, Galbraith paints a picture of power strikingly different from the traditional perspective. For the duration of this discussion, I will use Galbraith's terms *condign* and *compensatory power* rather than the traditional *coercive* and *reward.*

Conditioned Power

Galbraith's third instrument for wielding and enforcing power is not included in most traditional descriptions, but it's the key concept in his book. Conditioned power wins (or gains) submission to the will of others by what is thought to be the product of the individual's own moral or social sense, what he or she feels is right or good, acceptance of what the community and culture think right and virtuous that the individual comes to accept as inherently correct.

Whereas condign and compensatory power are visible and objective, and the individual is aware of submission, conditioned power is subjective and the individual may not be so aware. Wow! This is some heavy stuff! Think about this for a moment, because if taken too far in the wrong hands this is not just conditioning but brainwashing.

The objective of conditioned power is to make people take courses of action because they believe it's what they want to do. They have bought into the value system of their culture or organization and feel that what they are doing is not only the right course of action but an obligation they readily accept as a sense of duty. Conditioned power is the essence of leadership, winning submission by cultivating belief and gaining the individual's commitment to the group's or society's objectives. Properly applied, it makes kids choose not to do drugs because drugs are uncool, and they want to be like those cool persons who are drug-free. That's a whole lot more effective than punishing them if they get caught or bribing them with twenty bucks for passing the monthly drug screening. Properly applied, it makes an employee not steal from you because he or she believes stealing is wrong. Properly applied, it motivates a citizen to procure a designated driver because he or she considers it improper to put others at risk by driving drunk. Properly applied, soldiers put their lives on the line to defend their country and its way of life. Taken too far, it encourages young people to commit acts of mayhem in the name of their street gang or to commit suicide in an act of terrorism. Taken too far, it causes corporate executives to ignore or endorse procedures that will ultimately result in tremendous pain and hardship for employees, stockholders, and their families. Conditioned power is, far and away, the consummate instrument, one that can be employed for good or for evil. It is so pervasive and seductive that those who are using it for evil seldom recognize that to be the case until it is too late. Conditioned power, in many of its manifestations and implications, will be discussed through the remainder of the book.

THREE SOURCES OF POWER

Personality

Galbraith goes on to identify three sources of power, the first two of which closely parallel the traditional perspective. The first source is personality, tantamount to referent power, generally referring to persons associated with conditioned power and leadership. Galbraith makes an important distinction, however, between persons who exhibit conditioned power and leadership with a force of personality and those persons, such as politicians and corporate executives, who regularly deal with audiences already fully conditioned in their various and diverse beliefs. When such persons proceed to adjust their words to coincide with their audience's beliefs, those individuals are not really leaders, they are merely adept at identifying themselves with the conditioned will of the crowd. Implicit in Galbraith's commentary is that people who manage by opinion polls or do no more than go along with conventional thinking will not succeed as leaders or attain conditioned power.

This makes sense. As noted, a prerequisite of leadership is having vision and a dream of where to lead the followers. The concept of leadership necessitates moving somewhere, not sitting tight, not doing things the way everyone has always done them, and not using the same path most everyone else takes. Thus, leaders present to their audience the prospect of going somewhere or becoming something not previously envisioned or believed possible. Articulate your goal or vision, and if it's consistent with the value system the followers have bought into they may hop on board, but everyone gets the same message. Say what you think they want to hear and ultimately you'll lose the respect of your followers and your opposition alike.

Property

Galbraith's second source of power is property, the most forthright of the three sources, generally associated with the traditional concept of compensatory power. You own the factory so you can afford to hire the workers. Money is synonymous with property. If I've got the cash, I have the power to convince someone to spend the day washing my windows when he'd prefer to be at the beach. Galbraith makes an important point in suggesting that today the power of property is often associated with conditioned power. That is to say, wealth provides a person with more opportunity for visibility and influence and the use of persuasion. An example that quickly comes to mind is the large amount of money necessary to seek public office. Recent presidential candidates would never have been able to get their message out were it not for the fact that they spent many millions of their own dollars to fund their campaigns. One's dream of becoming a leader and attaining conditioned power in the U.S. Senate is made considerably more attainable if you have $60 million lying around to support your candidacy. On a smaller scale, we're all familiar with the old truism that fools and their money get a lot of attention from headwaiters.

The Organization

Just as conditioned power was an innovative concept as an instrument for wielding and enforcing power, so is his third and final source of power, which has been discussed throughout this book. As it's been such an essential context to everything discussed, this source is an easy one to overlook. But just as conditioned power is the key instrument, this is the key source. Galbraith's third and final source of power is the organization itself. The organization is not merely the structure, the buildings, and the resources. It is, in fact, an entity that exhibits and generates power. By definition, the organization implies legitimate power and authority, and it is the key to all the other sources and instruments of power. It creates condign power and compensatory power directly, and it is essential for any widespread applications of conditioned power. The power of personality is usually insignificant outside of an organizational context: how important are the media personalities without the networks; how far can political figures go without their party; who am I without the university; how powerful are you without your organization? The organization is a force, and it will succeed or fail depending on whether it is strong or weak, well or sick. An absolutely essential part of effective management, especially higher levels of management, is doing those things it takes to grow and nurture a healthy and powerful organization. It's the intangible foundation on which all the other intangibles are built, and it is the major theme of the remainder of this book.

Look at three quotes from Galbraith's (1983) *The Anatomy of Power,* which will lay the groundwork for where to go from here:

> The participants, in one degree or another, have submitted to the purposes of the organization in pursuit of some common purpose. . . . The individual submits to the common purposes of the organization, and from this internal exercise of power comes the ability of the organization to impose its will externally. . . . The organization wins submission to its purposes outside the organization only as it wins submission within. (pp. 55, 57, 56)

As you may have surmised in reading those quotations, a very thin line is being tread here. It is commonly agreed that in an environment of cooperation and teamwork each individual must give a little. Each person doesn't always get his or her way. Everyone has to perform unpleasant tasks. We might not care for some people with whom we must work. It's completely reasonable to expect people to put up with some personal inconveniences in the name of the greater good and the success of the organization. We can argue, yell, and scream, but ultimately we must come together and work toward common objectives. Anarchy is not an option, and an organization divided against itself is unlikely to succeed in the marketplace. When, ultimately, we work together as a team, we're more likely to win. If we exist in an environment of backstabbing and infighting, we're more likely to lose. But this ideal can go too far.

CREATING A POSITIVE ATMOSPHERE

Individuals submitting to the purposes of the organization have gone too far when such submission makes them slaves to conformity, when diversity is devalued, and when people are more concerned about getting along and not making waves than they are about meaningful accomplishment. Recognize the Organization Man syndrome? People shouldn't surrender their identities at the door and become mindless automatons. And as discussed in succeeding chapters, they shouldn't be asked to act in a manner inconsistent with their personal value system. But every individual *is* expected to give in on *some* personal preferences and pet ideas *some* of the time. At times we must quit complaining and just do what we have to do. Employees unwilling to do that are a detriment to the organization.

Employees will generally be willing to make the necessary sacrifices if they believe in the organization and its purposes. Management can do some simple things to help build that belief.

Cultivate Positive Beliefs and Goals

First and foremost, cultivate belief in the products and services you market as well as the quality and integrity of all your business relationships. If employees are convinced they earn their living helping people enjoy the benefits of your products and services, and that people like doing business with your organization and its people, they will be more supportive of management and the organization.

On a similar note, cultivate a belief in the values, goals, and influences the organization represents. Employees must view affiliation with the organization as part of a right and proper cause that helps them attain personal fulfillment they could not hope to achieve as individuals unaffiliated with the organization. As you may have noted, this is the foundation of conditioned power. Just as an individual makes a personal moral choice because of acceptance of a code which the culture considers right and virtuous, an employee submits to the will of an organization he or she perceives to be committed to a good and noble purpose. This is pure pragmatism: such values, integrity, and conditioned beliefs are essential to attracting and retaining the best employees.

THE GRAND MODEL OF MANAGEMENT

In Chapter 21, I integrated the ideas of Maslow, McGregor, and Hezberg to generate a model for motivation. Now, by adding the concepts of Galbraith, consider the Grand Model of Management as shown in Figure 22.1. Condign and compensatory power are content-based maintainers that address lower-level needs. By contrast, conditioned power motivates employees by helping them participate within an environment and value system, which helps them attain esteem and personal fulfillment as part of their affiliation with the organization. Leadership is, in effect, conditioned power, integrating individual and organizational objectives by motivating followers through upper-level needs.

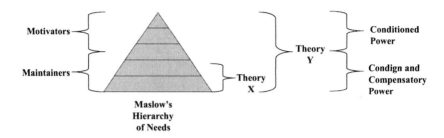

FIGURE 22.1. The Grand Model of Management

You'll recall that in Chapter 21 I asked you to consider your attitudes about employees to determine whether you held Theory X or Theory Y assumptions. At that time, the model for motivation suggested that a manager with Theory X assumptions, or, in its aggregate, an organization with a Theory X perspective, would be limited to lower-level needs and maintainers, incapable of meaningful motivation. Now, take that one step further: A manager or organization operating under a Theory X paradigm will be limited to the utilization of condign and compensatory power, will be unable to implement conditioned power, and is incapable of meaningful leadership.

The Mission Statement

You and your organization must adopt a Theory Y perspective or you will fail. In Chapter 21, I suggested the need to get out and get to know and appreciate employees at the point of encounter to help you understand your employees better and see them through Theory Y eyes. Now I'm going to suggest you and upper management do something else: take a look at your organization's mission statement. Please note that I did not say "Form a committee to explore the idea." Instead, assemble the two, three, at most four people who would be responsible for developing and signing off on the mission statement, have them assess what you have now, and revise and rewrite it as necessary. Do not allow this to take on a life of its own. The entire process should take no more than a few hours. Start first thing in the morning and permit no one to go to lunch, let alone home, until it's done.

The mission statement should be a very concise document—one page, two at the most—that states, in a very straightforward manner, what you are all about and what you stand for. It should be something employees look to with pride as representing the values and standards which make them want to affiliate with your organization as a vehicle for attaining their upper-level needs. It is the document upon which conditioned power is built. Employees should be proud to show it to customers and prospects.

The mission statement should be a series of short paragraphs no more than five or six lines each. Address the following in your mission statement:

1. Your products and services, their value and standards
2. Your organization, where you're seeking to take it, and how you propose to get there
3. The value system by which you treat suppliers, customers, and channel members
4. Your philosophy for treating employees and how you expect employees to treat one another
5. Standards by which persons are hired and retained by your organization
6. Your role in and relationship with the communities in which you do business

Remember just one more thing: Top management must fully buy into the mission statement and then walk the talk. This is one item that must be implemented top down.

Chapter 23

Norms

The past two chapters have addressed some familiar management issues—motivation, leadership, and power—and integrated them. As you see how those intangibles fit together, you should have an even better picture of what management is all about. Now, take the next step in the process and look at the implementation of those concepts in a plan of action, addressing the issue of norms in an organizational environment.

FUNCTIONAL AND DYSFUNCTIONAL CULTURES

Every organization has its norms that, in their aggregate, constitute what is called the normative culture. No two cultures are alike, further emphasizing the point that no single key will open every door, and a manager will be successful only to the extent that he or she is in sync with the normative culture. If there's a clash between the manager's view of how situations ought to be and how situations really are, the manager's potential will be severely limited. Thus, one of the first tasks for a new manager is to assess the normative cultures of the organization as a whole as well as that of the area of his or her direct responsibility. If a dysfunctional normative culture exists within the area of direct responsibility, one of his or her initial top priorities will be an application of the principles of leadership to make the necessary changes. Should there be a dysfunctional normative culture in the larger organizational entity that includes the area of direct responsibility, the manager may be doomed to failure. Attainment of a values-based normative culture can evolve only from the top down. If the executive suite is rotten, it won't be long before the rot pervades the entire organization. Thus, the farther up you are in the hierarchy, the more important it is to mold a normative culture and insist it trickle downward. If you're on the outside, considering affiliating with an organization, you might want to talk to employees at all levels, and thoroughly investigate the normative culture before you take the job. You might do well to avoid any organization with a dysfunctional culture above you. However, if the dysfunctional areas are within your scope of authority, you might want to take on the challenge, employing the tactics I will discuss in this and the final three chapters.

Normative Culture Defined

To be sure we're all on the same page, I will define what is meant by norms and a normative culture. Norms are consistent patterns of behavior, shared by the group, revealing the nature of management-employee relations. They are manifestations of the collective values and attitudes expected of employees if they are to be accepted, which are enforced by the group, and which pressure individual members to conform.

Whenever a new person arrives in any organizational environment he or she is immediately greeted by veteran employees and informed that "Around here, we do things this way" or "We don't bother to do this" or "In this department, we always do this." In a negative context, this constitutes belongingness, the requirements for loyalty and conformity, to the organization as a whole, a clique within it, or an ancillary entity such as a union. In a positive context, it may represent a statement of the commitment to excellence to which all persons are expected to adhere. In any context, norms represent general guidelines for behavior and attitude rather than specific policies and procedures. Thus the statement, "You must produce at least eighty units an hour" is a management standard, for which formal policies and procedures exist. By contrast, an employee norm could be "We never produce more than eighty-two units an hour" or "We never produce less than ninety units an hour," depending on the culture.

SYMBOLIC AND SUBSTANTIVE NORMS

Norms may be symbolic or substantive. A common symbolic norm is attire. In my own experience, years ago it was a norm that faculty in the College of Business wear a coat and tie, whereas the crowd in the Theatre Department wouldn't have been caught dead in such an outfit. Only recently, when some of our senior faculty began to dress down, did that norm begin to change. I'm one of the few holdouts who still wears a white shirt and tie, but I've deleted the sport coat and wear only comfortable cotton slacks. Though I never felt any direct pressure to conform, there's still a feeling of comfort in dressing at a level of formality close to that of my colleagues.

I noted the "never more than eighty-two never less than ninety" norm. I've seen the "never more than eighty-two" side of the coin in situations in which veteran employees tell a newcomer to slow down, lest management change the time standard for a particular task. New permanent employees always went along, but occasionally a summer temp worker would go all out, trying to make the piecework bonus in the short run, not caring about the long-term consequences for the permanent employees. It was always interesting to watch this play out. In very subtle ways, the permanent employees created time-consuming obstacles for these motivated people forcing them to slow down or stop for a few minutes at a time. Shop foremen, who knew whose loyalty was important to them, regularly changed the assignments of these people so that just when they were becoming proficient at a task and beginning to exceed the piecework rate, they would be moved to an entirely new and unfamiliar task.

On the "never less than ninety" edge of the sword, one colleague, against my advice and counsel, accepted an assignment at his company's office in Los Angeles. The manager there, as well as a couple of his chief lackeys, were devout workaholics with alcoholic tendencies, characteristics I'll explore in detail in Chapter 24. These guys would get to work about 9 a.m., stay at the office for about twelve hours, and then go out for an extended happy hour until 1 a.m. or so. To be part of the team, your presence was expected, and none of the other employees would take a stand and just go home at 5 or 6 p.m. This went on Monday through Saturday. My colleague described the environment as utter madness and called me after six weeks to say he couldn't take it anymore. Ultimately, he struck out of the culture, coming in a little before everyone else in the morning and leaving after a nine-hour day. Immediately, in a direct example of constructive termination, it was made clear he needed to seek employment elsewhere. Fortunately for him, his company transferred him back to corporate headquarters, an awkward move following less than three months in Los Angeles.

Consider another such experience, but with a diametrically opposite normative culture. Mr. E. took over as general manager of a direct store delivery company's distributor in a metro area where his company's market share was its second lowest in the nation. It didn't take him long to figure out why. Although all of the delivery vehicles were on the road by 6:30 or 7 a.m., returning around 5 p.m., all the managers were rolling in at about 9 a.m. and going home by 4 p.m. He never said a word, and he never had a policy about management office hours, but he just began getting in at 6 a.m. to talk to all the drivers before they headed out. In short order, one enlightened manager, hearing about this, began showing up at 6 a.m. as well. As a next step, Mr. E. began bringing in doughnuts and convening an "unofficial" staff meeting at 7 a.m. Though "unofficial," it quickly became the one and only staff meeting. The effect of all this was quick and decisive: managers either got in at 6 a.m. to talk to the drivers before the staff meeting at 7 a.m., or, in essence, they fired themselves, running to the job market.

Socializing

Another common norm in organizations revolves around expectations for socializing. One colleague speaks with pride about how his company is one big happy family, and about how their employees so enjoy getting together on weekend afternoons. Upon probing for details, it became clear that this normative culture was anything but fun for couples without children, let alone single employees who were expected to show up with a companion, of the opposite sex to boot. A variation on that theme was one of my own personal experiences: the first day on the job I was informed that on Thursday nights all the men got together to play poker. Since my idea of gambling is two-year treasury bonds, this was simply not going to happen. I never went and nothing was ever said, but I was never "in," either. Be fiercely independent at your peril.

Communication

Within the organization's day-to-day activities, communication style is one of the more pervasive norms. How does information get communicated around here? Is it formal, via memo or e-mail, or informal and face to face? What about meetings? Are they conducted with a formal agenda in the conference room or in casual conversations over lunch? I'm part of an organization where, thankfully, we have only one or two formal meetings a year, and those are often held in a private dining area at a casual dining buffet and grill. Usually, we all just get together at lunch and hash things over while digging into our Chateaubriands and washing them down with a little Chateau Lafite-Rothschild, 1949. One colleague, however, almost always lunches out on his own someplace. I mentioned to him once that he might wish to join us all for lunch occasionally, as it was there that important decisions were often made that affected him as well. Along the same lines, it's noteworthy whether managers apply an open-door policy or prefer more formality. In many organizations, you simply do not walk into a manager's office without an appointment.

What does the normative culture do about enforcing policies and procedures: it is by-the-book or lax? Does "no food or beverages in this room" mean eat and drink it before entering, or don't spill it on the chairs and floor? Does "no personal phone calls" mean keep it under two minutes? A sixty-five-mile-an-hour speed limit means keep it under seventy-two in southwest Virginia and keep it under ninety-five in Georgia.

Expenses

There are numerous manifestations of norms in organizations, but none so revealing of the nature of the employee-management relationship as the employees' actions regarding travel, entertainment, and other expenses. Is the norm that you spend the organization's money as if it were your own, or is the attitude one of getting all the goodies you can get and squandering their resources like a drunken sailor? What's the primary focus—personal convenience or the needs of the organization? In an earlier case study, I questioned whether an employee really needed to catch a 1:30 p.m. flight to go to a seminar, and whether there was really a legitimate business need to attend the seminar in the first place. I had a personal experience in which someone from corporate headquarters called me at our field sales office to schedule a meeting for the next week. After talking for a few moments, it became clear that a face-to-face meeting was unnecessary, and I told him so, but he insisted. I related this conversation to a colleague, who let me in on what was really going on: the guy's son lived in the area and he wanted to make a visit at company expense. That was bad enough, but the end of the story is worse. When this guy showed up at my office the next week, he opened up his briefcase only to discover that he'd left all his materials back at corporate headquarters, so he said, "Oh, well," and got up and left.

For my part in that organization, I was called in one day on an inquiry about my expense account. In this case, I was confronted about a zero expense for dinner on a given evening. I explained that I had consumed two first-class meals on the plane and did not have any further food or beverage after that. I was then informed that a zero expense for meals made everyone else look bad and was requested to refigure the expense account with at least a twenty-dollar meal charge. I complied then and from that point forward. I was also instructed to always expense equivalent cab fare to and from the airport, even when I had driven my own car and incurred only a two-dollar fee for parking.

In many cases, the normative culture pressures employees to spend the organization's expense monies with reckless abandon. If a convention is being held at a five-star hotel, you probably need to stay there. But spending $200 for a room the night before an appointment when a fifty-dollar room would have done just as well is not justified.

Some normative cultures condone or expect outright cheating. The previous examples are nothing compared to some of these. In one organization I dealt with, managers were playing a game tantamount to the lottery. About four or five of them would go out for dinner, and the deal was to split the tab equally. If, say, the five managers' tab came to a total of $100, including tip, everyone would kick in twenty dollars in cash except the winner, who would take the eighty dollars from his colleagues and put the whole $100 on his credit card. The losers would expense twenty dollars for dinner, but the winner would expense the $100 as customer entertainment and be reimbursed for the full amount. The managers would rotate the winner on a systematic basis.

Customer/Service Relationships

Norms that should be of the greatest concern to you are those having to do with customer service and relationships. Is the attitude, "We always do what we say we'll do" and "We do only the work that's necessary and never overcharge," or is it "Say whatever you have to say to get the order, then run like hell" and "They don't know any better and they can afford it." On an organizational level, do employees cooperate and work together, or is a territorial mentality evident, with fences around individual turfs? The key issue in all of this is control. Who's really in charge, you, the manager, or the normative culture? When you first take over any organizational entity, you can bet the normative culture is really running things. You're just kidding yourself, and doomed to frustration, if you think you can just walk in on Day 1 and take control. As described in great detail in Chapter 25, you'll need at least ninety days to get the lay of the land and figure out what's really going on. Much of that learning experience involves achieving a detailed understanding of the normative culture and developing a strategic plan for dealing with it and molding it into its appropriate form.

ESTABLISHING EFFECTIVE NORMS

First, identify all existing norms and the leaders and influencers behind those norms. All organizations have some combination of good norms and bad norms. Your objective is to build upon and establish norms you perceive to be good while minimizing the pervasiveness and influence of norms you perceive to be bad. You will not achieve perfection, even in silicon-based life-forms.

Determining Positive and Negative Influences

You'll need to take your time, listen aggressively, and use your street smarts, but within a few weeks you'll begin to get a sense of who is most strongly influencing the good norms, who is following those norms, and who is ignoring or attempting to sabotage them. Likewise, identify those persons influencing the bad norms, those who just sort of go along, and those who are trying to stand up in opposition to them. Those persons who are leaders and influencers behind the good norms are persons you'll want to reward and promote and who will be a part of your core team. On the other hand, beware of those persons you identify as leaders and influencers behind the bad norms, as they will likely become threats to you and your authority as you begin to modify the normative culture. They have the potential to cause you serious problems, and they will not go quietly, so move along casually and informally as you prepare all the groundwork for making all the organizational changes to be discussed in Chapter 25.

Motivating Employees

Next, concomitant with your assessment of the existing environment, determine those norms you wish to establish. You must achieve this through the group's acceptance of these as a moral imperative, with employees reacting to them with the thought, "This is right; this is what I want to do." If you've been paying attention, a little light should have just gone on in your head as you recognized leadership through conditioned power. That's exactly what I'm talking about here. With your Theory Y mind-set, you want to motivate employees through upper-level needs. You are doing so by molding a culture which corresponds to their inherent belief of what is right and good, which they regard as inherently correct. That is, "Around here, we work cooperatively in an environment of trust and respect. We are honest in all our dealings with one another and with the organization. We are committed to the highest quality in our goods and services. We are unsurpassed in customer service." That statement, which might be a good basis for a mission statement, is something most employees will want to believe in. If they do, you will have a much easier time commanding respect and leadership, though, of course, you must deal with those few people who don't buy in.

You cannot establish an effective normative culture with a Theory X mind-set through fear, rules, policies, and procedures. Anyone can get around rules, and such an approach may only lead to an us-versus-them mentality. Having said that, in certain cases in which inappropriate behavior was openly condoned or even demanded, some statement articulating specific standards and consequences is probably called for. As an example, I will revisit the issue of expense account abuse. In a situation such as was previously described, it would be inappropriate and unfair to suddenly lower the boom on someone doing nothing more than what everyone else has been doing, so some expense account policy statement is in order:

> Our organization will reimburse employees for all necessary expenses incurred in conducting business. We expect everyone to consider whether an expense is necessary and to spend the organization's money as if it were their own. It is absolutely unacceptable for an employee to expense an item and seek reimbursement for any expense not directly incurred.

Modify that as you wish. Now consider implementing such a policy, part of establishing the normative culture, in the postmemo period.

Violations

In some cases, employees may violate the spirit of the policy, perhaps to test the limits or to determine what you really mean and what you're going to do about it. That might include staying at the $150 downtown hotel when a forty-dollar motel outside of town might have done as well, or taking a thirty-dollar cab into town when rapid rail was available for a buck and a half and would have been faster. Here, at least the first time, just make a comment to the employee and ask that he or she consider alternatives in the future. Should that not do the trick, revert to the chapter dealing with performance problems.

But what if there's an egregious violation of both the spirit and letter of the law? I mentioned the lottery of people all going out to dinner, which should be easy to sniff out if you know something about who was with whom and doing what. Here are some variations on the theme, all of which demonstrate something any police veteran can tell you: criminals are stupid. For instance, assuming you know nothing about Chicago, an employee may claim twenty dollars in cab fare to go from the Palmer House to McCormick Place. Or he or she will bribe a waitress or a cab driver to give him or her a pad of blank receipts and then use them one at a time to claim reimbursements for expenses never incurred. The crafty employee takes rapid rail for a buck and a half and submits one of the cab receipts made out in the amount of thirty dollars, or eats at the Chinese buffet for five bucks and makes out a restaurant receipt to claim twenty-five dollars. What these idiots never seem to appreciate is that most of these blank receipts are sequentially numbered and, in any case, it's a bit suspicious to have the same receipt form from the same cab company in three different cities, or to have someone eating in the same restaurant chain wherever they go, particularly when, with the click of a mouse, you can determine that chain has no outlets in a particular location. Often, employees will submit no more than one of each kind of bogus receipt in any given week, hoping no one will notice, but it won't take you much time to compare and contrast the paperwork over a four-week span or so.

What do you do when you catch someone red-handed, which you will if you inherited a normative culture in which such behavior was previously rampant? Your memo notwithstanding, some employees will believe you don't really mean it or that you're too stupid to figure out what's going on. That was probably the case with their parents and teachers. It will not be the case with you. Almost inevitably, to terminate such a negative norm, you will have to fire someone.

Consider this carefully: What if the person you nail is a marginal employee you'd just as soon be rid of anyhow? Many managers believe such a person would represent a good place to make an example since their loss will have marginal impact on their organization. I disagree. To make your point effectively, you must come down on one of your better (or best) employees, and fire him or her on the spot. You'll get everyone's attention, employees will know you mean what you say, and ultimately your willingness to make such a decision to support ethical standards will command their respect.

The same principle applies to an employee who performs a $600 repair when a fifty-dollar procedure clearly would have done the job. First, immediately send the customer a $550 reimbursement with a note apologizing for a miscalculation in the bill. Then, see that the employee pays the cost of any unnecessary parts directly from his or her next paycheck and is not paid for the time that was billed. If that's unacceptable, the employee is free to leave.

A final point on these examples: If you're taking such decisive punitive action, be absolutely certain of your facts and confident you can withstand a challenge of wrongful termination. If you're in a union shop, work to establish mutually shared objectives with the union and reach an understanding of appropriate courses of action, including conditions under which you have the right to discipline or unilaterally terminate an employee.

Lead by Example

The third and final action you must take to establish the normative culture is the frosting on the cake: Lead by example, with consistency and equality between you and your employees. Don't expect your employees to embrace ethical standards if you're a crook. Don't expect them to stay at a motel in the boonies if you're living it up in a suite downtown unless a legitimate business reason demands that you do so. I was working for one boss who informed us that, due to budget cuts, we'd have to fly coach from then on rather than the front cabin. I didn't have a problem with that, feeling, frankly, that the difference in comfort and service didn't come close to justifying the cost. Until, that is, a few weeks later when I was peering over his secretary's desk and saw that he was still flying first class. His policy applied to *us,* but not to *him.* He had what he thought was an ironclad system in place to guarantee we were issued coach tickets and had no way to upgrade them to first class. I beat his game every time and never flew coach for my remaining years with his organization. As Andy Rooney (2000, p. 48) so succinctly reminds us in *My War,* ". . . they should keep in mind that there would always be one sonofabitch like me in their command."

Chapter 24

Addiction in Organizations

This chapter will take your thinking about intangibles to a whole new level regarding addiction in organizations, which may not be what you expect. Most discussions on addiction address the first three forms of addiction in organizations—important management issues to be sure, but nonetheless familiar issues concerning alcohol and drugs, or points previously addressed in this book. I tie some of those together to specifically document them within the context of addiction, but that will not be the major focus of this chapter.

THE ADDICTIVE SYSTEM

This chapter will concern itself with what I identify as the fourth form of addiction in organizations, a concept of immense importance to managers interested in those intangibles of leadership and motivation within a normative culture. The primary source for these ideas is Anne Wilson Schaef and Diane Fassel's (1988) *The Addictive Organization.* I'm confident that the concepts and ideas of this chapter will prove enlightening. If you agree, buy and read their book.

The preponderance of certain behavioral manifestations characterizes a system as addictive, not just the specific quantity of an addictive element. As a personal example—you've likely had a similar experience—I've had conversations with people in which I conveyed my opinion that they were alcoholics. Inevitably, in denial, their initial response was to cite a person, not considered to be an alcoholic, who drank more than they did. My observation, perhaps yours, too, was that alcohol affected them differently. Their personality changed and their lives were unmanageable.

Next, though we may tend to think of addiction in terms of substance addictions—alcohol, drugs, food—the manifestations are similar in process addictions such as work, sex, gambling, or philosophy. Many addictive individuals, rather than dealing with their addictive behaviors, merely switch over from less socially acceptable to more socially acceptable forms. Alcoholics may stop drinking but, instead of becoming sober, leap into philosophy addiction or immerse themselves in ninety-hour workweeks.

Addiction affects not only the individual but all those surrounding him or her. An addictive parent affects the entire family. An addictive manager affects the entire organization, or system. Take a look at those characteristics generally found in addictive systems. Not all of these will be found in every addictive system, but most of them will apply to a significant extent.

1. *Self-centeredness:* The "fix" is the center of everything else. An alcoholic is thinking about happy hour from the beginning of the day, and a social environment without alcohol is awkward and incomplete. He or she sits through the tea considering how soon to split and get out for a drink. Drug users think about little but getting high, and their conversations seldom go beyond reminiscing over drug-using experiences, discussions of who has what kind of dope and how good it is, and the agenda for procuring some stuff in the immediate future. Philosophy addicts cannot quietly live their beliefs, any more than an alcoholic can have two beers and stop, but remain in a frenzy twenty-four hours a day.

2. *Denial:* Addictive persons, until finally concluding that life is unmanageable, will deny that they have a problem, insisting that it's you, someone else, or the world that has a problem. For example, his drinking is not the issue, it's the fact that his wife is always complaining about him having "a couple of beers" after work and plotting to turn the kids against him. Closely related to denial is fabricated personality conflicts. The addicted person in denial blames other people and the attendant personality conflicts for mounting problems. Ultimately, of course, the addicted person's behavior may lead to actual difficulties in dealing with those others, further feeding the denial.

3. *Confusion and crisis orientation:* Addictive persons often aren't sure what they mean, and their perspective may shift often and suddenly. That, and the fact that life is unmanageable, leads to an ongoing crisis atmosphere. Closely related is the promise of the promise: This time, things will be different. This time, our strategy will impact

the market, knock over the competition, and save us from Chapter 11. This time life will change. I'll have this great job and we'll have a nice little house for ourselves. This time, I'll have no more than four beers and go home. Of course, the promise of the promise always falls through. Without a fundamental change of assumptions and behavior, this time will be the same as last time and every time before that.

4. *Perfectionism and the illusion of control:* It might seem inappropriate that perfectionism be a characteristic of addictive persons and systems. However, such attempts at perfectionism are illusions, mechanisms that feed denial that situations are actually becoming uncontrollable. An addictive parent will issue strict edicts directing his or her children's actions to stifle the reality that respect and authority has been lost. An addictive manager will institute rigid controls over employee actions and expenses, in denial that he or she doesn't know what to do and everything is crashing.

5. *Rigidity in thinking/black-and-white thinking:* This is a corollary to perfectionism and the illusion of control. There is no middle ground! This is it! This is right! Anything else is wrong! An addictive person, unable to think things through and see a number of sides to a question, unable to sustain relationships of teamwork to reach a consensus, grasps for the magic bullet. Such thinking extends into near paranoia with fabricated personality conflicts. You must agree with me or you're the enemy, plotting against me. You live your life the way I say you should or you're a failure or a bad person. If you don't agree with my views, you will inherit misery.

6. *Frozen feelings:* This may include a lack of respect for others' feelings, no trust or expression of feelings, an inability to feel anything or love anyone, or just feeling numb. Addictive persons do not believe themselves to exhibit frozen feelings. Especially with substance addictions, a partylike air of fun and fellowship surrounds the fix at the center. These feelings, however, are peripheral, not extending into personal closeness or emotional sharing and intimacy. Within process addictions, remember how the Gamesman was unable to share closeness and personal communication with his family, outside the context of the game in which people were pieces on a chessboard and relationships were illusory.

7. *Survival-level needs:* Addictive persons may delude themselves into thinking that they have self-esteem and are moving toward per-

sonal fulfillment, but it is an illusion. Particularly for substance addictions, all that really counts is the lower-level gratification of the fix, and it's not much different for process addictions such as sex or gambling. The person obsessed with scoring in the singles bar or winning big at the racetrack will ultimately hit bottom, not achieve personal fulfillment. The Gamesman, or other work-oriented addicts, obtain survival-level needs of power and money, but never get to the point at which, in a sense of satisfaction, they feel happy about where they are.

8. *Poor communication/triangular communication:* Addictive persons, and addictive systems, do not exhibit effective interpersonal communication, especially on a relationship level. With confusion and a crisis orientation, reality may change from minute to minute, and no one is ever sure what's really going on. Since people aren't relating to one another properly, there is a lack of frank one-on-one dialogue, often leading to triangular communication, in which individuals do not speak to one another but through intermediaries. Thus, if the mother is an alcoholic, she will not speak directly to the kids but will instruct the father to say something to them. Likewise, if the kids want to get a message to Mommy, they'll talk to Daddy and have him relay it to Mommy. The same concept exists on an organizational level. People hear about a personal problem with their addictive boss, likely a fabricated personality conflict, not from him or her directly but through a colleague who says, "I think you ought to know about this. The boss was talking about you the other day and said . . ."

9. *Ethical deterioration/spiritual bankruptcy:* Define *spiritual* for what it means to you, from the perspective of a person holding a deep, but not addictive, commitment to a traditional faith, or from the perspective of a deist, agnostic, or atheist. Numerous people walking around out there look alive, talk and maintain all their bodily functions, but are spiritually dead. You have certainly perceived this if you have ever encountered hard-core alcoholics or drug addicts, for whom all the twelve-step programs focus on an end to using as a first step to becoming alive again spiritually. Such spiritual deadness is the overriding factor in frozen feelings and poor communication, particularly poor relational communication, and the inability of a person to attain a sense of self-esteem and personal fulfillment. If you're spiritually dead, can ethical deterioration be far behind, in which a person compromises personal morality and experiences a loss of values and

a loss of concern for others? It's not surprising to see such character-istics among alcoholics and drug addicts. Why should it be surprising to see them manifested among pillars of the business establishment when they line their pockets at the expense of employees and share-holders? As illustrated by Schaef and Fassel, the same addictive char-acteristics manifest themselves in an addictive organization. Take a look, then, at their four forms of addiction in organizations, remem-bering that, as noted, the fourth form has the most important implica-tions for leadership through the normative culture.

THE FOUR FORMS OF ADDICTION

Form 1: Key Person Is an Addict

Form 1 occurs when a key person is an addict, with either a sub-stance or process addiction, and their addictive characteristics (the nine just noted) become the norms of the system. It was mentioned that addiction does not limit itself to the individual. On a personal level, it affects the entire family. On an organizational level, it affects the entire organizational system and its normative culture.

As a manager of a healthy culture, you may encounter an individ-ual employee with an addiction problem, which we addressed briefly under performance problems in Chapter 16. Though an issue of con-cern, addictive behavior of an individual employee is far less of a problem than such behavior on the part of the manager, especially when, as noted in Form 3, it takes on an ostensibly socially acceptable form, such as workaholism. Whereas a manager with alcohol or drug problems may ultimately be removed from his or her position, a man-ager with a process addiction, equally destructive to the organization, may actually be rewarded.

Form 2: ACOA/Codependent Carryover

Form 2 of addiction in organizations is when adult children of al-coholics (ACOAs) or codependents (those persons in a relationship with an addict and obsessed with the futile attempt to control the ad-dictive person's behavior) bring their problems to work with them. For ACOAs, participation in their families was a source of pain and fear, and thus they grew up isolated, since being alone was safer. Thus, they continue, to this day, to feel insecure about being "good enough." Consistent with the on-the-job training they inadvertently received within their families, these people are great at crisis handling but find relationships difficult and are often considered poor team players. If you encounter a person like this, you might be crossing over the legal line if you ask about his or her family history and childhood. Better to keep the individual in a task-oriented environment in which he or she can work alone with a minimum of interpersonal involvements.

Codependents will usually work long and hard without complaint, but they often get so involved in the lives and problems of others that they can't manage their own lives and work. I observed this in one divorced professional woman who was becoming seriously distracted at work because she was taking on the role of social worker and counselor to ten clerical workers in her office. Her ex-husband was paying to send their teenaged son to private school 500 miles away—*Good for him,* I couldn't help thinking—but when the kid came down with the flu she took two days off from work to drive up to the school, pick up her son, and drive him home so she could personally nurse him back to health. She shuttled back and forth between home and the office until the kid was better, and then killed another two days to drive him back. Soon thereafter, she suddenly took off on an "emergency" trip to see her father, a widower, in Montana. He was apparently seeing a woman—of his own age, of good repute, and having her own money, I might add—but she felt she had to be there to be sure he was all right and capable of handling the relationship. In her absence, her boss couldn't help but notice the increased productivity among the clerical staff, so upon her return she was fired.

As with Form 1, the implications of Form 2 vary depending on whether the problem affects an employee or a manager. At the employee level, the problems of an ACOA can be addressed, as noted, through a task-oriented work environment as long as the person's relationship deficiency is not disruptive. As in our example of the codependent, an application of performance standards can address a person who is being excessively distracted or distractive. Naturally, problems are exacerbated when the ACOA or codependent is a manager, but the organizational environment will not be as dysfunctional as Form 1, and not exhibit such severe manifestations of the nine characteristics of addictive systems. That is not to say that ACOAs or codependents are adequate managers, but that they will succeed to the extent that they recognize their situation and deal with it in a manner not unlike the process of an alcoholic or drug addict becoming a sober person.

Form 3: The Organization As "Fix"

Form 3 of addiction in organizations is a situation in which the organization itself is the "fix." There are three distinct ways in which this may occur.

Workaholism

Though seemingly socially acceptable, even admired, this form of addiction, in which work is the drug, is as dysfunctional as addiction to drugs and alcohol. Workaholics exhibit the same nine characteristics of addictive systems as do alcoholics and drug addicts. Though not exposed to the detrimental physical effect of alcohol and drugs, they nevertheless burn themselves out with stress and lack of rest. The Gamesman is a form of workaholic, multiaddicted to gambling with power and recognition as the prize. Workaholics are obsessed with work the same way alcoholics are obsessed with drinking. Relaxation and letting go are impossible. On vacation, they can't get off their cell phone and their minds never stop churning. They are having fantasies of market share and return on investment while making love. Just as food addicts live to eat rather than eat to live, for workaholics, work is the end in itself, not the means to an end. They climb one mountain and, rather than pause with a sense of satisfaction, are driven to climb another. Near the end of life, having conquered all the mountains and bought all the toys, they look around and ask themselves wistfully, "Is that all there is?" Or at age fifty-five, down for a few days for a triple bypass, there's a split second in which they realize they haven't talked to their spouse or kids for the past twenty years. It's a similar end for another version of workaholics, the Jungle Fighter, who in essence mirrors the addictive behavior of the Gamesman but without the charm. Both are so obsessed with the game and the job that they never move above the lower-level needs of gratification and conquest, power and control.

An advantage to being an alcoholic or drug addict, unappreciated until the individual becomes a sober person, is that social condemnation of the behavior puts the person into a downward spiral until the person hits bottom and, it is hoped, makes the decision to seek sobriety. By contrast, workaholics mistakenly perceive themselves to be on an upward spiral, often never realizing that they have failed to discover themselves as a person. Without that, of course, personal fulfillment is impossible and their mountain is an illusion.

Security

The second distinct way in which the organization is the "fix" is the situation in which an employee is hooked on and dependent on pay, benefits, and so-called "security." These people show up for work every day but have no sense of achievement or personal fulfillment. Lacking confidence and self-esteem, they have no dreams and won't take risks. They need the job for the steady paycheck, the medical benefits, and that pension they'll be getting in nine years, eleven months, and one day. As managers, these are often the Peter Principle types, long since past their level of competence. As employees, these are usually people someone should have fired years ago, but no one did. In the olden days of employment for life, these people were the ones living on the company welfare state, usually complaining about how lousy everything was but unwilling to quit or to learn how to do something of value outside the organization or within it. They stopped living years ago, but they're not dead yet. They don't exhibit the nine characteristics to any significant extent, and if they're pulling their weight there's a place for them.

Company Man Syndrome

The third and final way in which the organization is the "fix" is the Company Man syndrome: the individual's identity *is* the organization and its promise. As such, the Company Man has no real sense of "self," condemned to external referencing, making his or her choices on the basis of the perceptions and judgments of others rather than upon a personal system of values. From this perspective, belongingness constitutes an addictive relationship.

Form 3 enhances our appreciation of those personalities studied in Part I. Whyte's Organization Man/Maccoby's Company Man and

Maccoby's Gamesman and Jungle Fighter all come out looking unfulfilled or downright dysfunctional when studied from the perspective of addictive behavior. Only the Craftsman (the one of Maccoby's personalities who was happy) comes out looking good, but Craftsmen, as we observed, don't make good managers by and large.

Form 4: The Organization As Addictive System

By now, I believe you can appreciate the fact that effective management requires a whole different set of skills and personal characteristics, all directed toward establishing leadership to create a normative culture that motivates employees through the application of conditioned power. All we need to unify these many concepts and ideas is an understanding and appreciation of Schaef and Fassel's fourth form of addiction in organizations.

As a prelude, return to the days of yesteryear when, in your Economics 101 class, you were introduced to Adam Smith's analogy of the "invisible hand," which guided all the activities of production and consumption, supply and demand, leading all its participants to an optimum life through laissez-faire capitalism. Some proponents of such a concept may actually have been referring to some godlike entity that oversaw the world of commerce, but most, more realistically, interpreted the invisible hand to mean that human behavior, in its aggregate, was generally predictable in its actions toward satisfying needs. If prices were low, more product was demanded, if high, less. If a shortage of supply occurred, prices would go up and suppliers had incentive to enter the market. Pretty basic stuff, though in recent years the government has had to put some handcuffs on the hand to prevent it from raiding the cookie jar and taking everybody else's goodies for itself.

Schaef and Fassel (1988) have a concept closely related to the invisible hand, though it acts more like an iron fist. They theorize that, given certain management and organizational perspectives, a predictable normative culture will occur—*will,* not *may.* Studies of a wide variety of diverse organizational environments seem to support this theory. Schaef and Fessel's fourth form is not just a theoretical description; it's a law.

Form 4 of addiction in organizations is illustrated when the organization acts as an addictive system in which all nine of the addictive characteristics dominate the normative culture. That is to say, under certain conditions the organization's normative culture will be indistinguishable from one in which everyone in management is an active alcoholic or addicted to cocaine. Under these certain conditions, *nothing* can be done to establish a positive normative culture.

The organization will act as an addictive system when it lacks a *real* company mission. It benefits neither customers nor society, and the organization takes from and uses people and the environment, with no thought of a two-way mutual benefit. Under these conditions, the inevitable result will be that the way the organization treats customers and society will be reflected in the way the employees treat one another. As such, the normative culture will exhibit the same characteristics as an addictive system and *is* an addictive system.

In other words, there is no honor among thieves. If your organization, despite its lofty mission statement, is really out to dump and run, really out to take its customers for all it can get and give nothing in return, is really unconcerned about polluting the environment, and, after all is said and done, really produces products and services that are detrimental to its customers, the normative culture will act as an addictive system. Bring in the best-qualified management people you can find. Train them in all the latest leadership concepts. It will make no difference. You will have an addictive system.

CURING THE ADDICTIVE SYSTEM

These points cannot be ignored. Schaef and Fassel are not dealing in isolated theoretical concepts. In fact, their perspective unites all our ideas on leadership and motivation, the essential ingredient of which is conditioned power. As we've seen, conditioned power is predicated upon upper-level needs in which the individual is acting out of a sense of what is right and good, consistent with the value system of the community and large-scale culture. Conditioned power is impossible if the individual believes himself or herself to be acting in a manner harmful or detrimental to others. Conditioned power is irrelevant in an organization concerned solely with money and power.

The science of addiction has helped us understand that active alcoholics or drug addicts will never get beyond their lower-level needs. Only through sobriety can they find esteem and personal fulfillment, with meaningful interpersonal relationships. Now we understand how those same concepts are at work in organizations.

No one has ever accused me of being a touch-feely liberal, preaching about how everyone should treat everyone so nicely and be actively involved in societal and environmental interests. I am, with pride, known as "Bottom-Line Bob," believing that the primary objective of a for-profit organization is to maximize profits and shareholder wealth. But here's the bottom-line pragmatic truth: the only way your organization will maximize those profits and wealth is by being fully committed to those so-called touchy-feely liberal priorities.

Theory X and Theory Y Perspectives

Ask yourself, Why would a person wish to affiliate himself or herself with this organization? If you answer "Pay, fringes, and good working conditions," consider yourself exposed as a Theory X manager and go sit in a corner. By contrast, if you have a Theory Y perspective, desiring to lead and motivate, you realize that this person's ultimate interests are in satisfying upper-level needs. The most important reason, from a management perspective, for this person to affiliate with your organization is that by so doing, he or she can attain upper-level needs not possible alone. This is Galbraith's concept of power derived from the organization.

People will affiliate with your organization and commit themselves to work very hard for its success because they see it standing for high ideals and initiatives moving them as individuals toward personal fulfillment. Under such necessary conditions, effective management can create a positive normative culture through the proper implementation of all the necessary skills and functions that have been addressed.

If you're a business owner or hold a top management position in an organization of any size, take a moment to consider what you really stand for. Should that be no more than increasing sales, market share, and profits, you have some work to do. Start with your customers. Instead of specifying what you sell them, phrase your mission from the perspective of how you help them. Then, analyze your products, services, your Web site, all your policies and procedures, and consider all the ways to help your customers and to make it a pleasure doing business with you. On a regular basis, you want those customers telling your employees how your organization helped them and how it's nice working with you.

Look at the communities in which you do business. Instead of merely describing your company payroll, seek ways in which your organization can contribute to the enhancement of those communities and the environment. How can you make an impact? How can you make a difference? Routinely, you want citizens in the community mentioning to your employees how your organization has had a positive impact on them, the community, and the region.

Of course, look at your employees. Assuming you have the requisite Theory Y mind-set, you believe they really want to be the best they can be. What are you doing to help them improve themselves? Invest in training, and then establish an empowered teamwork environment in which they make the most of their potential. Regularly, you want employees to convey to managers the fact that they love working in your organization, even though they might make a little more money somewhere else. That's similar to what you want to hear from customers who say they like doing business with you even though they might be able to save a few bucks if they went with your competition.

The perspective of an organization which acts as an addictive system should be a loud and clear wake-up call for corporate leaders and managers in organizations of all sizes. Get out there and examine the normative culture. If you see many or most of the characteristics of addictive systems, you have high priorities that must be addressed before you can lay the foundation of your organization. It may be that merely a few individuals are creating a dysfunctional environment within their spheres of influence, or you may have an entire organization acting as an addictive system, one without any meaningful mission beyond lower-level needs. If such an addictive system has been around for some time, it has most likely attracted addictive individuals, particularly workaholics in the form of Gamesmen and Jungle Fighters. Some housecleaning will be in order.

You'll recall that among my sports analogies was the point that a failing team should hold a manager accountable for the team's performance, and that it was appropriate to fire a manager who didn't get results through the players. Let's amend that in light of the points just addressed. Some teams, like ones that lose 100 or more games in a season, are beyond the scope of effective management. They just haven't got the talent and won't become winners no matter who is at the helm. Maybe a management change is in order, but you also need a whole new group of players. The same principle applies to an organization. If you replace a mediocre manager with an effective manager in a healthy normative culture, you'll probably get a boost in performance. As an example, among many good managers, you may have a very few managers who are Company Men, hooked on their paycheck and benefits. Replace them, and improved performance may well result.

In a similar healthy environment, you may have an isolated workaholic with a concurrent substance addiction, such as the manager in Los Angeles cited earlier. Here, too, a management change may enhance performance unless the situation has progressed to the point where the entire cadre is addictive and all nonaddictive persons have been driven off before upper management acts.

Unfortunately you may face the necessity of finding not only a new manager but also a new coaching staff and then recruiting players with the requisite skills. If that doesn't give you enough to do, get to work on a mission statement and begin to formulate marketing and financial objectives for the upcoming season. Just remember that everything concerned with putting an organization in place—the structure and the people—must be implemented before a healthy normative culture begins to take shape and everyone can settle down to being productive. This may take considerable time, and it's time well spent.

In Chapter 25, you will look at the road map, your plan for getting there.

Chapter 25

Your Ninety-Day Plan: People, Personnel Assessment, and Training

You now have an objective to create a positive, nonaddictive normative culture in which employees and the organization have shared objectives. You, as coach and leader, empower individuals and teams with a sense of ownership. Employees feel pride in being affiliated with an organization committed to the best interests of the community, society, and environment. That's the destination, but you're not there yet. In all likelihood, the current organizational system and its players are not the ideal ingredients for the recipe you have in mind. Short-term changes must be made if the long-term dream is to become a reality. That's your ninety-day plan in which you address the issues of people, personnel assessment, and training.

ASSESSING THE ORGANIZATION

A few lead-in comments about the issue of people and organizations are necessary. No doubt, you've read numerous commentaries about why companies succeed or fail. Of course, as a given, you must have a product or service people want and are willing to pay for. You must deal within a marketing environment in which the competitive landscape and availability of alternatives is such that you can find a differential advantage and carve out a niche in which you can generate revenue and profits. It would take an entire book to explore all those concepts of marketing, so, since this is a book on management, I will stick with a situation in which those points are a given. So, within a viable industry, think about why some companies thrive whereas others fail. It isn't a question of costs, as generally companies face approximately the same costs of marketing their goods and services. To be sure, there are some economies of scale for larger companies, but on the other hand, smaller companies enjoy the advantages of having more flexibility, less overhead, and less bureaucracy. But just to be sure we're not comparing apples with oranges, consider comparably sized companies competing within the same viable industry. These firms all incur about the same costs for raw materials, production, manufacturing, packaging, and transportation. Likewise, their costs are mainly the same for office space and equipment, employee salaries and benefits, services, fees, taxes, and so forth. So why do some of these companies succeed and prosper while others wither on the vine and die? You already know the answer. It's people! Your organization *is* its people. As such, for a new manager coming into an organization, or even a veteran manager thinking about what needs to be done to reshape his or her current organization, your first and most important task is to evaluate your people and their potential. Very possibly you do not want some persons on your team, as their very presence has a detrimental effect on other employees and the normative culture. They must be dispensed before you can embark on the very first steps of your climb to the top of the mountain. Far more common are employees who are not fulfilling their potential, perhaps due more to the nature of their position and the organization than to any personal shortcomings. You may well find numerous persons of mediocre productivity who are dying to become heroes. It's your job, early on, to identify these people and act accordingly.

One more point: Before accepting any management position, clarify unequivocally that you have complete authority to hire and fire as you deem necessary. Stop, take a deep breath, and go back and read that last sentence again. You *must* have complete authority to hire and fire, or you are *not* a manager; you are staff. I have known dozens of people who accepted a so-called management position without that authority, and every one of them eventually regretted it. A manager cannot do his or her job if any or all of the employees know they can't be fired. You will not manage through fear and condign power, but they must be part of your arsenal if you are to be successful in any application of leadership and conditioned power.

It's not an insurmountable problem for you, by the way, if someone such as *your* boss says that the company cannot terminate certain employees for one reason or another, ranging from the fact that they are too old, a member of some other protected class, or the favorite nephew of the chairman of the board. Get an agreement that if *you* decide any of these people are undesirable or unnecessary, they need not be terminated but need only be taken off your budget. Someone else can figure out what to do with them and whose budget will be charged. Get this in writing as a condition for accepting the position.

If you're just coming into your management position, you should expect that every one of your employees will feel at least some sense of apprehension. That's a natural reaction to change and uncertainty. Most of them will be prepared to give you a chance even if they dearly loved your predecessor. Some will be sizing you up to see what they'll be able to get away with, perhaps a reflection of their role in existing negative norms. Some will be top dogs, some will have untapped potential, and some will be worthless or worse. You can look over all the records and evaluations before Day 1, but try as you might you know you're not going to figure out what's really going on until you get out there with all your people and, employing your best street smarts, determine what's actually happening and what you've got for a normative culture. This is your personnel assessment, which will culminate with the formulation of your new organizational structure.

Go slow. Get the facts. Get a feel for the situation. Don't even think of making significant organizational changes until you're completely confident you understand who's who and what's happening. With that in mind, hold a brief informal meeting with all employees as close to Day 1 as possible. Tell them simply that you're glad to be there and look forward to working with them. In this initial meeting, consistent with the principle of openly sharing information with employees, come right out and convey that you'll probably be making some changes at some point but that for the moment everything will continue as before. Assure them that no changes will be made until you've had the opportunity to meet with each of them individually. Proceed, then, to let them know that within a very short time, you will schedule a thirty-minute meeting to talk one-on-one about what they're doing, what they'd like to have the opportunity to do, and how you can help them, and to hear any suggestions they may have on any subject. If this sounds like an approach very similar to that of an employee performance review, it should. Of course, you're not evaluating their past performance against standards, but you most certainly are gaining input you'll use to set up position descriptions in the organizational structure you'll establish at the time changes are made. Employees should readily understand that these meetings provide them an opportunity for input on future events and their own fate, which should encourage them to prepare accordingly.

In your first weeks, between the individual employee meetings, also get out and do a little of the old management by walking around. Get a feel for the atmosphere and interactions in the office. Go out on the road with field sales reps and listen. Get a sense of how they think, how they feel, and their perceptions about the organization. Visit some of your customers and have them tell you what it's like doing business with your company and what you could do better. Throughout this whole process, take a lot of notes, as it may be some time before all these individual pieces begin to coalesce into a meaningful whole.

It will take at least sixty days to complete such a comprehensive personnel assessment in a moderately sized organization of approximately twenty employees, and you'll need at least a month after that before you'll be ready to implement changes in the organization structure, the culmination of your ninety-day plan. Don't let the tail wag the dog. Take the necessary time to do personnel assessment right, even if it means your "ninety-day plan" takes somewhat longer. Continue as before until you're totally ready to make your changes. It's better than making changes prematurely, not properly thought through.

THE FOUR CATEGORIES OF EMPLOYEES

As you go through this process of personnel assessment, quantify your thinking by categorizing each employee into one of four classifications. Category 1 employees are good employees who know their jobs and are doing them well. These folks are definitely on your team and will have a place in your restructured organization. Don't limit yourself to thinking of them in the context of their current positions. Ask yourself, Are they ready, with the potential, for new challenges? These are the people you'll look to promote to positions of greater responsibility at the time of restructuring, with important roles in the establishment of the normative culture.

Category 2 through 4 employees are not doing their job as they should and thus will be the focus of necessary changes of one kind or another. Category 2 employees are simply bad employees who won't work, who can't be motivated, who exhibit behaviors characteristic of addictive systems, and who are usually complainers, pointing to the organization, management, or anyone else they can find to blame for their personal shortcomings. These people are most responsible for those negative norms you need to eliminate to create a healthy organizational climate, and you can bet they'll do anything it takes to block your reforms. They will resist you, they will sabotage you, and, I hope not literally, they will assassinate you before they'll clean up their act and do an honest day's work. If you have any of these dark angels lurking within your organization, don't consider sensitivity training for them or for you. Ferret them out and fire them.

Category 3 employees are the Peter Principle types. They've been promoted to their level of incompetence and, though they try their best, just can't cut it. These people make management a tough job. It's easy to fire Category 2 employees who aren't producing, have a lousy attitude, and are a negative influence on other employees and the normative culture. It's a different story with the Category 3 Peter Principle types, who are usually longtime loyal employees who have a good attitude but simply can't carry their weight.

It's a tough reality of business life, but you cannot have employees who are a drain on the organization. You produce or you go. You are not running a welfare state. That's easy to say, but what do you do with a fifty-five-year-old employee who's dedicated thirty years to the company? Throw him or her out on the street? It's not ethical, potential legal liabilities notwithstanding. Something needs to be worked out.

Everything should be done to help a Peter Principle employee save face. Perhaps a demotion to a more useful level of competence would be a possibility he or she would welcome. The employee would likely be much happier, productive again, and out of your hair. If that can't be done, perhaps your company could tailor an early retirement package: a certain salary level to a certain age, reverting to a retirement income equal to a certain level. Here's the bottom line: You must get them out of your organizational sphere and off your budget. You cannot condone incompetence or pay people more than they produce. Here's where the need for unequivocal authority to hire and fire comes into play. You must be able to tell *your* managers that this individual will no longer be working for *you*. They can put this person on *their* budget if they wish. Someone—not you—can find another position for him or her. You are, as of the date of your organizational restructuring, removing the individual from your sphere and your budget, and you are sending him or her down to human resources for further instructions. This person may be a problem for the company, but he or she will not be a problem for you. You already have enough on your plate trying to achieve marketing and financial objectives with your competent people.

Category 4 employees are those persons who are underachievers but, unlike their Category 2 brethren, have the right attitude and appear to hold the potential for success. Here you have a performance problem in which you need to identify causes for the failure to meet standards. First determine whether the employee has the requisite competencies. If not, deal with this training need when you revise the structure. On the other hand, if this employee is properly trained and qualified, it's possible a management or supervisory problem exists, so address this when you determine whether you need to replace that person's manager or provide that manager with managerial training. Certainly you should uncover why any person with the right attitude and potential is not producing and why nothing has yet been done to rectify the problem.

REVISING THE ORGANIZATIONAL STRUCTURE

Once you've completed employee classifications, you're ready to get down to business. Now, and only now, can you set out to construct your revised organizational structure and the attendant position descriptions. Among current employees, you know who will take what place in the structure and who will no longer be part of your team. Very possibly, you will discover that some positions remain unfilled at this time, in which case you'll be initiating the hiring function to identify, interview, and hire new employees. For all of this, you'll need to work very closely with human resources to ensure that every detail has been handled by the time you announce the revised organizational structure. All conversations between you and human resources must be held in the strictest confidence. Employees will sense that change is afoot, but that's all right. You've already communicated to them that some modifications are in store. It's a whole different game when rumors start floating around that this person will be fired and so-and-so is being exiled to the Aleutians. Once the rumor mill cranks up, it takes on a life of its own and you can forget about anything getting done in the foreseeable future. Even worse is spreading out terminations and relocations over time. It is absolutely essential that you make all these changes at once, as productivity will remain near zero from the moment of the initial change until the time when employees are satisfied that the upheaval is at an end. Thus, in one fell swoop, you will make *all* organizational and personnel changes and immediately set a course and initiate specific actions which will put the organization in motion and heading where you want it to go. The day this happens will be one of the most stressful and challenging days of your life.

Most managers historically choose a Friday to do the deed, believing this gives everyone a weekend to let reality set in before getting down to business on Monday. I've heard some managers say such actions should be spread across the week lest employees be conditioned into emotions of fear every Friday, wondering who's going to get the ax this week. Personally, I go with the Friday school, since, as I've noted, this is a one-time major reorganization and not something to be spread over a number of weeks.

Downsizing versus Termination

Much about what I discussed concerning firing an employee will apply here, though with some modifications. The most significant difference between this scenario and terminating an individual employee is that a high probability exists that your organizational restructuring will reflect downsizing. Frankly, this makes your life a whole lot easier. You can avoid all the steps of documenting performance problems for those Category 2 employees you simply want to lose. You can sidestep all the complications of terminating a marginal-to-poor employee with a series of okay performance evaluations who is a leader or influencer behind negative norms. Within bounds, you can rid yourself of incompetent Peter Principle types. Just don't fire everyone over fifty and, as noted, cover your bases up front to be sure that someone other than you will find a way to reach a satisfactory agreement with these people concerning their future.

You can, plainly and simply, restructure your organization and eliminate their positions entirely, which is much easier and cleaner than firing for specific cause. As always, be sure you're on firm legal ground. Because of the understanding about your authority to fire, however, you're transferring those babies to someone else's doorstep.

Have no illusions. Try as you might to be fair and equitable and to treat all those affected with respect, this event will be Black Friday, even though it's really the beginning of a much better organization with a more positive culture. The fact that this event was the end of the line for many employees, some of whom had friendships and ties with their fellow employees, will not soon fade from memory. Even the survivors being promoted to positions of greater responsibility will come out of the event not unlike soldiers receiving a battlefront promotion. The old reality and the illusion of security will have been shattered. But it's the moment in which you take command and seize the opportunity to assume the leadership role your organization needs you to take.

The Action Plan

Your action plan gets under way late Thursday afternoon or Thursday evening, when all employees receive notification of a meeting they need to attend on Friday. Some will be invited to an organizational meeting in the early afternoon, others will be scheduled for a fifteen-minute meeting with you or your immediate staff beginning early Friday morning. Proper execution of these employee contacts is essential. You must be absolutely certain everyone has been contacted late Thursday. If you do this by e-mail, request a reply to confirm. Otherwise, contact everyone by phone. To do this right, in an organization of even modest size, you may wish to procure the services of secretarial support from inside your company or through an outsourcer.

It will soon become apparent to all employees that those invited to the afternoon program still have jobs and those invited to a morning meeting do not. Employees will quickly begin contacting one another, and very quickly patterns will emerge about who's been invited to what. Contributing to this will be the fact that all employees being terminated will have lost all computer access and had their company phone, pager, and credit cards deactivated just before contacts and invitations began. Keep that in mind when you implement those contacts. You can e-mail employees who are retained, since they will get your message and be able to reply confirmation in plenty of time for the afternoon meeting. But you'll likely need a personal contact for those being terminated since they will have been cut off from the company's e-mail server.

All expectations, suspicions, and fears will be confirmed first thing Friday morning after the initial fifteen-minute meeting with a terminated employee. For this meeting, walk through the steps of the termination meeting from the chapter on firing. Get straight to the point: Business conditions necessitate we make changes, and we need to let you go. If you are facing several to many such meetings, you might wish to hold them away from your office, perhaps in the human resources department. It might also be a good idea to enlist the participation of human resource persons who can explain all postseparation benefits and procedures. Thus, your role in the meeting could be limited to nothing more than explaining the situation before turning the remainder over to the human resources person. For those persons not being terminated but merely taken off your budget, you need only let them know that they will no longer be working in your sphere. Then, introduce them to the person who will be the contact point in determining what their future disposition will be.

No productive work will be accomplished on Black Friday, so plan accordingly. People will be standing around in small groups, sharing information about what has happened to whom. There will be awkward consolations for those persons preparing for a 10:00 a.m. meeting they know means sayonara. People will compare and contrast separation packages as bits and pieces come out. Emotions from sadness to anger will pervade the atmosphere as terminated employees pack their personal belongings and leave. Those invited to the afternoon session will feel a mixture of relief and apprehension.

TAKING COMMAND OF THE NEW ORGANIZATION

For you, unless you're a Jungle Fighter who enjoys this sort of thing, it's going to be a long, hard morning; but someone must do what needs to be done, even with those Category 2 employees merely getting their just deserts. Do what you have to do. Then, in the afternoon, stand up and assume command of your new organization, giving them a show they won't forget. More than that, direct those employees who remain toward specific action.

Put yourself in the shoes of those remaining employees walking into the afternoon meeting, full of apprehension and uncertainty. They'll be walking in quietly, perhaps murmuring a few words to a fellow survivor. The air will be so thick you can cut it with a knife. At this moment, your first act as manager of the revised organization, dramatically shift the atmosphere to one of excitement and fun.

Shifting the Atmosphere

How you do this will depend on how many employees are involved. If the number is twenty or more, hold the meeting in a large room and hire an outside supplier to set up a light show with high-quality stereo sound. That will immediately get everyone's attention and jump-start the mood of Black Friday to that of the first day of the rest of their lives. With all the tension, no one probably ate much for lunch, and the atmosphere of excitement and fun might begin to spark people back to life and regenerate their appetites. Since one of your first messages to the troops is that those people who play a role in the achievement of marketing objectives will be appropriately rewarded, this is a nice place to demonstrate what those rewards are all about. Don't be a cheapskate. Spring for the jumbo shrimp, strawberries to dip in chocolate, and mini eclairs. Oysters Rockefeller also add a nice touch.

If your meeting is only for five or six employees, all the aforementioned trappings may be a bit much, but you can still brighten up the room with *something* and better music than a boom box playing Abba cassettes. Do whatever is best for you and your situation, but don't lose sight of the fact that it's imperative to create a mood of excitement from the start.

When it's time for the meeting to start, open up with a hearty welcome and let everyone know how glad you are to have them on the team. Give them an overview of the overall structure of the revised organization and show them where they fit. Depending on the size of the meeting, you may be able to describe the specific roles and responsibilities of individuals in key positions.

During the period of your one-on-one employee meetings, you had the opportunity for dialogues about their interests and aspirations. Now, as you present the new structure, each individual can see his or her new role, likely to be somewhat different from what he or she is doing now or had expressed an interest in. If that difference is relatively minor, you need only note that you, his or her immediate supervisor, or some other designated person will be meeting with that person soon to clarify expectations and answer any questions. What you *don't* want in the meeting, however, is for someone to see for the first time that he or she has been given a radically different position or is being relocated. In those situations, someone needs to have an earlier conference with that person to confirm receptivity to the new assignment. At the prior meeting, the employee could be told that the current position might be eliminated and, were that to happen, would he or she be receptive to an alternative position in either St. Louis or Kansas City? If the employee were amenable, the meeting would then merely confirm which of the possible alternatives would occur. On the other hand, had the employee been unwilling to consider a relocation, he or she would have been aware of a possible position elimination and been able to consider taking action to seek employment elsewhere. Fair enough.

Depending on the size of the organization and the extent of changes being made, you will conduct this meeting in a manner appropriate to your unique circumstances. But one thing is absolute: when employees walk out of that meeting on Friday afternoon, they should have a pretty clear picture of the situation on Monday morning. You can't have them walking out thinking, "Gee, that sounded nice. I wonder what it means to me and what I'm going to do." An action plan must be in place, a likely cornerstone of which is training.

Training Programs and Schedules

Before you implemented organizational and personnel changes, you would have had to assess each employee's current competencies in relation to those of the revised position description. In many or most cases, employees do not already possess all the requisite competencies of their new position, something they're bound to realize immediately. Thus, a key component of your action plan will be to promptly provide employees with all details of their respective training programs and schedules. This will get them into motion and begin to build their confidence in soon being able to handle the requirements of their new position.

It will take a lot of work to prioritize your overall training needs and then to determine training programs and schedules and procure all necessary resources. First address those areas that represent the greatest need to the greatest number, then work in specialized training needed by a very few.

I've stressed the importance of meeting bottom-line financial objectives and spending the company's money wisely. That said, don't be penny-wise and pound-foolish when it comes to training. Your sales managers can probably put their reps through a daylong sales training program for nothing, but an outside specialist might have skills and expertise well worth paying for. They might well enhance the credibility of a program over that which would be possible with a program conducted by one of your employees with limited experience in skills training. Along the same lines, don't just hold the activity in some spare room you're not using. Get your people out and away from the familiarity of your office and conduct it at a nice hotel or conference center, which makes people feel special and feel that the program is special. Face it: your employees are not going to jump up and down at the thought of spending a day or two in a training activity, even when they know it will help them perform better and help them make more money. It just reminds them of all the things they didn't like about school. That change of scenery will cost more than doing it in your conference room and ordering out pizza for lunch, but you'll get a good return on your investment.

To extend this point, look for an opportunity to conduct some important program that will involve all your people over about a three-day period. You can use it for training, brainstorming, or strategic planning, whatever you wish, but as important as anything else it can serve as a team-building activity. After Black Friday, those who remained are bound to be a bit shocked and apprehensive. Getting people involved in training and initiating project teams and cross-functional activities with colleagues outside your sphere will get the ball rolling. Now, build the momentum by bringing all your people together at a remote location such as a resort hotel where everyone can enjoy a combination of working hard and relaxing in a first-class environment. Here's a generalized example that you can customize to your unique situation.

Employees all arrive on location Wednesday night at their convenience. That evening no formal activities are planned, but a hospitality suite with food and refreshments is open. Close down the suite about 10 p.m. since there's a busy day ahead tomorrow. You can't prohibit people from hitting the bar after that, but you can communicate that it is discouraged by having no managers present and specifying that any such expenses are personal. Thursday morning, make breakfast available from 7 to 8 a.m., meetings/training/planning until 3 p.m., with a break for lunch. After 3 p.m. they are on their own, with use of the facilities—from golf to paddleboats—paid for by the company. Dinner may be expensed, but refreshments are not.

Plan a similar schedule for Friday until 3 p.m. by which time, if they've had an hour for lunch, everyone will have been in sessions for two six-hour days. That's about the limit. I know of companies who put their people through four- and five-day programs which, with night assignments, add up to sixteen-hour days, but I don't recommend it. You really hit a point of diminishing returns after six hours of this sort of thing in one day, and people begin to lose focus in Day 3. If you really need more time than this, you might want to consider spreading it out over a number of weeks, considerations for employee travel and scheduling notwithstanding. Plus, for this initial special program designed to bring people together in an atmosphere of team building, you want it to be fun. So by Friday at 3 p.m. the work should be essentially over. At that point, a significant other or the family may join them with all the property's facilities available and paid for by the company. That evening, a dinner banquet for everyone, friends and families included, should be on the company's tab.

Saturday morning, assemble all employees for a meeting around 9 a.m. to tie together any loose ends and give them any necessary information, materials, etc. Handle the Saturday session as you deem necessary. It will likely be two hours or less since significant others and families are waiting on them. You may wish to delete the Saturday session entirely. In any case, checkout time is noon, or thereabouts, and employees and their companions are invited to enjoy the facilities for the rest of the day at company expense.

I can hear what you're thinking: This will cost a lot of money. Yes, but it's the same principle noted in the past several pages. Consider what it costs to hire, employ, and retain a good employee. Now consider how important it is that an employee feel good about his or her affiliation with your organization. I realize we're not dealing with upper-level needs of personal fulfillment here, just mixing in some fun and socializing with work. But, especially early on, that's the foundation upon which all the other intangibles will be built. It won't hurt you to be reputed as someone who treats employees with style when those employees meet and exceed standards. Consider this, too: Friday and Saturday afternoons, as your employees are socializing and teaming over a round of golf or refreshments at the pool, they'll be talking to one another about the organization, where it's been, and where they think it's going. Your name is bound to come up. Won't it be nice to have them say they're feeling good about the job, and about you, who are leading them where they are going?

Chapter 26

Your Long-Term Strategy:
Molding the Normative Culture

This is the end of our journey together, but it's just the beginning for you and your organization.

FACING AND OVERCOMING HURDLES

As noted, effective management is not only what you do but who and what you are. Beyond that, it requires the building of an organizational culture committed to high standards and values. Getting this done may seem straightforward, as I have addressed the tasks and issues step by step. But it won't be as easy as pressing a few buttons and watching everything fall into place. Impediments must be dealt with.

A potentially serious issue involves the necessity of removing employees who, for whatever reason, cannot be viable and productive colleagues. With this accomplished, and the establishment of an organizational structure with the right people in the right positions, it may still take some time to get the ball rolling.

Resistance to Change

One major hurdle you will face is resistance to change, even in the face of an unsatisfactory situation. Many employees will experience fear of change, even when they logically perceive it to be necessary. Thus, you need to sell employees on the benefits of doing things differently. But go beyond that. Communicate to everyone that continuing along as before is not an option and will lead the organization toward atrophy and ultimate destruction. Share the information that demonstrates a compelling need for change, and help employees understand the necessity of everyone working together toward shared objectives.

In addition, you are likely to encounter cynicism, even among your best employees, who have lived through buzzwords and management fads which, after they had played themselves out, left everything essentially the same. They will be very skeptical at the promise of the promise that "this time it will be different." Over time they will come to realize that, son of a gun, this time it *is* different—but don't expect this to happen on Day 1.

Distrust and Mindless Obedience

Extending that point, in some organizations it's very possible that you will inherit a culture in which management has generated open distrust between themselves and employees. Initially, your overtures of working as a team to achieve mutual objectives may be interpreted as merely a ploy to manipulate the employees one more time. In such a situation, you'll need to demonstrate your security and integrity for a period of time before being able to establish a foundation of credibility.

In many organizations, especially those obsessed with the illusion of control, you may encounter an intriguing paradox. On one hand, there will be a lack of clearly articulated standards of performance for achieving marketing and financial objectives. Then, on the other hand, there will be a morass of policies and procedures, accompanied by all the attendant reports and forms. This sort of culture has whipped employees into a mindless obedience of fulfilling requirements for paperwork rather than focusing on meaningful accomplishment. When it's time to go home, they may pride themselves on having cleared their desks of a whole pile of work but have no idea of what any of it actually contributed to the organization or its customers. Such an attitude may satisfy a good employee's work ethic and provide a certain sense of comfort, but it's killing the achievement of bottom-line objectives. So, when you take over start delving into all your paperwork, policies, and procedures with the objective of eliminating every one that is crushing individual initiative and responsibility and taking time away from genuine achievement. Then, simultaneously, establish a system of standards that focuses on results within boundaries and a specific time frame. Get people working together in an empowered environment in which they take ownership of a task and its quantifiable results. Consider such activities as you proceed through personnel assessment and training, creating specific activities and programs, along with the rewards and recognition, for putting their training to work.

Establishing a Positive Values System

Another apparent paradox you'll face will be in the establishment of the normative culture. As we've described, you cannot do this through the implementation of directives and policies, but you must have employees come to see that the organization stands for accomplishments that are right and good, consistent with their value systems. Having said that, you must still issue explicit standards addressing expectations for dealing with customers, the organization, and one another. Your objective is to have employees deal with customers in the mind-set of an entrepreneur, doing their utmost to optimize customer satisfaction consistent with your organizational objectives. You want employees to think, and to think like an owner: weighing the costs of getting and keeping a customer in balance with the best interests of your organization's long-term profitability. You want them to take action and assume responsibility for that action, not blindly follow a manual of procedures. To get them to that point, you'll need to provide explicit guidelines for decision making and, especially in the short run, be there to provide help and suggestions.

Monitoring Expenses

Similarly, you want employees to spend the organization's money as if it were their own, which it is, actually. Faced with a proposed expense, you want them to make a decision about the expected payoff of the expenditure and act accordingly. This is easily said; however, the fact remains that you must monitor expenses, particularly at first, to ensure that employees are complying with the spirit of the law. In some situations, this will necessitate pointing out that a free cocktail hour does not really justify staying at a motel priced fifty dollars higher than one across the street. In more egregious circumstances, it will demand swift and decisive action to demonstrate that you mean business and will not tolerate dishonesty.

Empowering Employees

Most of all, your potential for success will depend upon whether you really follow through in implementing an empowering system of management. The first time you hand your employees or your teams a project and tell them you're giving them authority and ownership, expect to hear a collective "Yeah, right." But then, as they perceive that you really *are* going to let them make decisions and, within boundaries, you'll go with whatever they decide, their attitudes will change. Initially, there may be a glimmer of hope and the feeling that "Well, I'll be. I'm really going to be allowed to do this!" Then some trepidation may set in as they begin to fear making a mistake and being led to slaughter. Steeped in a tradition of performing tasks but not actually assuming responsibilities, they are likely to come back to you and attempt to reverse delegate their decision. That will be another moment when you must walk a fine line. Give the team members advice and coaching, helping them determine how to make their decision, but do not let them delegate it back to you. They must decide. For them to do that and do it right, they must feel confident that you are not the police officer on the corner, ready to punish them for making the inevitable mistake. On the contrary, as their coach, you will help them critique their decisions and the process they employed to formulate them, allowing those persons to discover for themselves how to be more effective in taking on more complex decisions, with more significant implications, in the future. Having made mistakes, they will now know how to avoid such pitfalls in the future.

Leading by Example

Finally, in everything you say and do, be a person who commands respect and trust. Lead by example. Treat your employees the way you want them to treat one another and the way you want them to treat your customers. Be true to your word. Represent your employees to your manager, and fight for their best interests. Once your employees understand that you are their advocate, you begin to become their leader. When they see that you and the organization are dedicated to serving the best interests of customers and society, you will begin to build the loyalty and commitment necessary for a positive normative culture motivated to achieve excellence through the application of conditioned power. Organizations that respect and empower their employees in this manner will create a teamwork environment with potential for success. Those that do not will not survive in today's competitive environment. You know what must be done and where you need to go. Now take the first step of that journey.

Bibliography

Blanchard, Kenneth H. and Johnson, Spencer (1982). *The One Minute Manager.* New York: Berkley Books.

Galbraith, John Kenneth (1983). *The Anatomy of Power.* Boston: Houghton Mifflin Company.

Glatthorn, Allan and Adams, Herbert (1983). *Listening Your Way to Management Success.* Glenview, IL: Scott Foresman and Company.

Herzberg, Frederik, Mausner, Bernard, and Snyderman, Barbara (1959). *The Motivation to Work.* New York: John Wiley & Sons.

Iacocca, Lee (1984). *Iacocca: An Autobiography.* New York: Bantam Books.

Jacobs, T. O. (1971). *Leadership and Exchange in Formal Organizations.* Alexandria, VA: Pippin.

Maccoby, Michael (1976). *The Gamesman: The New Corporate Leaders.* New York: Simon and Schuster.

Mackay, Harvey (1988). *Swim with the Sharks Without Being Eaten Alive.* New York: Fawcett Columbine.

McCormack, Mark H. (1984). *What They Don't Teach You at Harvard Business School.* New York: Bantam Books.

McCormack, Mark H. (1996). *On Managing.* Los Angeles: New Star Press.

McGregor, Douglas (1960). *The Human Side of Enterprise.* New York: McGraw-Hill

Peter, Laurence J. and Hull, Raymond (1969). *The Peter Principle: Why Things Always Go Wrong.* New York: William Morrow and Company, Inc.

Peters, Thomas J. and Waterman, Robert H. (1982). *In Search of Excellence: Lessons from America's Best-Run Companies.* New York: Warner Books.

Rooney, Andy (2000). *My War.* New York: PublicAffairs.

Schaef, Anne Wilson and Fassel, Diane (1988). *The Addictive Organization.* San Francisco: Harper & Row.

Walton, Mary (1986). *The Deming Management Method* (Foreword by W. Edwards Deming). New York: Dodd, Mead, & Company.

Whyte, William H. Jr. (1956). *The Organization Man.* New York: Simon & Schuster.

Index

Page numbers followed by the letter "f" indicate figures; those followed by the letter "t" indicate tables.

Order a copy of this book with this form or online at:
http://www.haworthpress.com/store/product.asp?sku=5208

THE BOOK ON MANAGEMENT

_____in hardbound at $39.95 (ISBN: 0-7890-2500-0)

_____in softbound at $22.95 (ISBN: 0-7890-2501-9)

Or order online and use special offer code HEC25 in the shopping cart.

COST OF BOOKS_____	☐ **BILL ME LATER:** (Bill-me option is good on US/Canada/Mexico orders only; not good to jobbers, wholesalers, or subscription agencies.)
	☐ Check here if billing address is different from shipping address and attach purchase order and billing address information.
POSTAGE & HANDLING_____ *(US: $4.00 for first book & $1.50 for each additional book)* *(Outside US: $5.00 for first book & $2.00 for each additional book)*	
	Signature_____
SUBTOTAL_____	☐ **PAYMENT ENCLOSED:** $_____
IN CANADA: ADD 7% GST_____	☐ **PLEASE CHARGE TO MY CREDIT CARD.**
STATE TAX_____ *(NJ, NY, OH, MN, CA, IL, IN, & SD residents, add appropriate local sales tax)*	☐ Visa ☐ MasterCard ☐ AmEx ☐ Discover ☐ Diner's Club ☐ Eurocard ☐ JCB
FINAL TOTAL_____	Account # _____
(If paying in Canadian funds, convert using the current exchange rate, UNESCO coupons welcome)	Exp. Date_____
	Signature_____

Prices in US dollars and subject to change without notice.

NAME_____

INSTITUTION_____

ADDRESS_____

CITY_____

STATE/ZIP_____

COUNTRY_____ COUNTY (NY residents only)_____

TEL_____ FAX_____

E-MAIL_____

May we use your e-mail address for confirmations and other types of information? ☐ Yes ☐ No We appreciate receiving your e-mail address and fax number. Haworth would like to e-mail or fax special discount offers to you, as a preferred customer. **We will never share, rent, or exchange your e-mail address or fax number.** We regard such actions as an invasion of your privacy.

Order From Your Local Bookstore or Directly From
The Haworth Press, Inc.
10 Alice Street, Binghamton, New York 13904-1580 • USA
TELEPHONE: 1-800-HAWORTH (1-800-429-6784) / Outside US/Canada: (607) 722-5857
FAX: 1-800-895-0582 / Outside US/Canada: (607) 771-0012
E-mailto: orders@haworthpress.com

For orders outside US and Canada, you may wish to order through your local sales representative, distributor, or bookseller.
For information, see http://haworthpress.com/distributors

(Discounts are available for individual orders in US and Canada only, not booksellers/distributors.)
PLEASE PHOTOCOPY THIS FORM FOR YOUR PERSONAL USE.
http://www.HaworthPress.com   BOF04